Philly Jocks

The Best Philadelphia
Pro Athletes of Our Time

Foreword by
Jody McDonald

To an avid Philly sports fan —
Enjoy the book!
And how about those 2008
Phillies!

Camino Books, Inc.
Philadelphia

Manufactured in the United States of America

1 2 3 4 5 10 09 08 07

Library of Congress Cataloging-in-Publication Data

Brown, David W. (David Wesley), 1960-
    Philly jocks : the best Philadelphia pro athletes of our time / by Dave
Brown ; foreword by Jody McDonald.
        p. cm.
      ISBN-13: 978-1-933822-09-9 (alk. paper)
1. Professional athletes—Pennsylvania—Philadelphia—Biography. I. Title.
    GV697.A1B77 2007
    796.04'40922—dc22
    [B]   2007020269

Cover and interior design: Jerilyn Bockorick

This book is available at a special discount on bulk purchases for promo-
tional, business, and educational use.

Publisher
Camino Books, Inc.
P.O. Box 59026
Philadelphia, PA 19102

www.caminobooks.com

Contents

Acknowledgments

As always, I'm indebted to numerous people, whom I would like to thank.

My brother Doug and longtime agent John Sammis assisted me considerably when I was developing the idea for the book. Sadly, John passed away in the middle of the project, and this book is dedicated to him.

It took some doing to find 100 people to compile a list of best Philadelphia athletes for the book. John Mitchell, Stacy Smith, Dave Bristowe and his wife Kathy were especially helpful in rounding up diehard fans to respond to my survey.

My able research assistant Kevin Kent lent a big hand in digging up the statistics for the 100 players featured, while my MVP mother-in-law Diane Minch went beyond the call of duty, spending countless hours formatting the stats section for the book.

The typing of the manuscript was a team effort. Peggy Gryga was the laboring oar, but co-workers Eileen Berky, Kathy McCarthy, Jen Keller and Nicole Francisco, along with Kim McLaughlin, contributed substantially as well.

I am much obliged to Edward Jutkowitz, Publisher of Camino Books, who had faith in the project from the beginning.

Finally, I extend a heartfelt thanks to the people who were the lifeblood of this book: the Philadelphia sports fans and individuals from the Philly sports business who graciously took the time to complete lists and enthusiastically answer my questions about their picks. My name is on the cover, but these folks really wrote the book.

Foreword by Jody McDonald

Lists. They are not just for bringing to the grocery store anymore. I'm not sure when, how or why we became obsessed with lists but they are now a societal must. We can debate the "why." Is it our need for a neat, orderly way of looking at things? The desire to make things easier to comprehend and catalogue?

Who are the 100 hottest chicks on the planet? Who are the 50 hottest chicks between the ages of 20 and 40? Who are the 20 hottest over the age of 50? Who are the 10 hottest who make over 10 million dollars a year? (Added value is also a new societal obsession.) Who are the five hottest females who have starred in a movie with Kevin Bacon? (We can get pretty compartmentalized with our lists.)

Or is the "why" the debate? My list probably won't match your list, which almost definitely won't match your father's list. That's the rub and that's the fun! These all-important deliberations used to take place at the corner tavern. Now they take place on talk radio and in chat rooms: a little less personal but just as passionate nonetheless.

Which brings us to sports, a topic we can get quite passionate about these days. Philadelphia fans take their sports as seriously as a heart attack. Inside these pages you will find a tally of the top professional athletes who have toiled here for their teams in the "city of brotherly shove" for the past half-century. The author has compiled the opinions of some of the most respected Philly sports chroniclers and ardent fans to compile his list. Who are the top 50? How is Hal Greer not in the top 20? Who is number one? Doc? Schmidty? Or "the Big Dipper"? Let the debate begin!

One piece of advice before you start your trip down memory lane of the best to play in Philly over the past five decades. Get out a pen and piece of paper and assemble your own ordering. I believe you'll find it's harder than you think. Either way, you will realize that we've had some sensational, spectacular athletes come through Philadelphia since 1955, despite a paucity of championships. As a matter of fact, the capturing of the ultimate accomplishment seems to have an elevating effect on the members of this list. The ring is still the thing here in Philly.

Enjoy and let the disputes commence!

Introduction

Since the late 1960s, when my father began to take my brother Doug and me to Connie Mack Stadium and Franklin Field for Phillies and Eagles games, I have been an avid Philadelphia sports fan. And I'm very proud of it. Philadelphia sports fans have gotten a bad rap over the years for doing inappropriate things like pelting Santa Claus with snowballs and cheering when Cowboys receiver Michael Irvin lay injured on the Veterans Stadium turf. But we are also regarded as among the most loyal, passionate and knowledgeable sports fans in the country. Whether our beloved teams are winning or losing, we never lose the enthusiasm for watching, rooting for and talking—sometimes arguing—about them.

No doubt, we have endured countless suffering—last-place fin-ishes, underachieving teams, agonizing postseason losses—but every so often we have experienced the thrill of attending a championship parade. In December 1960, two months after I was born, the Eagles capped an incredible season by beating Vince Lombardi's power-house Packers for the NFL title. In '67, the Sixers, who had moved from Syracuse four years earlier, assembled a juggernaut that rolled to the NBA championship. The Flyers, who kicked off play as an expansion team that fall, ascended to the top of the hockey world in a few short years by winning back-to-back Stanley Cups in '74 and '75. The Phillies had deprived their fans of a World Series triumph since the fall classic began in 1903, but finally they came through in 1980 to win it all. And the Sixers returned to the winner's circle in '83 with a decisive sweep of the Lakers in the NBA Finals to avenge some near misses in previous years.

We Philly fans also have had the privilege of watching some of the finest athletes ever to step on a baseball diamond, football field, basketball court or hockey rink. Who, I wondered, have been the very best athletes to play for our teams? I decided to try and find out by putting together a list of the top athletes for our city's four major sports teams over the last 50 years.

To compile the list, I polled 100 people and asked them to provide me with their top 50 professional athletes in Philadelphia over the last half-century. My survey participants included 15 experts—individuals who work in some facet of the Philadelphia sports business. (One is retired.) My esteemed panel included broadcasters from our local teams, sportswriters from our city and suburban newspapers, sportscasters and anchors from our local TV stations, a sports producer and a sports radio host, Jody McDonald. (A complete list of the experts, along with their biographies, follows this introduction.)

My pollsters also included 84 diehard Philly sports fans from throughout the Delaware Valley; some have moved away, but have remained faithful to our Philadelphia teams. (A complete list of the fans also follows this introduction.) The fans who participated are from all walks of life, from lawyers (sorry about that) and postal workers to ministers and accountants. When I was collecting surveys, Jody McDonald featured "the Philly Top 50" on his radio show, and listeners gave their picks, five players per day; the collective list of the WPEN listeners comprised the 100th list.

I provided each of the participants with a ballot consisting of 180 of the best players for the Phillies, Eagles, Sixers, Warriors (for those of you asking who are the Warriors, they were Philadelphia's first NBA franchise; they played in our city for 14 years before moving to San Francisco in 1962) and Flyers since 1955, and guidelines for the voters to follow when making their picks. Here are the guidelines which the participants received:

Please consider only athletes who played professionally for one of the four major sports teams in Philadelphia over the last 50 years. Thus, the only athletes under consideration are those who played (or are still playing) for the Phillies, A's (under certain limited circumstances described below), Eagles, Warriors, Sixers and Flyers since 1955. If an athlete played at least one year in Philadelphia since 1955, you should consider all the years he played in Philadelphia, even the years prior to 1955 (like Richie Ashburn, who played for the Phillies from 1948 to 1959). Do not consider athletes' performances for non-Philadelphia teams. For example, when evaluating Charles Barkley, only consider his play with the Sixers; do not consider his play with the Houston Rockets and Phoenix Suns.

I am well aware that by imposing these time period limitations, some great players from the Phillies (such as Chuck Klein), A's (such as Lefty Grove), Eagles (such as Steve Van Buren), and Warriors (such as Joe Fulks) are excluded from consideration. I used 1955 because with all the great athletes who have played for Philadelphia teams over the last half-century, it's a difficult task to consider them and rank the top 50. The task would become even more daunting if the athletes who played for our teams during the first half of the twentieth century had to be considered as well.

Furthermore, I realize that our local high school and college teams have produced star athletes in several sports, but please don't consider their accomplishments. Thus, when sizing up athletes who starred for local teams at the high school or college level and professional level (such as Chuck Bednarik and Wilt Chamberlain), consider only their accomplishments for the professional teams in Philadelphia.

Likewise, many outstanding athletes grew up in the Philadelphia area (including Reggie Jackson, Marvin Harrison and Rasheed Wallace), but because they didn't play here professionally, they should not be considered. Please also do not consider athletes who excelled in sports other than one of the four major sports. Philadelphian Joe Frazier is, of course, one of boxing's best ever, but because this book is only about baseball, football, basketball and hockey players, Smokin' Joe, as well as athletes who hailed from Philly and starred in other sports, should not be on your list.

There have been three franchise changes involving Philadelphia teams which I want to address briefly:

▸ The Warriors played in Philadelphia from 1949 to 1962 and then moved west to become the San Francisco Warriors and later the Golden State Warriors. Even though Wilt Chamberlain, Tom Gola and others were playing for the same franchise when the team went to San Francisco, only consider their play for the Philadelphia Warriors.

▸ The Syracuse Nationals moved to Philadelphia and became the 76ers at the start of the 1963-64 season. Therefore, when assessing basketball players who saw action for both the Nationals and Sixers (such as Hal Greer), only consider their play for the Sixers.

▸ The Philadelphia A's moved to Kansas City following the 1954 season. Therefore, because of the 1955 cutoff, no A's player should be considered unless he played for the Phillies since

1955 and also for the A's prior to 1955, in which case you would consider his play for both the A's and Phillies. I did not include any players in this category on the ballot, but if you think any are worthy, please include them on your list.

I don't mean to be hypertechnical with these guidelines, but because this book is being written for Philadelphia pro sports fans, I want to make sure that everybody is voting based solely on the play of the athletes whom the fans have watched and cheered for.

Criteria

In ranking the athletes please use the following criteria, giving each criterion the weight you believe it deserves: overall performance, dominance in his sport, ability to perform in the clutch, awards won, championship teams played for, All-Star Game selections, Hall of Fame induction, whether his team retired his number, appeal among Philadelphia fans, and length of service.

With regard to the length of service factor, I'm imposing a three-year minimum. Thus, don't consider an athlete unless he played or has played at least three full years for a Philadelphia team. Also, when evaluating active players, please refrain from projecting into the future what you think they will accomplish; only consider their accomplishments to date.

Based on the foregoing guidelines, using the enclosed form, please rank the players from best (50 points) to 50th best (1 point). If you feel that two or more athletes are tied for a certain slot, indicate so with a T. (For example, if you believe that two players should be tied for ninth and tenth places, put a T next to both of their names and each will receive $41^{1}/_{2}$ points.)

When I received the top 50 lists from the 100 participants, I tallied the votes and ranked the athletes from 1 through 100. I then interviewed the participants and asked them questions about how they arrived at their choices. What set Wilt Chamberlain apart from the rest of the great athletes? Why did you put Randall Cunningham higher than Allen Iverson? Lenny Dykstra made your list, but Garry Maddox didn't—what was your thinking there? How come you put Reggie Leach higher than John LeClair? I didn't see Scott Rolen or Andrew Toney on your list—why didn't they make the cut?

The answers I received—from the experts and the fans—were sometimes humorous and sarcastic, often controversial, and always insightful and thought-provoking. It's fascinating—and fodder for great sports debate—how differently people viewed the various athletes. Many felt that Pete Rose was "the missing piece" who taught the Phillies how to win, and without him there would have been no world championship in 1980. Other voters thought that Rose's contributions paled in comparison to those of Schmidt, Carlton and McGraw. Donovan McNabb has been one of the NFL's best quarterbacks of the new millennium in the eyes of a lot of voters; however, to others he's an overrated player who consistently has failed to win the big game. Charles Barkley was a better player than Iverson or Erving, according to some. His detractors considered him a big mouth who never led the Sixers beyond the Eastern Conference Semifinals. Eric Lindros? His supporters insisted that he was an awesome force and that in his prime for the Flyers, he was one of the NHL's elite players. Many, however, vehemently disagreed, describing Eric as a selfish whiner who never reached his potential. I used the comments by my very quotable group of experts and fans and wove them into short biographies that I wrote for each of the 100 athletes featured. I also have included, for each player, the survey results (how many people voted for him, the number of first-place votes, second-place votes, etc. that he received), his year-by-year regular season statistics, and major awards that he won.

Sprinkled throughout the book are sidebars in which the participants have described memorable Philadelphia games that they attended. Ray Didinger chronicled the 1960 NFL Championship Game which riveted him, a high school freshman at the time, from his endzone seat. Terry Bickhart recalled the '62 game when Wilt, then with the Warriors, scored 78 points in a triple-overtime thriller against the Lakers. Adam Kimelman captured in detail the night that the Wachovia Center crowd was louder than he's ever heard them: Game 1 of the 2004 Eastern Conference Semifinals when the Flyers beat the Maple Leafs 3-1. Jim Kent described the thrill of attending the Eagles-Cowboys NFC Championship Game in January 1981 when Wilbert Montgomery had the game of his life, helping the Birds advance to their first Super Bowl. My brother Doug summed up the Phillies game in 1970 that I joined him for, in which fan favorite Tony Taylor hit a grand slam in the bottom of the ninth inning to erase a three-run deficit and beat the Giants 7-6.

So Philly fans, start reading. See how the survey turned out and what our voters had to say about the best Philadelphia pro athletes over the last half-century. You're not always going to agree, but I hope you'll be entertained for hours.

Biographies
of Experts

Ray Didinger ▶ Ray is a senior producer with NFL Films in Mt. Laurel, New Jersey. Prior to joining NFL Films, he spent 27 years as a sportswriter for the Philadelphia *Bulletin* and the *Philadelphia Daily News*. He was named Pennsylvania Sportswriter of the Year five times and in 2006, he was the first sportswriter inducted into the Philadelphia Sports Hall of Fame. In 1998, Ray won the Dick McCann Memorial Award for long and distinguished coverage of the National Football League and his name was added to the Writers Honor Roll at the Pro Football Hall of Fame in Canton, Ohio.

Merrill Reese ▶ Merrill has been the Voice of the Eagles since 1977. He has the longest continuous tenure in the NFL. He is a graduate of Temple University and served in the U.S. Navy as a Public Affairs Officer.

Chris Wheeler ▶ "Wheels" has been broadcasting Phillies games since 1977 and has worked for the Phils' organization since 1971. He is a 1963 graduate of Marple-Newtown High School and a 1967 graduate of Penn State University.

Jody McDonald ▶ Jody "Mac" has been part of the Philadelphia sports talk scene for the past 16 years, logging almost 10 years at WIP, four years as the host of the Eagles pregame show on WYSP (with three championship games and one Super Bowl appearance in those four years) and now is the afternoon drive host on Sports Radio 950. Jody has been engrossed in sports since he was a wee little guy going back to the 1960s when his dad, Joe Sr., was in major league baseball serving as General Manager of the New York Mets, St. Louis Cardinals and Detroit Tigers.

Andy Musser ▶ Andy was play-by-play announcer for the Phillies for more than 25 years. Upon leaving the booth in 2001, he became the eastern representative for Anchor Brewing Company of San Francisco. Andy also was heard on 76ers radio and TV broadcasts periodically from the 1960s through the 1990s. He also did four years of Eagles play-by-play on their radio network beginning in 1965 and starting in 1988, he spent 10 years broadcasting Villanova basketball. Andy and his wife, Eun Joo, have two grown children and four grandchildren. They reside in Wynnewood, Pennsylvania.

Michael Barkann ► Since 1997, Michael has filled many roles on Comcast SportsNet — Philadelphia's first 24-hour sports network — as host, anchor and reporter. Most often, he hosts the *Daily News Live* and the *Post Game Live* programs for the Flyers, Sixers and Eagles. When not sitting in the host's chair, he assumes the role of anchor and reporter for *SportsNITE*. Prior to joining Comcast SportsNet, Michael was the sports director at WLVI-TV in Boston from 1992 to 1997. He was also sports anchor/reporter at KYW-3 in Philadelphia from 1987 to 1991. Michael has also covered three Olympic Winter Games for CBS: in Albertville, France; Lillehammer, Norway; and Nagano, Japan. In August 2007, he covered his 17th U.S. Open Tennis Championship for USA Network. He has been recognized with five Mid-Atlantic Emmy Awards, and he was selected as Pennsylvania's Sportscaster of the Year in 1999, 2001-04 and 2006. The East Brunswick, New Jersey, native is a graduate of S.I. Newhouse School of Public Communication at Syracuse University.

Mark Eckel ► Mark has been covering the NFL as a sportswriter for more than 20 years. He currently writes for *The Trenton Times* and also fills in as a sports radio host for WIP. He co-authored a book, *It's Gooooood!* with Merrill Reese.

Steve Bucci ► Winner of the 2005 local Emmy Award for Best Sports Anchor and currently a weekend sports anchor, Steve joined CBS 3's Eyewitness News team as a sports reporter in 1997. As part of CBS 3's sports team, he has covered some of the biggest stories in Philadelphia sports history, including the Eagles' appearance in Super Bowl XXXIX and the 76ers' run to the 2001 NBA Finals. Steve is at home in any sport, covering everything from major league baseball to bass fishing in a career that has spanned 20 years. He also co-hosted the Philadelphia Eagles pregame show on sister station 94 WYSP in 2003 and 2004. Before coming to Philadelphia, Steve served as a sports anchor on NewsChannel 8 in Washington, D.C. While there, he first earned a local Emmy Award. Steve was also the weekend sports anchor at WRIC-TV in Richmond, Virginia, and at WJHL-TV in Johnson City, Tennessee, where he began his career in 1984. A native of Providence, Rhode Island, Steve was raised in Allentown, Pennsylvania, and now resides in Center City Philadelphia. He is a graduate of Shippensburg University and holds a Bachelor of Arts degree in Communications/Journalism.

John Clark ▶ John joined the NBC News team in September 2001 as a weekend sports anchor. During his time as a sports reporter for NBC 10, John has earned two nominations for Mid-Atlantic Emmy Awards. In 2004, he won the award for Outstanding Individual Achievement for Reporter/Sports. John was again honored in 2005 as the reporter for "Philadelphia's Paraolympians," which was nominated for Outstanding Sports News/Features or Series. While growing up in Wallingford, Pennsylvania, John used to imitate legendary Phillies announcer Harry Kalas. He graduated from Strath Haven High School and Temple University.

Steve Kennedy ▶ Steve has been part of the Philadelphia sports media since 1996. Since then he has been involved in a wide variety of sports-related activities, including on-air appearances and radio production, Internet writing and television production. In the past 10 years, Steve has worked closely with such sports personalities as Big Daddy Graham, Lou Tilley, Anthony Gargano, Glen Macnow and Gregg Murphy. In the past three years, Steve has earned three nominations for Mid-Atlantic Emmy Awards. In 2004, he won the award for Best Show as a producer for *Lou Tilley's Sports Connection*. Steve grew up in Ridley, Pennsylvania. He graduated from Cardinal O'Hara High School and Temple University.

Terry Bickhart ▶ A graduate of Spring-Ford High School (1965) and Temple University (1969), Terry has lived in suburban Philadelphia his entire life. He has been a member of *The Reading Eagle* sports department since 1969, serving as Sunday sports editor from 1983 to 1999 and as sports editor since 1999.

Gordie Jones ▸ Gordie has been a journalist for 25 years and currently is a sports columnist for *The Morning Call* in Allentown. He is co-authoring a book with ex-Sixers general manager Pat Williams, which is due out in November 2007.

Adam Kimelman ▸ Adam has been a sportswriter for *The Trenton Times* since 1998. He has covered the Flyers since the start of the 2002-03 season, and also covers the Trenton Titans (ECHL).

Mike Sielski ▸ A graduate of La Salle University and Columbia University, Mike is the sports columnist for *The Bucks County Courier Times, The Burlington County* (New Jersey) *Times* and *The Intelligencer.* The Newspaper Association of America has named him one of the 20 best newspaper people under age 40 in the nation, and he is the co-author of *How to Be Like Jackie Robinson: Life Lessons from Baseball's Greatest Hero.*

Michael Beirne ▸ Michael has been a Philadelphia sports fan for more than 40 years, and because of that, his aging process has been ratcheted up to somewhere in his 60s. He's stuck with his teams, though. He has been a sportswriter and editor for suburban Philadelphia newspapers and trade magazines for more than a decade, had the unique perspective of seeing many games from just feet away during his decade as a security guard and usher, and has attended more than 700 sporting events in the Philadelphia area, according to his vast (and very geeky) ticket collection. Michael Jack Schmidt, Eddie Jones and his daughter are his favorite three athletes of all time. His favorite team is the 2045 Phillies, the second and final World Series champion in Philadelphia.

List of Fans

Bob Anderson
Jim Angelichio
Ralph Antonelli
Gregg Asman
Randy Axelrod and Steve Danawitz
Dave Beck
Sean Bergin
John Bergmann
Ken and David Berky
Rob Betts
Bob Bookbinder
Dennis Brady
Dave Bristowe
Mark Bristowe
Ed Brittingham
Michael Brophy
Dan Brown
Doug Brown
Joe Brown
Bob Chazin
Bob Cinalli
Chuck Cutshall
Bryan Davis
Mike DiColla
Patrick Dooley
Ed Dougherty
Andy Dziedzic
Rob Elias and Jason Garber
Joe Fee
Harvey Feldman
Lee Fiederer
Marianne Gallagher
Fran Garvin
Greg Geier
Joe Geier
Neil Goldstein
Joe Gribb
Jon Grisdale
Jack Guziewicz
Ned Hark
Bill Jakavick
Bob Kelly
Jim Kent

Kevin Kent
Ryan Kent
Mike Koob
Paul Lalley
Paul Lightkep
Mike Mastalski
Dan McCarthy
Bill McClain
Jerry McDonough
Bill McElroy
Ken Miller
Frank Minch
John Mitchell
Dave Myers
Rob Neducsin
Cliff Patterson
Andy Paul
Mike Rad
Jim Robinson
Jim and Stacy Rosen
Andy Salayda
Brent Saunders
Dave Sautter
Jim Schloth
Fred Schumacher
John Senkow
Jeff Skow
Rod Smith
Wayne Smith
Dick Streeter
John Surbeck
John Tobin
Paul Troy
Steve Van Allen
Greg Veith
Ryan Vogel
Mark Voigt
Tom Walter
Fred Warren
Chuck Wolf
WPEN callers
Glenn Young

**The Best Philadelphia
Pro Athletes of Our Time**

1 Wilt Chamberlain

RANK	POINTS	VOTES RECEIVED
1st	50	56
2nd	49	15
3rd	48	3
4th	47	2
5th	46	6
6th	45	3
7th	44	2
8th	43	2
9th	42	3
10th	41	1
11th	40	1
12th	39	0
13th	38	1
14th	37	1
15th	36	1
16th	35	1
17th	34	0
18th	33	0
19th	32	1
20th	31	0
21st	30	0
22nd	29	0
23rd	28	0
24th	27	0
25th	26	0
26th	25	0
27th	24	0
28th	23	1
29th	22	0
30th	21	0
31st	20	0
32nd	19	0
33rd	18	0
34th	17	0
35th	16	0
36th	15	0
37th	14	0
38th	13	0
39th	12	0
40th	11	0
41st	10	0
42nd	9	0
43rd	8	0
44th	7	0
45th	6	0
46th	5	0
47th	4	0
48th	3	0
49th	2	0
50th	1	0
Not on List	0	0

TOP 10 VOTES	93
2ND 10 VOTES	6
3RD 10 VOTES	1
4TH 10 VOTES	0
5TH 10 VOTES	0
TOTAL VOTES	100
TOTAL POINTS	4776

▼ TEAM
Warriors / Sixers

▼ YEARS PLAYED
1960–1962, 1965–1968

▼ POSITION
Center

The numbers were mind-boggling—100 points in a game, 55 rebounds in a game, 50.4 points per game in a season; the accomplishments were astounding—seven NBA scoring titles, 11 rebounding titles, four MVPs; and the accolades which Wilt "the Big Dipper" Chamberlain received from the voters were of the highest order. "He totally dominated the sport. He is the greatest NBA player ever (Oscar Robertson is the second best)" (Andy Musser). "He was a larger than life figure...Shaq [Shaquille O'Neal] is not even close to Wilt" (Steve Bucci). "He was a player of incredible historical significance. He is a transcendent player who changed his sport. He was bigger than the sport" (Ray Didinger). "He is the best Philadelphia athlete by far; he revolutionized the game of basketball" (Jody McDonald). "Nobody will touch the records that he set" (Adam Kimelman). "He was the single most dominant player in the history of the NBA—more dominant than Michael Jordan" (Merrill Reese). "He had strength, finesse, endurance, and power—he was devastating" (Michael Barkann).

A few of the voters pointed out that Wilt was so dominant that the NBA enacted several rule changes, including the widening of the lane and the three-second clock, to control his dominance.

Nobody disputed Wilt's greatness, but some voters, including Dave Beck and Paul Lalley, moved "the Stilt" down a few notches because he spent a fair amount of his professional career outside of Philadelphia. "When I envision Wilt," said Dave Beck, "I see him in a Lakers uniform, not a Philly uniform." Wilt's 1972 world champion Lakers are remembered for their NBA record, 33-game winning streak. Ken Miller felt that Wilt didn't win the big game enough and that his arch-rival for the Celtics, Bill Russell, seemed to be one up on him most of the time. Wilt squared off against Russell's Celtics six times in the playoffs while he was in Philadelphia—three times with the Warriors, and three with the Sixers. Wilt's team came out on the short end of the stick every time except 1967 when the Sixers beat the Celtics in the Eastern Conference Finals en route to the world championship.

Dave Myers thought that Wilt's 100-point game, although very impressive, generated more hoopla than it deserved. "Too much weight was given to that game. It's just one game, not a compilation of his entire career."

No, I wasn't among the eight billion who were at Hershey the night in March 1962 when Wilt Chamberlain scored 100 points. But I was with a few thousand others at Convention Hall in Philadelphia three months earlier.

It was the second game of a doubleheader, an NBA custom as quaint as the times. The Chicago Packers lost to the Detroit Pistons in the opener. My dad and I sat in the second row of the rickety wooden chairs along the one baseline, just a few feet behind the basket. Through the haze of cigarette smoke, the Philadelphia Warriors and Los Angeles Lakers went at each other through three overtimes. When it was over—no, the smoke hadn't cleared, but the Lakers had won 151-147 behind Elgin Baylor's 64 points. Wilt scored 78 that night, the most in league history. It would remain the league record for only three months, but it stayed at No. 2 for more than 44 years when Kobe Bryant scored 81.

For one 14-year-old kid it was a defining moment.

—TERRY BICKHART

Year	Team	Lg	G	Min	FGM	FGA	FGP	FTM	FTA	FTP	AST	REB	Pts	PPG
1959–60	Warriors	NBA	72	3338	1065	2311	.461	577	991	.582	168	1941	2707	37.6
1960–61	Warriors	NBA	79	3773	1251	2457	.509	531	1054	.504	148	2149	3033	38.4
1961–62	Warriors	NBA	80	3882	1597	3159	.506	835	1363	.613	192	2052	4029	50.4
1962–63	San Francisco	NBA	80	3806	1463	2770	.528	660	1113	.593	275	1946	3586	44.8
1963–64	San Francisco	NBA	80	3689	1204	2298	.524	540	1016	.531	403	1787	2948	36.9
1964–65	San Francisco	NBA	38	1743	636	1275	.499	208	500	.416	117	893	1480	38.90
1964–65	Sixers	NBA	35	1558	427	808	.528	200	380	.526	133	780	1054	30.1
1965–66	Sixers	NBA	79	3737	1074	1990	.540	501	976	.513	414	1943	2649	33.5
1966–67	Sixers	NBA	81	3682	785	1150	.683	386	875	.441	630	1957	1956	24.1
1967–68	Sixers	NBA	82	3836	819	1377	.595	354	932	.380	702	1952	1992	24.3
1968–69	L.A. Lakers	NBA	81	3669	641	1099	.583	382	857	.446	366	1712	1664	20.5
1969–70	L.A. Lakers	NBA	12	505	129	227	.568	70	157	.446	49	221	328	27.3
1970–71	L.A. Lakers	NBA	82	3630	668	1226	.545	360	669	.538	352	1493	1696	20.7
1971–72	L.A. Lakers	NBA	82	3469	496	764	.649	221	524	.422	329	1572	1213	14.8
1972–73	L.A. Lakers	NBA	82	3542	426	586	.727	232	455	.510	365	1526	1084	13.2
Warriors/Sixers Totals			508	23806	7018	13252	.530	3384	6571	.515	2387	12774	17420	34.3
Career Totals			1045	47859	12681	23497	.540	6057	11862	.511	4643	23924	31419	30.1

NBA Rookie of the Year (1960)
NBA MVP (1960, 1966–68)
NBA Finals MVP (1972)
NBA All-Star (1960–69, 1971–73)
Member of NBA Champions (1967, 1972)
Number 13 retired by Warriors, Sixers and Lakers
Basketball Hall of Fame (1979)

2 Mike Schmidt

RANK	POINTS	VOTES RECEIVED
1st	50	14
2nd	49	31
3rd	48	18.5
4th	47	11
5th	46	4.5
6th	45	5
7th	44	6
8th	43	0
9th	42	3
10th	41	1
11th	40	2
12th	39	1
13th	38	0
14th	37	0
15th	36	1
16th	35	0
17th	34	0
18th	33	0
19th	32	0
20th	31	0
21st	30	1
22nd	29	0
23rd	28	0
24th	27	0
25th	26	0
26th	25	0
27th	24	0
28th	23	0
29th	22	0
30th	21	0
31st	20	0
32nd	19	0
33rd	18	0
34th	17	0
35th	16	0
36th	15	0
37th	14	0
38th	13	0
39th	12	0
40th	11	0
41st	10	0
42nd	9	0
43rd	8	0
44th	7	0
45th	6	0
46th	5	0
47th	4	0
48th	3	0
49th	2	0
50th	1	0
Not on List	0	1

TOP 10 VOTES	94
2ND 10 VOTES	4
3RD 10 VOTES	1
4TH 10 VOTES	0
5TH 10 VOTES	0
TOTAL VOTES	99
TOTAL POINTS	4672

▼ TEAM
Phillies

▼ YEARS PLAYED
1972–1989

▼ POSITION
Third Baseman

In 1941, Ted Williams had one of his best seasons in a long and illustrious career: he hit .406 with 37 home runs and 120 RBIs. But one writer detested Williams so much that he snubbed the Red Sox great by leaving him off his American League MVP ballot. Likewise, Jon Grisdale's disdain for Michael Jack Schmidt compelled him to omit the first-ballot Hall of Famer from his top 50 list. Jon had a few interactions with Schmidt at the Vet before games where fans congregated for autographs and at a couple banquets. Jon's assessment of Schmidty: "He was a standoffish jerk." Jon also thought Schmidt was an overrated player, pointing to his modest lifetime average, loads of strikeouts (1883, which puts him high on the all-time list), and poor performance in some postseasons (.182 average with no home runs and four RBIs in 1976, 1977 and 1978 playoff losses). Jon also recalled a play in one of the Phillies' most heartbreaking losses ever: Game 3 of the '77 National League's League Championship Series against the Dodgers. The series was tied at one, and the Phillies carried a 5-3 lead into the ninth inning at Veterans Stadium. L.A. scored three runs to win the game, and then won Game 4 to take the series. While most Phils fans remember Greg Luzinski misplaying a flyball into a triple, Jon was quick to point out that in the next play, Schmidt failed to field Davey Lopes' groundball cleanly, allowing the tying run to score.

Jon was the only voter who criticized Schmidt's on-the-field performance, but a handful of others rated him low in the "fan appeal" category. Merrill Reese: "Mike Schmidt was a tremendous player. His only failing was that he could not connect with the fans." Terry Bickhart: "Philadelphia fans rooted for Mike; they didn't love him."

Most voters, though, overlooked Schmidt's aloofness when making their picks. Paul Lalley: "He may not be the most loved Philly pro athlete of all time, but he is still the greatest. Much of the credit for the Phils' success in the late 1970s through 1983, especially 1980, belongs to Schmidty." Ed Brittingham: "He established himself as the

7

best player in baseball and best ever at his position when Philly was a baseball town. He did it all as a Phillie; he did not have prime years with other organizations." Ed explained why he picked Schmidt first over Chamberlain: "I don't think any basketball player has ever captivated the Philly fans the way a baseball or football player has. He played a crucial role in bringing Philadelphia perhaps its most cherished championship ('80 MVP, game-winning home run vs. the Expos to clinch the N.L. East, World Series MVP)."

Kevin Kent relied on Schmidt's awesome arsenal of stats: all-time Phillies leader in home runs (548), RBIs (1595), hits (2234), runs (1506), walks (1507), and games played (2404); three-time MVP, 10-time Gold Glove winner, and 12-time All-Star. "He redefined the third-base position by being both a power hitter and an excellent fielder and is thought by many to be the best third baseman of all time."

I was a senior at Albright College and was lucky enough to have secured a ticket to Game 1 of the 1980 World Series. Yes, I was actually walking into a World Series game at the Vet and my team was playing. All those years of running home from school to catch the games or seeking a listen on the transistor radio in the men's room at Hebrew school because it was the World Series, so big, so important, yet my team never had a shot of being there.

I have been to many big games, including the Super Bowl in Jacksonville. But I will never have the same feeling that I had that October night as a 21-year-old Phillies fan who had grown up with bad teams so that a World Series could only be a dream. But now my team grew up and the whole world was going to watch a game that they were playing in my town and I would be there. We all know that the Phillies won that night—they scored four runs in the eighth inning to beat the Royals 6-4; Mike Schmidt had the game-winning hit. Six nights after that Tug leapt into our hearts forever.

I also had a ticket for Game 7. I did not need that ticket. I went to Game 3 in 1993 and that was nice, but not the same. My hope is that someday my sons will walk up to our new ballpark to a World Series game and have the same feeling that I had on that night.

—NED HARK

Year	Team	Lg	G	AB	R	H	HR	RBI	SB	Avg	SLG
1972	Phillies	N.L.	13	34	2	7	1	3	0	.206	.294
1973	Phillies	N.L.	132	367	43	72	18	52	8	.196	.373
1974	Phillies	N.L.	162	568	108	160	36	116	23	.282	.546
1975	Phillies	N.L.	158	562	93	140	38	95	29	.249	.523
1976	Phillies	N.L.	160	584	112	153	38	107	14	.262	.524
1977	Phillies	N.L.	154	544	114	149	38	101	15	.274	.574
1978	Phillies	N.L.	145	513	93	129	21	78	19	.251	.435
1979	Phillies	N.L.	160	541	109	137	45	114	9	.253	.564
1980	Phillies	N.L.	150	548	104	157	48	121	12	.286	.624
1981	Phillies	N.L.	102	354	78	112	31	91	12	.316	.644
1982	Phillies	N.L.	148	514	108	144	35	87	14	.280	.547
1983	Phillies	N.L.	154	534	104	136	40	109	7	.255	.524
1984	Phillies	N.L.	151	528	93	146	36	106	5	.277	.536
1985	Phillies	N.L.	158	549	89	152	33	93	1	.277	.532
1986	Phillies	N.L.	160	552	97	160	37	119	1	.290	.547
1987	Phillies	N.L.	147	522	88	153	35	113	2	.293	.548
1988	Phillies	N.L.	108	390	52	97	12	62	3	.249	.405
1989	Phillies	N.L.	42	148	19	30	6	28	0	.203	.372
	Phillies Totals		2404	8352	1506	2234	548	1595	174	.267	.527
	Career Totals		2404	8352	1506	2234	548	1595	174	.267	.527

National League All-Star (1974, 1976–77, 1979–84, 1986–87, 1989)
National League Gold Glove (1976–84, 1986)
National League MVP (1980–81, 1986)
World Series MVP (1980)

Member of World Champions (1980)
Number 20 retired by Phillies
Baseball Hall of Fame (1995)

3 ▶ Julius Erving

RANK	POINTS	VOTES RECEIVED	RANK	POINTS	VOTES RECEIVED
1st	50	9	31st	20	0
2nd	49	17	32nd	19	0
3rd	48	16	33rd	18	0
4th	47	9.5	34th	17	0
5th	46	12.5	35th	16	0
6th	45	15	36th	15	0
7th	44	6	37th	14	0
8th	43	5	38th	13	0
9th	42	3	39th	12	0
10th	41	2	40th	11	0
11th	40	3	41st	10	0
12th	39	1	42nd	9	0
13th	38	0	43rd	8	0
14th	37	0	44th	7	0
15th	36	0	45th	6	0
16th	35	0	46th	5	0
17th	34	0	47th	4	0
18th	33	0	48th	3	0
19th	32	0	49th	2	0
20th	31	0	50th	1	0
21st	30	1	Not on List	0	0
22nd	29	0			
23rd	28	0			
24th	27	0			
25th	26	0			
26th	25	0			
27th	24	0			
28th	23	0			
29th	22	0			
30th	21	0			

TOP 10 VOTES	95
2ND 10 VOTES	4
3RD 10 VOTES	1
4TH 10 VOTES	0
5TH 10 VOTES	0
TOTAL VOTES	100
TOTAL POINTS	4623.5

▼ **TEAM**
Sixers

▼ **YEARS PLAYED**
1977–1987

▼ **POSITION**
Forward

In the summer of 1976, the ABA folded after nine years, and four of its teams, including the New York Nets, joined the NBA. Because of financial difficulties, the Nets' best player was expendable, and in October, the Sixers brass jumped at the opportunity to purchase his contract. The player's name: Julius Erving. Over the next 11 years, Dr. J. dazzled Philly fans as he led them to a winning season and berth in the playoffs every year, which included four trips to the NBA finals and the cherished 1983 championship.

Football, of course, is Merrill Reese's sport, but he ranked Doc second overall, higher than any Eagle. "He was in a league of his own. He was a dominating player who took over games. And he was a spectacular performer who defied gravity." Nine people put Julius at the top of their list, and they had nothing but praise for number 6. "He was the centerpiece of the Sixers" (Jim Robinson). "He brought the game to a new level by playing above the rim" (Fred Warren). "He never had an off day" (Mike Rad). "He was an ambassador to basketball" (Frank Minch). "He was out of this world. No other Philadelphia athlete did the things he could do" (Paul Troy).

But even the legendary Dr. J., first-ballot Hall of Famer, perennial All-Star and league MVP, whose number was retired by the Sixers, did not escape criticism from the voters. "He was very exciting," acknowledged Mark Eckel, "but he was not a complete player. He was an average shooter and average defensively." Erving squeaked into Mark's top 10 at tenth. Tom Walter (seventh) and Rob Neducsin (eighth) downgraded Dr. J. somewhat because they didn't think he was dominant enough. "He was a fantastic player, but he did not dominate a game like Lefty [Carlton] or Parent," opined Rob. Tom added, "As good as Doc was with the Sixers, he was not as dominant in the NBA as he was when he was playing for the Nets in the ABA." Fred Schumacher's comments about Julius were the harshest. "He was a 'one-trick pony.' He played less defense than Iverson. He was more of a showman than a basketball player."

Year	Team	Lg	G	Min	FGM	FGA	FGP	FTM	FTA	FTP	AST	REB	Pts	PPG
1973–74	N.Y. Nets	ABA	84	3398	914	1785	.512	454	593	.766	434	899	2299	27.4
1974–75	N.Y. Nets	ABA	84	3402	914	1806	.506	486	608	.799	462	914	2343	27.9
1975–76	N.Y. Nets	ABA	84	3244	949	1873	.507	530	662	.801	423	925	2462	29.3
1976–77	Sixers	NBA	82	2940	685	1373	.499	400	515	.777	306	695	1770	21.6
1977–78	Sixers	NBA	74	2429	611	1217	.502	306	362	.845	279	481	1528	20.6
1978–79	Sixers	NBA	78	2802	715	1455	.491	373	501	.745	357	564	1803	23.1
1979–80	Sixers	NBA	78	2812	838	1614	.519	420	534	.787	355	576	2100	26.9
1980–81	Sixers	NBA	82	2874	794	1524	.521	422	536	.787	364	657	2014	24.6
1981–82	Sixers	NBA	81	2789	780	1428	.546	411	539	.763	319	557	1974	24.4
1982–83	Sixers	NBA	72	2421	605	1170	.517	330	435	.759	263	491	1542	21.4
1983–84	Sixers	NBA	77	2683	678	1324	.512	364	483	.754	309	532	1727	22.4
1984–85	Sixers	NBA	78	2535	610	1236	.494	338	442	.765	233	414	1561	20.0
1985–86	Sixers	NBA	74	2474	521	1085	.480	289	368	.785	248	370	1340	18.1
1986–87	Sixers	NBA	60	1918	400	850	.471	191	235	.813	191	264	1005	16.8
Sixers Totals			836	28677	7237	14276	.507	3844	4950	.777	3224	5601	18364	22.0
Career Totals			1243	45227	11818	23370	.506	6256	8052	.777	5176	10525	30026	24.2

ABA All-Star (1972–76)
ABA MVP (1974–76); ABA co-MVP (1975)
ABA Playoffs MVP (1974, 1976)
Member of ABA Champions (1974, 1976)
NBA All-Star (1977–87)
NBA MVP (1981)
Member of NBA Champions (1983)
Number 32 retired by Nets; number 6 retired by Sixers
Basketball Hall of Fame (1993)

4 Steve Carlton

RANK	POINTS	VOTES RECEIVED
1st	50	7
2nd	49	3
3rd	48	21
4th	47	12
5th	46	19
6th	45	15
7th	44	5
8th	43	6
9th	42	5
10th	41	3
11th	40	1
12th	39	0
13th	38	1
14th	37	1
15th	36	0
16th	35	0
17th	34	0
18th	33	1
19th	32	0
20th	31	0
21st	30	0
22nd	29	0
23rd	28	0
24th	27	0
25th	26	0
26th	25	0
27th	24	0
28th	23	0
29th	22	0
30th	21	0

RANK	POINTS	VOTES RECEIVED
31st	20	0
32nd	19	0
33rd	18	0
34th	17	0
35th	16	0
36th	15	0
37th	14	0
38th	13	0
39th	12	0
40th	11	0
41st	10	0
42nd	9	0
43rd	8	0
44th	7	0
45th	6	0
46th	5	0
47th	4	0
48th	3	0
49th	2	0
50th	1	0
Not on List	0	0

TOP 10 VOTES	96
2ND 10 VOTES	4
3RD 10 VOTES	0
4TH 10 VOTES	0
5TH 10 VOTES	0
TOTAL VOTES	100
TOTAL POINTS	4587

▼ TEAM
Phillies

▼ YEARS PLAYED
1972–1986

▼ POSITION
Pitcher

The Phillies have fielded some hapless teams over the last half-century, but the 1972 squad was among the worst. With a starting rotation that included Ken Reynolds (2-15), Billy Champion (4-14) and Woody Fryman (4-10), the Phils stumbled to a 59-97 last-place finish; in games in which their ace, Steve Carlton, did not get a decision, the Phillies were a wretched 32-87, rivaling the '62 Mets for futility. But as Mike DiColla said, on days when "Super Steve" took the ball, the '72 Phillies were a "World Series team." Carlton, who had been acquired in the off-season from the Cardinals in a trade for Rick Wise, went 27-10, and during one torrid stretch over the summer, he won 15 straight games. Lefty won his first of four Cy Young Awards in '72, which he captured during his outstanding 15-year career with the Phillies.

Bob Anderson explained why he chose Carlton first. "He redeemed the Phillies. Take him away and they would have continued to flounder. He carried the franchise. No other Philadelphia athlete was as significant for that long a period of time. He made others around him better; Wilt did not. Palmer and Seaver were great; Carlton was intimidating." Doug Brown also went with the big lefthander as his top pick and offered this in support: "He brought the team up two notches whenever he pitched. He was one of the best pitchers of all time." He was, no doubt. Among pitchers who started their careers after 1900, Carlton ranks sixth with 329 wins. Carlton's ability to dominate also earned him a first-place vote from Rob Neducsin. "When Steve was on, the Phillies would not lose." Rob's friend Paul Lightkep focused on the intangibles: "He was a great competitor; he had an incredible workout routine. He kept himself in top mental and physical shape."

But like his teammate Mike Schmidt, Carlton lost some points in the popularity and personality department. "He was detached" (Merrill Reese). "He never talked to anybody" (Joe Geier). "He kept to himself—other players did more for the city than he did" (Frank

Minch). Carlton's attitude incensed Bob Bookbinder so much that he ranked Steve 18th despite his outstanding accomplishments as a pitcher. "His attitude took some of the fun out of watching him."

Michael Barkann downgraded Carlton for a different reason: "As a starting pitcher who played every fourth or fifth day, he was not as good an all-around athlete as other players such as Wilt Chamberlain and Mike Schmidt."

One of my favorite baseball memories was witnessing Steve Carlton throw his 3000th strikeout. It occurred on April 29, 1981, a Wednesday night, and even better a school night (not to mention my brother's birthday). It was a year in which my brothers and I were still heavy into baseball cards, and with the introduction of competition to Topps a year earlier, there were plenty of cards to collect. That said, the cards in those times were our means of getting year-end stats. We used the cards to rate and judge players. Maybe someone in the neighborhood had a *Baseball Digest* that featured the season-ending stats, but it was the cards that told the story for us. As the 1980 season ended, both Carlton and Tom Seaver were in a heat to get to 3000 first. Both were roughly under 30 strikeouts away to reach that magic plateau, Seaver maybe closer. We wanted Carlton to get there first—obviously.

As the 1981 season began, Carlton chipped away, getting closer to the mark in his first three games. He seemed to be on fire the beginning of that season. Seaver reached 3000 a week earlier (unfortunately for us), while Carlton was within a game's reach.

My dad was onto this and was able to get tickets to Carlton's next game, a game where we *knew* he'd break the record (the folks at the Vet had the same amount of confidence as well, as you'll read in a second). He took my brothers and me to see the Phillies play the Montreal Expos at the Vet on April 29, 1981. Steve Carlton versus Steve Rogers. Lefty needed just three strikeouts—that's all that mattered. Everyone in the crowd knew it, there was no doubt. As Carlton came to the mound to start the game, the crowd went absolutely nuts, screaming and cheering. Everyone was there to see history be made, but not just history, rather another achievement toward Carlton's long-deserved lock into the Hall of Fame. He had been the pitcher so closely branded to the Phillies during that era. He was "pitching excellence" on a team that had rarely had such a pitching asset. Tim Raines, the Expos' fast-running lead-off batter, came to the plate and quickly became strikeout number 2998. Jerry Manual was the second batter and number 2999. The stadium seemed like it was shaking with the crowd cheering so loudly. It seemed like Carlton was feeding off of the crowd, which was awesome, especially when it seemed so unlike Lefty to do so. Tim Wallach, batter number three, became Carlton's 3000th. That was it—one, two, three. The crowd erupted. It sounded like thunder within the Vet. It was the strangest thing—it was so loud you could not hear a thing for the cheering. Deafening. I am sure anyone who has been at the Vet, or anywhere for that matter, to see something similar can relate. It was not difficult for Carlton to get 30,000 fans so pumped up. It had to be a solid five minutes of cheering (as I remember) as he made his way back to the dugout. What I can't remember, but seem to want to recall, was that in those three strikeouts, he may have only thrown nine pitches, and it may have been just that that really threw the crowd into a screaming frenzy. I also think that in the second inning he struck out another three in a row. The crowd was still going crazy with excitement.

Later in the game, around the sixth or seventh inning, workers at the Vet came down each row and handed out preprinted light red and white certificates. They had Carlton's picture on them, with the date of the game, and stated that we witnessed his 3000th strikeout. It is a keepsake that I still have today. The Phillies management knew, the team knew and the crowd knew that April 29, 1981 was going to be the day that Carlton threw his 3000th strikeout! He did not let us down. He finished the game with nine strikeouts, still on fire—Lefty style. But what a first inning! One I will never forget!

—DAVE BRISTOWE

Year	Team	Lg	G	W	L	CG	SH	IP	H	BB	SO	ER	ERA
1965	St. Louis	N.L.	15	0	0	0	0	25	27	8	21	7	2.52
1966	St. Louis	N.L.	9	3	3	2	1	52	56	18	25	18	3.12
1967	St. Louis	N.L.	30	14	9	11	2	193	173	62	168	64	2.98
1968	St. Louis	N.L.	34	13	11	10	5	232	214	61	162	77	2.99
1969	St. Louis	N.L.	31	17	11	12	2	236	185	93	210	57	2.17
1970	St. Louis	N.L.	34	10	19	13	2	254	239	109	193	105	3.72
1971	St. Louis	N.L.	37	20	9	16	4	273	275	98	172	108	3.56
1972	Phillies	N.L.	41	27	10	30	8	346	257	87	310	76	1.98
1973	Phillies	N.L.	40	13	20	18	3	293	293	113	223	127	3.90
1974	Phillies	N.L.	39	16	13	17	1	291	249	136	240	104	3.22
1975	Phillies	N.L.	37	15	14	14	3	255	217	104	192	101	3.56
1976	Phillies	N.L.	35	20	7	13	2	253	224	72	195	88	3.13
1977	Phillies	N.L.	36	23	10	17	2	283	229	89	198	83	2.64
1978	Phillies	N.L.	34	16	13	12	3	247	228	63	161	78	2.84
1979	Phillies	N.L.	35	18	11	13	4	251	202	89	213	101	3.62
1980	Phillies	N.L.	38	24	9	13	3	304	243	90	286	79	2.34
1981	Phillies	N.L.	24	13	4	10	1	190	152	62	179	51	2.42
1982	Phillies	N.L.	38	23	11	19	6	295.2	253	86	286	102	3.10
1983	Phillies	N.L.	37	15	16	8	3	283.2	277	84	275	98	3.11
1984	Phillies	N.L.	33	13	7	1	0	229	214	79	163	91	3.58
1985	Phillies	N.L.	16	1	8	0	0	92	84	53	48	34	3.33
1986	Phillies	N.L.	16	4	8	0	0	83	102	45	62	57	6.18
1986	San Francisco	N.L.	6	1	3	0	0	30	36	16	18	17	5.10
1986	Chisox	A.L.	10	4	3	0	0	63.1	58	25	40	26	3.69
1987	Cle.-Minn.	A.L.	32	6	14	3	0	152	165	86	91	97	5.74
1988	Minnesota	A.L.	4	0	1	0	0	9.2	20	5	5	18	16.76
Phillies Totals			499	241	161	185	39	3696	3224	1252	3031	1270	3.09
Career Totals			741	329	244	252	55	5216	4672	1833	4136	1864	3.22

National League All-Star (1968–69, 1971–72, 1974, 1977, 1979–82)
National Cy Young Award (1972, 1977, 1980, 1982)
Member of World Champions (1967, 1980)
Number 32 retired by Phillies
Baseball Hall of Fame (1994)

5 Bobby Clarke

RANK	POINTS	VOTES RECEIVED		RANK	POINTS	VOTES RECEIVED
1st	50	8		31st	20	0
2nd	49	8		32nd	19	0
3rd	48	15		33rd	18	0
4th	47	19		34th	17	0
5th	46	16		35th	16	0
6th	45	13		36th	15	0
7th	44	4		37th	14	0
8th	43	6		38th	13	0
9th	42	0		39th	12	0
10th	41	2		40th	11	0
11th	40	3		41st	10	0
12th	39	1		42nd	9	0
13th	38	0		43rd	8	0
14th	37	1		44th	7	0
15th	36	0		45th	6	0
16th	35	0		46th	5	0
17th	34	0		47th	4	0
18th	33	1		48th	3	0
19th	32	0		49th	2	1
20th	31	0		50th	1	0
21st	30	0		Not on List	0	1
22nd	29	0				
23rd	28	0				
24th	27	0		TOP 10 VOTES		91
25th	26	0		2ND 10 VOTES		6
26th	25	0		3RD 10 VOTES		1
27th	24	0		4TH 10 VOTES		0
28th	23	0		5TH 10 VOTES		1
29th	22	0		TOTAL VOTES		99
30th	21	1		TOTAL POINTS		4494

▼ **TEAM**
Flyers

▼ **YEARS PLAYED**
1970–1984

▼ **POSITION**
Center

As summer wound down in 1973, things were looking mighty bleak for Philadelphia sports fans. The Sixers had completed a wretched 9-73 season in the spring. The Phillies were putting the finishing touches on their third straight season in the basement, and the Eagles were going nowhere, about to stumble to their 11th losing season out of the previous 12. But there was hope. The Flyers, a first-year expansion team just a few years earlier, were on the rise. In the 1972-73 season, they finished second in the Western Division and then beat Minnesota in the quarterfinals, before falling to Montreal in the semifinals. They headed into the 1973-74 season with high expectations. As Wayne Smith aptly stated, "The Flyers stepped up when the city needed it." Indeed, the "Broad Street Bullies" captivated Philadelphia fans by winning back-to-back Stanley Cups in 1974 and 1975.

In the opinion of seven voters, Clarke's integral role in the Cup-winning years and his outstanding 15-year career with the Flyers earned him the number one slot. John Surbeck summed up Clarkie succinctly: "He was the ultimate leader and team player." Dave Beck provided this reasoning in support of his pick: "Philly is a 'blue collar' city. Those glory years of the Flyers were among Philadelphia's best and since Clarke spent his entire career here and was the heart and soul of the team, I went with him." Glenn Young's rationale: "Bobby Clarke was on another level than everyone else. How many other Philadelphia athletes led their team to consecutive championships?" (No Philly team, of course, has won consecutive championships since; the last team to do it before the Flyers was the Eagles, led by Pete Pihos and Steve Van Buren, who won it all in 1948 and 1949.) It wasn't just that Clarke was a winner, Glenn stressed; it was how he won. "He was small, sickly, gasping for air, toothless, but totally tough and seemingly willing to literally risk killing himself to help his team win." Joe Fee placed much importance on Clarke's winning three MVPs in four years; Chamberlain is the only other Philadelphia athlete who has accomplished this feat.

Bryan Davis praised Clarke's superb leadership skills and added another key point: "Wilt, Bednarik and some others were born to be pro athletes. Clarke was a skinny kid from Flin Flon with diabetes." Bryan gave Clarke high marks for *not* being a great natural athlete, but through hard work and tenacity, he became a great hockey player. On the other hand, Paul Lightkep's decision to exclude Clarke from his list was based largely on Clarke's not being superior athletically. "I considered athleticism high when I picked my top 50. I didn't think much of Clarke as an athlete. He succeeded mainly because he was a dirty player. If I were picking a role model for my kids, it wouldn't be Clarke." Paul's dislike of Clarke became more intense with his handling of Eric Lindros' situation. "Clarke and the Flyers ruined Lindros. They tried to make him into a leader when he wasn't cut out to be one."

Year	Team	Lg	Gm	G	A	Pts	PM
1971–72	Flyers	NHL	78	35	46	81	87
1972–73	Flyers	NHL	78	37	67	104	80
1973–74	Flyers	NHL	77	35	52	87	113
1974–75	Flyers	NHL	80	27	89	116	125
1975–76	Flyers	NHL	76	30	89	119	136
1976–77	Flyers	NHL	80	27	63	90	71
1977–78	Flyers	NHL	71	21	68	89	83
1978–79	Flyers	NHL	80	16	57	73	68
1979–80	Flyers	NHL	76	12	57	69	65
1980–81	Flyers	NHL	80	19	46	65	140
1981–82	Flyers	NHL	62	17	46	63	154
1982–83	Flyers	NHL	80	23	62	85	115
1983–84	Flyers	NHL	73	17	43	60	70
	Flyers Totals		1144	358	852	1210	1453
	Career Totals		1144	358	852	1210	1453

NHL All-Star (1970–75, 1977–79)
NHL MVP (1973, 1975–76)
Member of Stanley Cup Champions (1974–75)
Number 16 retired by Flyers
Hockey Hall of Fame (1987)

6 Bernie Parent

RANK	POINTS	VOTES RECEIVED		RANK	POINTS	VOTES RECEIVED
1st	50	1		31st	20	0
2nd	49	4		32nd	19	0
3rd	48	6		33rd	18	0
4th	47	7		34th	17	1
5th	46	6		35th	16	0
6th	45	6		36th	15	0
7th	44	11		37th	14	0
8th	43	12		38th	13	0
9th	42	10		39th	12	1
10th	41	8		40th	11	0
11th	40	3		41st	10	0
12th	39	3		42nd	9	0
13th	38	3		43rd	8	0
14th	37	2		44th	7	0
15th	36	1		45th	6	0
16th	35	2		46th	5	0
17th	34	1		47th	4	0
18th	33	1		48th	3	0
19th	32	2		49th	2	0
20th	31	1		50th	1	0
21st	30	1		Not on List	0	1
22nd	29	2				
23rd	28	0				
24th	27	2				
25th	26	0				
26th	25	2				
27th	24	0				
28th	23	0				
29th	22	0				
30th	21	0				

TOP 10 VOTES	71
2ND 10 VOTES	19
3RD 10 VOTES	7
4TH 10 VOTES	2
5TH 10 VOTES	0
TOTAL VOTES	99
TOTAL POINTS	4071

▼ **TEAM**
Flyers

▼ **YEARS PLAYED**
1968–1971, 1974–1979

▼ **POSITION**
Goalie

Since the 1950s, winning back-to-back world championships has been accomplished dozens of times by teams throughout the country in the four major sports. Philly fans don't like to admit it, but only one of those teams hailed from Philadelphia. In describing Bernie Parent's role in the Flyers' winning consecutive Stanley Cups, Michael Brophy made a compelling argument to support his first-place vote for Bernie: "If the ultimate measure of a professional athlete's success is winning championships, then I select Bernie Parent as the greatest professional athlete to play in Philadelphia. In a city starved for championships, athletes who have won them should be given the greatest consideration. The four major sports are all team sports; even Steve Carlton could only account for one-fifth of the Phillies' successes from the 1970s and 1980s. The great Dr. J. was one part of a great team. In hockey, especially playoff hockey, goaltending is, and has always been, the key to winning. In hockey, the goalie stands alone, every night. By the nature of his position, Bernie Parent can be given more credit than any other athlete for bringing two world championships to Philadelphia. TWO! And world championships remain the ultimate measure of greatness in sports."

Bernie also earned some second-place votes from those who completed the survey, including Andy Salayda, Ken Miller and Bill Jakavick, each of whom described Parent as the most critical member of the Flyers' Cup-winning teams. Bill: "He had more impact in the big picture than Bobby Clarke. If you put Clarke on another team, he wouldn't have made as much of a difference as Bernie did." Rob Neduscin and John Mitchell also voted Parent number two. Rob emphasized Bernie's ability to dominate: "When he was on, the Flyers wouldn't lose." John said that Parent's postseason goaltending is some of the best he has ever seen. In the 1974 and 1975 postseasons, Bernie was 22-10 with six shutouts (including the clinching game of the finals both years) and a 1.96 goals against average.

Mark Voigt's rationale for not including Bernie on his list was interesting: "I consider goalies sort of one-dimensional players like designated hitters or kickers." Chuck Wolf acknowledged Parent's greatness as a goalie, but Chuck puts a lot of stock in what a player does away from the game, and he felt that Bernie needed more civic leadership and charitable appearances to be higher on his list. Bernie battled some major injuries: a back injury which required surgery and forced him to miss most of the 1976 season, and an eye injury in 1979 which ended his career at the age of 33. His second tour of duty with the Flyers was limited to less than six full seasons. Bernie lost some points from John Senkow and Jim Robinson because his career was not longer.

Year	Team	Lg	Gm	W	L	T	Sh	Avg
1965–66	Boston	NHL	39	11	20	3	1	3.69
1966–67	Boston	NHL	18	4	12	2	0	3.64
1967–68	Flyers	NHL	38	16	17	5	4	2.48
1968–69	Flyers	NHL	58	17	23	16	1	2.69
1969–70	Flyers	NHL	62	13	29	20	3	2.79
1970–71	Flyers	NHL	30	9	12	6	2	2.76
1970–71	Toronto	NHL	18	7	7	3	0	2.65
1971–72	Toronto	NHL	47	17	18	9	3	2.56
1973–74	Flyers	NHL	73	47	13	12	12	1.89
1974–75	Flyers	NHL	68	44	14	10	12	2.03
1975–76	Flyers	NHL	11	6	2	3	0	2.34
1976–77	Flyers	NHL	61	35	13	12	5	2.71
1977–78	Flyers	NHL	49	29	6	13	7	2.22
1978–79	Flyers	NHL	36	16	12	7	4	2.70
	Flyers Totals		486	232	141	104	50	2.42
	Career Totals		608	271	198	121	54	2.55

NHL All-Star (1970, 1974–75, 1977)
Vezina Trophy (1975); co-winner of Vezina Trophy (1974)
Conn Smythe Trophy (1974–75)
Member of Stanley Cup Champions (1974–75)
Number 1 retired by Flyers
Hockey Hall of Fame (1984)

Chuck Bednarik

RANK	POINTS	VOTES RECEIVED		RANK	POINTS	VOTES RECEIVED
1st	50	1		31st	20	0
2nd	49	8		32nd	19	0
3rd	48	8		33rd	18	0
4th	47	11		34th	17	0
5th	46	6		35th	16	0
6th	45	7		36th	15	0
7th	44	5		37th	14	0
8th	43	9		38th	13	0
9th	42	6		39th	12	0
10th	41	6		40th	11	1
11th	40	6		41st	10	0
12th	39	4		42nd	9	0
13th	38	2		43rd	8	0
14th	37	3		44th	7	0
15th	36	0		45th	6	0
16th	35	2		46th	5	0
17th	34	3		47th	4	0
18th	33	0		48th	3	0
19th	32	0		49th	2	0
20th	31	1		50th	1	0
21st	30	1		Not on List	0	6
22nd	29	0				
23rd	28	2				
24th	27	0		TOP 10 VOTES		67
25th	26	0		2ND 10 VOTES		21
26th	25	1		3RD 10 VOTES		5
27th	24	1		4TH 10 VOTES		1
28th	23	0		5TH 10 VOTES		0
29th	22	0		TOTAL VOTES		94
30th	21	0		TOTAL POINTS		3981

▼ TEAM
Eagles

▼ YEARS PLAYED
1949–1962

▼ POSITION
Linebacker/Center

Since his retirement from football, Chuck Bednarik has become cynical and bitter, scoffing at players of this generation who have made millions, but in his view, don't play the game with the skill and tenacity that he did. Bednarik's biggest supporter in the survey, Fred Schumacher, the only voter to rank "Concrete Charlie" first, felt the same way. "He was a real football player who played both ways and always gave it his all. There have been better centers and better linebackers, but none who played both ways. Besides, he put that hated Giant [Frank Gifford] out for awhile, didn't he?" Yes, he did. In a key game in the 1960 championship season, Bednarik buried Gifford with a hit, which gave the future *Monday Night Football* broadcaster a concussion and knocked him out for the season. Gifford did not return to the NFL until 1962. That famous play, as Jim Angelichio put it, is "the stuff of Eagles legend." "Bednarik embodied the heart and soul of Philadelphia sports," said Jim. "When I think of Philadelphia Eagles football, he is one of the first people that comes to mind. Local guy. University of Pennsylvania. Hard-nosed. Played both ways." Adam Kimelman ranked Bednarik second and summed him up with three adjectives: mean, tough and durable. Neil Goldstein, who like Fred Schumacher is from the old school, said of number 60: "He had guts that today's players don't have. Today's players may be faster than Bednarik, but he was better."

In ranking Bednarik second only to Wilt, Ray Didinger mentioned the big hit on Gifford, noting that he forced a fumble, helping the Eagles beat the Giants 17-10, and improve their record to 7-1. Ray talked about some of Bednarik's career accomplishments—he played 14 seasons, a lot both ways, and was the best in the league at two positions. But he focused a lot on the memorable 1960 season and Bednarik's enormous contribution to the Birds' title. "He was the oldest man on the team (35), playing 58 minutes per game. [In addition to the big hit on Gifford], he knocked Paul Hornung out of the Championship Game, and made the legendary stop on Jim Taylor at the end of the game." (Ray attended that game, which he eloquently describes below.)

But was Bednarik one of those rare athletes who was "larger than life"? Jim Rosen didn't think so. Among Philadelphia athletes, he believed that only Chamberlain belongs in that very exclusive category.

Although Bednarik made attempts to smooth things over with the Eagles organization in 2006, for years he harbored ill-will toward his old team. Mike Koob moved him down several notches because of his attitude. "He had a chip on his shoulder. He disavowed himself to the Eagles."

For most Philadelphians—and certainly for me—1960 was the year Christmas Day felt like Christmas Eve. That's because the Eagles played Green Bay for the NFL Championship on Monday, December 26th, so we opened our presents and ate our turkey on the 25th as usual, but we were really looking forward to making the trip to Franklin Field the next day. Whatever Santa Claus delivered, it could not compare to what the Eagles delivered in their 17-13 win over the Packers. I was 14 years old, a high school freshman, sitting with my parents and grandparents in Section EE, behind the end zone. We were season ticket holders, so we sat there for every home game, but I never experienced anything like the energy in Franklin Field that day. They installed temporary bleachers on the track, which boosted the official capacity to 67,325, but there were more than a few gate crashers. I know because in our row we were jammed together like rush-hour commuters on the Market Street Subway.

My two most vivid memories were plays that happened right in front of me. The first was Tommy McDonald, my favorite player, catching a touchdown pass from Norm Van Brocklin and tumbling into a snowbank behind the end zone. The second was the great Chuck Bednarik tackling Jim Taylor at the eight-yard line and pinning him to the turf as the final seconds ticked away. In the 60th minute of play, number 60 brought down the curtain on the Eagles' last NFL championship. It was both fitting and unforgettable.

—RAY DIDINGER

Year	Team	Lg	G	Int	Yds	TD
1949	Eagles	NFL	10	0	0	0
1950	Eagles	NFL	12	1	9	0
1951	Eagles	NFL	12	0	0	0
1952	Eagles	NFL	12	2	14	0
1953	Eagles	NFL	12	6	116	1
1954	Eagles	NFL	12	1	9	0
1955	Eagles	NFL	12	1	36	0
1956	Eagles	NFL	12	2	0	0
1957	Eagles	NFL	11	3	51	0
1958	Eagles	NFL	12	0	0	0
1959	Eagles	NFL	12	0	0	0
1960	Eagles	NFL	12	2	0	0
1961	Eagles	NFL	14	2	33	0
1962	Eagles	NFL	14	0	0	0
	Eagles Totals		169	20	268	1
	Career Totals		169	20	268	1

Pro Bowl (1950–57, 1960)
Member of NFL Champions (1949, 1960)
Number 60 retired by Eagles
Pro Football Hall of Fame (1967)

8 ▶ Reggie White

RANK	POINTS	VOTES RECEIVED
1st	50	1
2nd	49	7
3rd	48	3
4th	47	8
5th	46	6
6th	45	12
7th	44	7
8th	43	9
9th	42	8
10th	41	2
11th	40	2
12th	39	4
13th	38	6
14th	37	3
15th	36	1
16th	35	3
17th	34	0
18th	33	0
19th	32	0
20th	31	1
21st	30	0
22nd	29	2
23rd	28	2
24th	27	0
25th	26	0
26th	25	1
27th	24	1
28th	23	1
29th	22	1
30th	21	3

RANK	POINTS	VOTES RECEIVED
31st	20	0
32nd	19	0
33rd	18	0
34th	17	0
35th	16	2
36th	15	0
37th	14	0
38th	13	1
39th	12	0
40th	11	0
41st	10	1
42nd	9	0
43rd	8	0
44th	7	0
45th	6	0
46th	5	1
47th	4	0
48th	3	0
49th	2	0
50th	1	0
Not on List	0	1

TOP 10 VOTES	63
2ND 10 VOTES	20
3RD 10 VOTES	11
4TH 10 VOTES	3
5TH 10 VOTES	2
TOTAL VOTES	99
TOTAL POINTS	3920

▼ **TEAM**
Eagles

▼ **YEARS PLAYED**
1985–1992

▼ **POSITION**
Defensive End

Reggie White was an awesome force on the Eagles' defensive line, starting in 1985, Marion Campbell's last year as the Birds' head coach, through Buddy Ryan's turbulent five-year reign, and extending two years into Rich Kotite's four-year run as coach. After playing eight seasons with the Eagles, Reggie then signed with the Packers as a free-agent, and that decision did not sit well with many of the Philly faithful. Rob Neducsin was so incensed that he chose not to include White on his list. "His leaving Philadelphia because God told him to left a very bad taste in my mouth." Rob added, "I think he benefited from the Eagles' style of defense as well as all the other good players around him." Bryan Davis, who acknowledged Reggie's greatness, would have ranked "the Minister of Defense" much higher than 35th had it not been for the circumstances under which he left. "He was a traitor," fumed Bryan. "He left for the money."

Jody McDonald had a different take on White's signing with the Packers. "Reggie didn't screw the Eagles. Norman Braman [the Eagles' owner at the time] never made Reggie an offer because he didn't think Reggie would accept it. The Packers made him an offer, and he accepted." Jody ranked White fourth, hailing him as the best defensive end in NFL history. Mark Eckel and Merrill Reese ranked Reggie second and third, respectively. "He was the greatest player I've ever covered, offense or defense," said Mark. "He dominated a game like no other player. It was actually a story in a game in which Reggie did *not* get a sack." Merrill had similar praise for the Hall of Famer. "He changed how offenses had to play. They had to be aware of where Reggie was on every single snap. It took a good part of the week of the offensive coordinator [for the Eagles' upcoming opponent] to figure out how to cope with Reggie."

It was Reggie's ability to dominate a game that earned him high marks from many others, most notably football fanatic Dave Myers, who gave Reggie his only first-place vote. "Year in and year out, he was the best, most dominant defensive lineman in the NFL. His 'body of work' for the Eagles was incredible. He played hurt. He made his other teammates better." Dave framed his final point in the form of a question: "Can you name me a more well-respected player than Reggie White?" (Editor's note: How about T.O.?) Rob Betts, who placed only Chamberlain ahead of White, noted, "He was a more dominant player than Schmidt, Carlton or Dr. J."

While most voters focused on either White's dominance in ranking him high or his exit to Green Bay in ranking him low, Andy Paul, who rated Reggie 27th, had a different perspective. "He didn't make as strong an impression on Philadelphia fans as other superstars. He made more of an impression on Packers fans and did more for the Packers than for the Eagles." It's hard to argue with Andy's last point: he and Brett Favre led the Pack to a Super Bowl victory in the '96 season, but the Birds won a lone playoff game during Reggie's eight years in town. Dave Myers, though, quickly came to Reggie's defense. "You can't blame him that the Eagles didn't make it to the Super Bowl."

Year	Team	Lg	G	Int	Yds	TD	Sacks
1986	Eagles	NFL	16	0	0	0	18
1987	Eagles	NFL	12	0	0	1	21
1988	Eagles	NFL	16	0	0	0	18
1989	Eagles	NFL	16	0	0	0	11
1990	Eagles	NFL	16	1	33	0	14
1991	Eagles	NFL	16	1	0	0	15
1992	Eagles	NFL	16	0	0	1	14
1993	Green Bay	NFL	16	0	0	0	13
1994	Green Bay	NFL	16	0	0	0	8
1995	Green Bay	NFL	15	0	0	0	12
1996	Green Bay	NFL	16	1	0	0	8.5
1997	Green Bay	NFL	16	0	0	0	11
1998	Green Bay	NFL	16	0	0	0	16
2000	Carolina	NFL	16	0	0	0	5.5
	Eagles Totals		121	2	33	2	124
	Career Totals		232	3	33	2	198

NFL Pro Bowl (1986–98)
Member of NFL Champions (1996)
Number 92 retired by Eagles and Packers
Pro Football Hall of Fame (2006)

9

Richie Ashburn

RANK	POINTS	VOTES RECEIVED
1st	50	1
2nd	49	0
3rd	48	2.5
4th	47	2.5
5th	46	3
6th	45	5
7th	44	10
8th	43	8
9th	42	7
10th	41	11
11th	40	8
12th	39	5
13th	38	2
14th	37	5
15th	36	6
16th	35	4
17th	34	2
18th	33	2
19th	32	2
20th	31	1
21st	30	2
22nd	29	1
23rd	28	0
24th	27	0
25th	26	1
26th	25	1
27th	24	1
28th	23	0
29th	22	0
30th	21	1

RANK	POINTS	VOTES RECEIVED
31st	20	0
32nd	19	0
33rd	18	0
34th	17	1
35th	16	1
36th	15	0
37th	14	1
38th	13	1
39th	12	0
40th	11	0
41st	10	0
42nd	9	0
43rd	8	0
44th	7	0
45th	6	1
46th	5	0
47th	4	1
48th	3	0
49th	2	0
50th	1	0
Not on List	0	0

TOP 10 VOTES	50
2ND 10 VOTES	37
3RD 10 VOTES	7
4TH 10 VOTES	4
5TH 10 VOTES	2
TOTAL VOTES	100
TOTAL POINTS	3795.5

▼ TEAM
Phillies

▼ YEARS PLAYED
1948–1959

▼ POSITION
Outfielder

In 1995, more than 30 years after he retired, Richie "Whitey" Ashburn was elected to the Baseball Hall of Fame by the Veterans' Committee. Jon Grisdale, who voted his boyhood idol first, thought Whitey's Hall of Fame election was a long time coming. Jon insisted that Ashburn should have been a first-ballot Hall of Famer. "He would have been if he played in New York or Boston." Jon cited two key stats to support his argument that Whitey was one of the premier players of his time: "In the 1950s [the Golden Era of baseball, according to Jon], he had the most putouts and hits of any player." Jon remembered Ashburn playing a shallow center field, but because he was so fast, he could track down balls over his head. Jon also recalled Ashburn saying that he never went into a slump because he could always bunt for a base hit. That brings to mind Ashburn's classic response when Harry Kalas asked "His Whiteness" during a broadcast who was the best bunter he ever saw. Ashburn's matter-of-fact answer: "Me. I beat out 35 bunts one year."

Terry Bickhart also thought that Ashburn should have made it to Cooperstown sooner. "He was very smooth with his hitting, fielding and base running. He had style. He was better defensively than Maddox or Dykstra. He was underappreciated; he was overshadowed by Mantle, Aaron and Mays. He epitomized Philadelphia."

Other voters gave Whitey similar accolades. "He came to play every day—and he didn't do it for the money or glory" (Bob Chazin). "He was an underrated center fielder. He just bled Philadelphia" (Jim Robinson). "He was a champion on and off the field" (Chuck Wolf).

Jim Angelichio fondly recalled Ashburn playing great defense in center field and slapping the ball all over the park and in so doing always contending for the batting title. He won two National League batting titles and finished second to the Cardinals' great Stan Musial twice.

The eminently likable Ashburn was the subject of some criticism. Jerry McDonough bumped him a few notches because his arm was not first-rate and he didn't have much power. (He never hit more than four home runs in a season for the Phillies.) John Bergmann thought Ashburn was overrated. "He was a very nice player, but not great and not someone who could carry a team." Jeff Skow went into considerable detail explaining why he ranked Ashburn 20th, lower than almost all of the voters. "His stats are good and I am not knocking him, but the guys in front of him [on my list] were not only great Philadelphia athletes, but well-documented super stars in their sport. I ranked dominance ahead of consistency or likability. Ashburn's name would never come up in a discussion of the giants of his sport. He didn't get into the Hall of Fame until 30 [actually 33] years after his retirement. The 19 guys [I] ranked ahead of him, with the exception of Eric Lindros, went to the Hall with ease, should be in the Hall (Rose) or are shoo-ins when eligible [such as Iverson]. Whitey well represented the city but his likability in my opinion swayed people over performance. The other factor is he never played on a championship team."

There are many great baseball stories Rich Ashburn used to tell, but here are two in which I participated.

Having been a position player, Whitey never cared much for pitchers. One of his great lines was, "I'd never let my daughter marry a pitcher!" One night Whitey was on an especially severe rant about how dumb pitchers are and how he didn't trust any of them. "I don't know a pitcher I like," he said. Knowing they were actually close friends, I said, "Whitey, how about Robin Roberts?" He snapped, "I'm not even too sure about him!"

Whitey always taped his pregame radio interview. One day in San Francisco, he went to the Giants' booth and asked Hank Greenwald, the Giants' announcer, to be his guest. Busy at the moment, Hank agreed to do it if Whitey would come back in half an hour. Thirty minutes later, Whitey returned with his recorder and began the show: "Hi everybody, this is Rich Ashburn on the Phillies' pregame show and my special guest today is . . . is," at which point he feigned a coughing fit, so much that he turned off the recorder and said he needed to get a cough drop. He came back to the Phillies' radio booth, turned to me and asked, "What's the name of the guy I'm interviewing? I can't remember!"

—ANDY MUSSER

Year	Team	Lg	G	AB	R	H	HR	RBI	SB	Avg	SLG
1948	Phillies	N.L.	117	463	78	154	2	40	32	.333	.400
1949	Phillies	N.L.	154	662	84	188	1	37	9	.284	.349
1950	Phillies	N.L.	151	594	84	180	2	41	14	.303	.402
1951	Phillies	N.L.	154	643	92	221	4	63	29	.344	.426
1952	Phillies	N.L.	154	613	93	173	1	42	16	.282	.357
1953	Phillies	N.L.	156	622	110	205	2	57	14	.330	.408
1954	Phillies	N.L.	153	559	111	175	1	41	11	.313	.376
1955	Phillies	N.L.	140	533	91	180	3	42	12	.338	.448
1956	Phillies	N.L.	154	628	94	190	3	50	10	.303	.384
1957	Phillies	N.L.	156	626	93	186	0	33	13	.297	.364
1958	Phillies	N.L.	152	615	98	215	2	33	30	.350	.441
1959	Phillies	N.L.	153	564	86	150	1	20	9	.266	.307
1960	Chi. Cubs	N.L.	151	547	99	159	0	40	16	.291	.338
1961	Chi. Cubs	N.L.	109	307	49	79	0	19	7	.257	.306
1962	N.Y. Mets	N.L.	135	389	60	119	7	28	12	.306	.393
Phillies Totals			1794	7122	1114	2217	22	499	199	.311	.388
Career Totals			2189	8365	1322	2574	29	586	234	.308	.382

National League All-Star (1948, 1951, 1953, 1958, 1962)
Number 1 retired by Phillies
Baseball Hall of Fame (1995)

10

Allen Iverson

RANK	POINTS	VOTES RECEIVED		RANK	POINTS	VOTES RECEIVED
1st	50	0		31st	20	1
2nd	49	3		32nd	19	0
3rd	48	0		33rd	18	1
4th	47	6		34th	17	1
5th	46	3		35th	16	0
6th	45	4		36th	15	0
7th	44	11		37th	14	1
8th	43	3		38th	13	0
9th	42	12		39th	12	0
10th	41	6		40th	11	2
11th	40	6		41st	10	0
12th	39	4		42nd	9	0
13th	38	5		43rd	8	0
14th	37	2		44th	7	0
15th	36	3		45th	6	0
16th	35	4		46th	5	0
17th	34	1		47th	4	0
18th	33	2		48th	3	0
19th	32	3		49th	2	0
20th	31	2		50th	1	0
21st	30	0		Not on List	0	6
22nd	29	0				
23rd	28	1				
24th	27	0		TOP 10 VOTES		48
25th	26	3		2ND 10 VOTES		32
26th	25	3		3RD 10 VOTES		8
27th	24	0		4TH 10 VOTES		6
28th	23	1		5TH 10 VOTES		0
29th	22	0		TOTAL VOTES		94
30th	21	0		TOTAL POINTS		3571

▼ TEAM
Sixers

▼ YEARS PLAYED
1997–2006

▼ POSITION
Guard

Since Charles Barkley left town in 1992, there has been a dearth of star-caliber players who have graced the Sixers' lineup. There is one very notable exception: future Hall of Famer Allen Iverson. Steve Kennedy, who ranked Iverson fourth, had these thoughts: "He revolutionized what we now know as the hip-hop movement in the NBA. A.I. won a league MVP, and has changed our idea of what a two-guard should or could be. Also, [he has won] scoring titles, All-Star Game MVPs....Why [did] the Sixers draw so well on the road [when Iverson was a Sixer]? The answer: 'The Answer.'"

Dave Bristowe explained why he picked Iverson second over Chamberlain, Erving and Barkley: "A.I. brings more character to the game than other Sixers—different than Barkley, Wilt and Julius. To me he seems more focused than [those three]. He seems more athletic in an overall sense, more intense, better overall and can hang in for the whole game. Disadvantaged by not having natural height like Dr. J. or Wilt, or natural leadership skills, he makes up for it with scrappiness, intensity, hustle, and a keep-up-with-me-attitude—150% of the time."

A few voters put Iverson near the top of their lists because of what he has accomplished despite being only 6'0". "He has Jordon's killer instincts without his size" (Brent Saunders). "He is unstoppable, so good despite being so small. He never had a great sidekick [with the Sixers]" (Michael Beirne). "He is amazing for his size—he looks 5'5" compared to the other players. He has to fight and battle the big guys" (Bob Chazin). "He delivers more excitement with less physical gifts [than Dr. J.], and he never had the supporting cast Dr. J. had [with the Sixers]" (Mark Voigt).

Ryan Kent also offered his ardent support for A.I.: "I will probably never see a better Sixer in my lifetime. Iverson, year in, year out, is in the top three in scoring, steals and minutes. He defines the word competitor. He battles through injuries like it is his job. You would have to shoot him in the leg in order for him to sit out a game. He plays with so much passion and heart every night. No one in the NBA wants to win more than he does."

Iverson always had his detractors—in the media, and especially on talk radio—and he had his share among the voters. "He is not a team guy," said Steve Van Allen. "He just doesn't get it." Dick Streeter acknowledged that Iverson is a magnificent player, but moved him down several notches because he is not a good role model, especially compared to Dr. J. Jim Robinson never cared for Iverson's attitude when he was a Sixer, dating back to the days of Larry Brown when A.I displayed a lackadaisical attitude toward practice. Ralph Antonelli opened both barrels when firing shots at Iverson. "Other Sixers, like Dr. J., Bobby Jones and Doug Collins were better team players. Iverson is not a great leader; leaders have to create an atmosphere for their teammates." Ralph also criticized Iverson for shooting too much and being a crybaby at times.

Year	Team	Lg	G	Min	FGM	FGA	FGP	FTM	FTA	FTP	AST	REB	Pts	PPG
1996–97	Sixers	NBA	76	3045	625	1504	.416	382	544	.702	567	312	1787	23.5
1997–98	Sixers	NBA	80	3150	649	1407	.461	390	535	.729	494	296	1758	22.0
1998–99	Sixers	NBA	48	1990	435	1056	.412	356	474	.751	223	236	1284	26.8
1999–00	Sixers	NBA	70	2853	729	1733	.421	442	620	.713	328	267	1989	28.4
2000–01	Sixers	NBA	71	2979	762	1813	.420	585	719	.814	325	273	2207	31.1
2001–02	Sixers	NBA	60	2622	665	1669	.398	475	585	.812	331	269	1883	31.4
2002–03	Sixers	NBA	82	3485	804	1940	.414	570	736	.774	454	344	2262	27.6
2003–04	Sixers	NBA	48	2040	435	1125	.387	339	455	.745	324	178	1266	26.4
2004–05	Sixers	NBA	75	3174	771	1818	.427	656	786	.835	596	299	2302	30.7
2005–06	Sixers	NBA	72	3101	815	1822	.447	675	829	.814	532	232	2377	33.0
2006–07	Sixers	NBA	15	640	151	366	.413	154	174	.885	109	41	468	31.2
Sixers Totals			697	29079	6841	16253	.421	5024	6457	.778	4283	2797	19583	28.1
Career Totals			697	29079	6841	16253	.421	5024	6457	.778	4283	2797	19583	28.1

NBA Rookie of the Year (1997)
NBA All-Star (2000–07)
NBA MVP (2001)

11 Robin Roberts

RANK	POINTS	VOTES RECEIVED
1st	50	0
2nd	49	1
3rd	48	2
4th	47	2
5th	46	2
6th	45	1
7th	44	7
8th	43	3
9th	42	2
10th	41	7
11th	40	7
12th	39	3
13th	38	10
14th	37	5
15th	36	8
16th	35	4
17th	34	4
18th	33	3
19th	32	3
20th	31	1
21st	30	3
22nd	29	1
23rd	28	1
24th	27	0
25th	26	0
26th	25	0
27th	24	1
28th	23	0
29th	22	2
30th	21	0

RANK	POINTS	VOTES RECEIVED
31st	20	1
32nd	19	1
33rd	18	1
34th	17	0
35th	16	0
36th	15	1
37th	14	0
38th	13	0
39th	12	0
40th	11	0
41st	10	1
42nd	9	1
43rd	8	0
44th	7	1
45th	6	1
46th	5	0
47th	4	0
48th	3	0
49th	2	1
50th	1	0
Not on List	0	8

TOP 10 VOTES	27
2ND 10 VOTES	48
3RD 10 VOTES	8
4TH 10 VOTES	4
5TH 10 VOTES	5
TOTAL VOTES	92
TOTAL POINTS	3257

▼ TEAM
Phillies

▼ YEARS PLAYED
1948–1961

▼ POSITION
Pitcher

When you look at Steve Carlton's stats from the early 1970s through the early 1980s, it's hard not to be awed. A perusal of Robin Roberts' numbers from the early to mid-1950s should evoke a similar reaction. From 1950 to 1955, Roberts *averaged* 23 wins, 27 complete games, 323 innings pitched and a 2.93 era. His 28 wins in 1952 are the most for a National League hurler since 1934.

Several voters, including Bob Anderson, Fred Schumacher and Jon Grisdale, put Roberts in their top five, and in so doing compared him to some of the game's great pitchers. Bob: "He was one of the best pitchers in baseball for about 10 years. Roberts, Warren Spahn, Bob Lemon and Bob Feller were the best pitchers of that era. He carried a Phillies pitching staff that didn't have much else. He was dignified, competitive and a class act. His control was amazing." Roberts' impeccable control was one of the keys to his success; he walked less than two batters per nine innings over his career. Fred: "He is the model for today's 'number one' pitcher. He went out every fourth (not fifth) day and if he did not win, it was from lack of support. He was much like 'the Rocket' [Roger Clemens] is today. I would say that he was better than Spahn or Lemon but not as good as Bob Gibson or Sandy Koufax." Jon: "He was a great pitcher on a last-place team. He was better than Whitey Ford."

Mark Bristowe also placed Robin in his top five, not only because of his "hugely impressive" stats, but because he was a role model and genuine person, and doesn't have a chip on his shoulder.

Mark Voigt is well aware of all of the wins and complete games that Roberts racked up, but couldn't overlook his numbers in another category. "I know he is a Hall of Famer, but it is hard to put a pitcher who lost 250 games [245 to be exact] in your top 50 list." Robby is in the top 15 on the career losses list, and he finished in the top five in defeats in the National League seven times while he was a Phillie. Much of that is attributable to the poor teams he pitched on—the Phillies had a winning record just four of the 14 seasons that

Roberts was in town. Other voters, including Joe Brown, Rod Smith and Andy Paul, downgraded Roberts in part because while he did a lot of good pitching, it was for bad Phillies teams.

Year	Team	Lg	G	W	L	CG	SH	IP	H	BB	SO	ER	ERA
1953	Phillies	N.L.	44	23	16	33	5	346.2	324	61	198	106	2.75
1954	Phillies	N.L.	45	23	15	29	4	336.2	289	56	185	111	2.97
1955	Phillies	N.L.	41	23	14	26	1	305	292	53	160	111	3.28
1956	Phillies	N.L.	43	19	18	22	1	297.1	328	40	157	147	4.45
1957	Phillies	N.L.	39	10	22	14	2	249.2	246	43	128	113	4.07
1958	Phillies	N.L.	35	17	14	21	1	269.2	270	51	130	97	3.24
1959	Phillies	N.L.	35	15	17	19	2	257.1	267	35	137	122	4.27
1960	Phillies	N.L.	35	12	16	13	2	237.1	256	34	122	106	4.02
1961	Phillies	N.L.	26	1	10	2	0	117	154	23	54	76	5.85
1962	Baltimore	A.L.	27	10	9	6	0	191.1	176	41	102	59	2.78
1963	Baltimore	A.L.	35	14	13	9	2	251.1	230	40	124	93	3.33
1964	Baltimore	A.L.	31	13	7	8	4	204	203	52	109	66	2.91
1965	Baltimore	A.L.	20	5	7	5	1	114.2	110	20	63	43	3.38
1965	Houston	N.L.	10	5	2	3	2	76	61	10	34	16	1.89
1966	Chi. Cubs	N.L.	24	5	8	2	1	112	141	21	54	60	4.82
Phillies Totals			529	234	199	272	35	3739.1	3661	718	1871	1437	3.45
Career Totals			676	286	245	305	45	4688.2	4582	902	2357	1774	3.41

National League All-Star (1950–56)
Number 36 retired by Phillies
Baseball Hall of Fame (1976)

Charles Barkley

RANK	POINTS	VOTES RECEIVED
1st	50	0
2nd	49	0
3rd	48	0
4th	47	0
5th	46	3
6th	45	3
7th	44	7
8th	43	2
9th	42	1
10th	41	11
11th	40	3
12th	39	4
13th	38	2
14th	37	9.5
15th	36	5.5
16th	35	3
17th	34	3
18th	33	3
19th	32	3
20th	31	3
21st	30	3
22nd	29	3
23rd	28	2
24th	27	0
25th	26	2
26th	25	0
27th	24	3
28th	23	2
29th	22	1
30th	21	1
31st	20	2
32nd	19	1
33rd	18	1
34th	17	1
35th	16	0
36th	15	0
37th	14	0
38th	13	0
39th	12	1
40th	11	1
41st	10	1
42nd	9	0
43rd	8	1
44th	7	1
45th	6	0
46th	5	0
47th	4	0
48th	3	0
49th	2	1
50th	1	0
Not on List	0	6

TOP 10 VOTES	27
2ND 10 VOTES	39
3RD 10 VOTES	17
4TH 10 VOTES	7
5TH 10 VOTES	4
TOTAL VOTES	94
TOTAL POINTS	3146.5

▼ **TEAM**
Sixers

▼ **YEARS PLAYED**
1985–1992

▼ **POSITION**
Forward

As a player, analyst and author, Charles Barkley has never been shy about expressing his opinions. Voters in the survey didn't hesitate to voice their opinions about Sir Charles. Not all of them were positive.

"He was a great talent," said John Mitchell, "but what did he accomplish here? Not much, plus he wanted out. The Sixers weren't really good, fun or interesting during his time here." John declined to put Barkley in his top 50, while Bob Kelly put Charles low on his list. "He never won a thing [in Philly]; he was somewhat overrated." In Barkley's eight years in Philadelphia, the Sixers never advanced beyond the Eastern Conference Semifinals, although Charles did his part: he finished in the top 10 in the NBA scoring five times, and in the top five in rebounding five seasons. Mike Rad thought Barkley was a good ballplayer, especially for his size, but didn't respect Charles for some of his off-the-court behavior. "He was outspoken, big-mouthed, and [exhibited] some rude behavior."

It didn't matter a lick to many voters that Charles didn't lead the Sixers to the promised land in Philadelphia or that he offended some people with his words and actions. Michael Barkann rated Barkley fifth, citing his "indomitable spirit" and "unbelievable will." "He left it all on the court," said Michael. "He didn't take crap from anybody." "Day in and day out, he was a more valuable player than Dr. J.," said Tom Walter. "He carried the Sixers' teams while he was there, and got some of them into the playoffs." Randy Axelrod gave Barkley the edge as an all-around player over Iverson.

The most ringing endorsement for Charles as a player and person was offered by Gordie Jones: "He is one of the most unique players and personalities ever to roll through Philadelphia—a guy who was under 6'5" but rebounded fiercely. He was a guy who spoke freely, if not always wisely. He was just a refreshing guy in so many ways. Former Sixers publicist Dave Coskey once said that while there are several players who are bad guys who want you to think they are good guys, Charles was just the opposite—a good guy who wanted you to think he was a bad guy. That summed him up."

Year	Team	Lg	G	Min	FGM	FGA	FGP	FTM	FTA	FTP	AST	REB	Pts	PPG
1984–85	Sixers	NBA	82	2347	427	783	.525	293	400	.733	155	703	1148	14.0
1985–86	Sixers	NBA	80	2952	595	1041	.572	396	578	.685	312	1026	1603	20.0
1986–87	Sixers	NBA	68	2740	557	937	.594	429	564	.761	331	994	1564	23.0
1987–88	Sixers	NBA	80	3170	753	1283	.587	714	951	.751	254	951	2264	28.3
1988–89	Sixers	NBA	79	3088	700	1208	.579	602	799	.753	325	986	2037	25.8
1989–90	Sixers	NBA	79	3085	706	1177	.600	557	744	.749	307	909	1989	25.2
1990–91	Sixers	NBA	67	2498	605	1167	.570	475	658	.722	284	680	1849	27.6
1991–92	Sixers	NBA	75	2881	622	1126	.552	454	653	.695	308	830	1730	23.1
1992–93	Phoenix	NBA	76	2859	716	1376	.520	445	582	.765	385	928	1944	25.6
1993–94	Phoenix	NBA	65	2298	518	1046	.495	318	452	.704	296	727	1402	21.6
1994–95	Phoenix	NBA	68	2382	554	1141	.486	379	507	.748	276	756	1561	23.0
1995–96	Phoenix	NBA	71	2632	580	1160	.500	440	566	.777	262	821	1649	23.2
1996–97	Houston	NBA	53	2009	335	692	.484	288	415	.694	248	716	1016	19.2
1997–98	Houston	NBA	68	2243	361	744	.482	296	397	.746	217	794	1036	15.2
1998–99	Houston	NBA	42	1526	240	502	.478	192	267	.719	192	516	676	16.1
1999–00	Houston	NBA	20	620	106	222	.477	71	110	.654	63	209	289	14.5
Sixers Totals			610	22761	4965	8722	.569	3920	5347	.733	2276	7079	14184	23.3
Career Totals			1073	39330	8375	15605	.537	6349	8643	.809	4215	12546	23757	22.1

NBA All-Star (1987–97)
NBA MVP (1993)
Number 34 retired by Sixers and Suns
Basketball Hall of Fame (2006)

13 Moses Malone

RANK	POINTS	VOTES RECEIVED		RANK	POINTS	VOTES RECEIVED
1st	50	0		31st	20	2
2nd	49	0		32nd	19	2
3rd	48	2		33rd	18	0
4th	47	0		34th	17	1
5th	46	1		35th	16	0
6th	45	1		36th	15	0
7th	44	4		37th	14	0
8th	43	2		38th	13	4
9th	42	1		39th	12	0
10th	41	2		40th	11	0
11th	40	7		41st	10	0
12th	39	3		42nd	9	3
13th	38	5		43rd	8	0
14th	37	6		44th	7	0
15th	36	4		45th	6	0
16th	35	4		46th	5	0
17th	34	2		47th	4	0
18th	33	5		48th	3	1
19th	32	1		49th	2	0
20th	31	4		50th	1	0
21st	30	3		Not on List	0	7
22nd	29	6				
23rd	28	1				
24th	27	2		TOP 10 VOTES		13
25th	26	1		2ND 10 VOTES		41
26th	25	4		3RD 10 VOTES		26
27th	24	2		4TH 10 VOTES		9
28th	23	1		5TH 10 VOTES		4
29th	22	3		TOTAL VOTES		93
30th	21	3		TOTAL POINTS		2904

45

▼ TEAM
Sixers

▼ YEARS PLAYED
1983–1986, 1994

▼ POSITION
Center

In the off-season following the gut-wrenching loss to the Celtics in the 1982 Eastern Conference Finals, the Sixers made a monumental free-agent signing: Moses Malone. And as voters said again and again and again, Moses was the difference when the Sixers went 65-17 the next season and then steamrolled over the Knicks, Bucks and Lakers in the postseason ("Fo, Fo and Fo") to win the NBA championship.

"He was the missing element for the Sixers," said Wayne Smith. "Caldwell Jones and George McGinnis couldn't win it all. Moses won the championship, not Dr. J." Other voters, including Joe Gribb and Sean Bergin, used the "missing piece" phrase to describe Moses. "He changed the whole dynamics of the team," said Sean. "Without Moses, the Sixers would have never overcome the Celtics and Lakers," added John Mitchell, "and Dr. J. and company would still owe us."

While Moses was a good scorer, averaging almost 25 points per game in the championship season, it was his rebounding that drew the most raves. As Paul Troy emphasized, Moses was an especially adept rebounder on the offensive end. "He cleaned up other players' mistakes off the glass." Indeed, Moses is the NBA's all-time leader in offensive rebounds. Ned Hark felt that the '83 Sixers were "light years better than the '82 Sixers" and Moses was the main reason. "He was a workhorse with talent. He wore opponents down emotionally and physically. He was a 'lunch pail' type player."

Not everybody credited Moses with being the catalyst of the Sixers' championship run. "He was not great; he just had great players around him," said Bill McElroy. Bob Bookbinder and John Bergmann pointed to Malone's lack of longevity. "He had a small window in Philadelphia," noted Bob. Moses played pro ball for 21 years, but only five of those seasons were with the Sixers; during one of those seasons, 1993-94, Moses was a seldom-used backup. Malone's best years arguably were with the Rockets. He won the MVP in '79 (averaging nearly 18 rebounds per game) and '82, averaging 31.1 points a game to rank second in the league. "If we were able to consider his non-Philadelphia years," said John, "he would definitely be near the top of my list."

Year	Team	Lg	G	Min	FGM	FGA	FGP	FTM	FTA	FTP	AST	REB	Pts	PPG
1974–75	Utah	ABA	83	3205	591	1035	.571	375	591	.635	82	1209	1557	18.8
1975–76	St. Louis	ABA	43	1168	251	490	.512	112	183	.612	58	413	614	14.3
1976–77	Buff.-Hou.	NBA	82	2506	389	810	.480	305	440	.693	89	1072	1083	13.5
1977–78	Houston	NBA	59	2107	413	828	.499	318	443	.718	31	886	1144	19.4
1978–79	Houston	NBA	82	3390	716	1325	.540	599	811	.739	147	1444	2031	24.8
1979–80	Houston	NBA	82	3140	778	1549	.502	563	783	.719	147	1190	2119	25.8
1980–81	Houston	NBA	80	3245	806	1545	.522	609	804	.757	141	1180	2222	27.8
1981–82	Houston	NBA	81	3398	945	1822	.519	630	827	.762	142	1188	2520	31.1
1982–83	Sixers	NBA	78	2922	654	1305	.501	600	788	.761	101	1194	1908	24.5
1983–84	Sixers	NBA	71	2613	532	1101	.483	545	727	.750	96	950	1609	22.7
1984–85	Sixers	NBA	79	2957	602	1284	.469	737	904	.815	130	1031	1941	24.6
1985–86	Sixers	NBA	74	2706	571	1246	.458	617	784	.787	90	872	1759	23.8
1986–87	Washington	NBA	73	2488	595	1311	.454	570	692	.824	120	824	1760	24.1
1987–88	Washington	NBA	79	2692	531	1090	.487	543	689	.788	112	884	1607	20.3
1988–89	Atlanta	NBA	81	2878	538	1096	.491	561	711	.789	112	956	1637	20.2
1989–90	Atlanta	NBA	81	2735	517	1077	.480	493	631	.781	130	812	1528	18.9
1990–91	Atlanta	NBA	82	1912	280	598	.468	309	372	.831	68	667	869	10.6
1991–92	Milwaukee	NBA	82	2511	440	929	.474	396	504	.786	93	744	1279	15.6
1992–93	Milwaukee	NBA	11	104	13	42	.310	24	31	.774	7	46	50	4.5
1993–94	Sixers	NBA	55	618	102	232	.440	90	117	.769	34	226	294	5.3
1994–95	San Antonio	NBA	17	149	13	35	.371	22	32	.688	6	46	49	2.9
	Sixers Totals		357	11816	2461	5168	.476	2589	3320	.780	451	4273	7511	21.0
	Career Totals		1455	49444	10277	20750	.495	9018	11864	.760	1936	17834	29580	20.3

ABA All-Star (1975)
NBA MVP (1979, 1982–83)
NBA Finals MVP (1983)
Member of NBA Champions (1983)
NBA All-Star (1978–83, 1985–89)

Number 24 retired by Rockets
Basketball Hall of Fame (2001)

14 ▸ Donovan McNabb

RANK	POINTS	VOTES RECEIVED
1st	50	0
2nd	49	1
3rd	48	1
4th	47	2
5th	46	4
6th	45	5
7th	44	3
8th	43	5
9th	42	3
10th	41	0
11th	40	3
12th	39	8
13th	38	1
14th	37	2
15th	36	7
16th	35	1
17th	34	3
18th	33	2
19th	32	3
20th	31	1
21st	30	4
22nd	29	0
23rd	28	3
24th	27	2
25th	26	2
26th	25	3
27th	24	1
28th	23	1
29th	22	2
30th	21	0

RANK	POINTS	VOTES RECEIVED
31st	20	0
32nd	19	1
33rd	18	0
34th	17	2
35th	16	1
36th	15	0
37th	14	5
38th	13	0
39th	12	1
40th	11	2
41st	10	0
42nd	9	2
43rd	8	0
44th	7	1
45th	6	0
46th	5	1
47th	4	0
48th	3	0
49th	2	0
50th	1	0
Not on List	0	11

TOP 10 VOTES	24
2ND 10 VOTES	31
3RD 10 VOTES	18
4TH 10 VOTES	12
5TH 10 VOTES	4
TOTAL VOTES	89
TOTAL POINTS	2878

▼ TEAM
Eagles

▼ YEARS PLAYED
1999–Present

▼ POSITION
Quarterback

The Eagles are in the throes of the longest world championship drought among the four Philadelphia pro sports teams, but arguably no Philly team since the 1950s has been as good over a several-year period as Andy Reid's Birds were from 2001 to 2004 when they advanced to the NFC Championship Game four straight years, culminating in a trip to Jacksonville to square off against the Patriots in the Super Bowl. Depending on your viewpoint, Donovan McNabb is either the player deserving of the most credit for the Eagles' string of successful seasons, or he is an overrated quarterback whose tendency not to rise to the occasion in big games has cost the Birds and their fans that long-awaited first Super Bowl victory.

John Clark was one of Donovan's fiercest supporters, ranking him sixth. "He was almost a combination of Randall and Jaws. He has the athletic ability of Randall and the game smarts of Jaws. Number five has won so many games with so little help around him and always played through pain. There are not too many quarterbacks in the NFL that I would rather have." Dave Sautter and Dave Myers both ranked McNabb in their top 10, anointing him as "one of the best quarterbacks in the NFL." Stacy and Jim Rosen, as well as Mike Sielski, sized up the Eagles' signal-callers over the years and concluded that Donovan is the king. Jim said that Norm Van Brocklin and Sonny Jurgensen were very good, but they had major successes with other teams. Mike cited an impressive accomplishment by Donovan—he became the first quarterback in history to throw 30 or more touchdowns and less than 10 interceptions in one season (2004). Bob Bookbinder rated Donovan high largely because of the Eagles' success with him at the helm, but Bob's review of Donovan's performance was mixed. "He is one of the greatest athletes and competitors that Philadelphia has had. That being said, I don't think he is one of the greatest quarterbacks. He struggles with touch, accuracy, reading defenses and getting it done."

For some voters, though, three consecutive championship-game losses and the Super Bowl defeat stick in their craw. John Senkow, Rob Neducsin and Brent Saunders excluded McNabb, characterizing him as overrated. John ripped him for "choking at critical times"; Rob said that he has not consistently won the big game; and Brent criticized McNabb for "not having the killer instinct of Iverson."

The father-son duo of Ken and David Berky rattled off some plaudits for McNabb—incredible athlete, great role model and ambassador to the NFL—but those attributes were not enough to justify a spot on their top 50. David explained Donovan's shortcomings: "He was beaten by a less capable quarterback (Brady) in the Super Bowl, who thrives on pressure. McNabb cannot handle the pressure. McNabb has to win the big game for him to be taken seriously." Sean Bergin and Rod Smith also felt that McNabb has not measured up to other star quarterbacks. Sean: "He doesn't have the intensity level of Montana, Aikman or Elway." Rod: "Young or Montana would have won two Super Bowls if they were the Eagles' quarterback during the glory years." John Mitchell had some specific criticisms of Donovan's skill as quarterback: "Before the Super Bowl meltdown and the T.O. debacle, I recognized McNabb for what he is: a guy who builds up nice stats throwing five-yard slants who has never consistently been able to put the ball where he needs to on the downfield throws. He never seems to hit the receiver in stride; he always seems to throw the ball at the receiver's feet. Plus he doesn't want to take advantage of his running ability."

A final note of interest about Donovan: in Ron Jaworski's 10 years in town, he led the Birds to three postseason victories, while Randall Cunningham quarterbacked the Birds to just one postseason win in his decade here. When the Eagles beat the Falcons on that cold day in January 2005 to win the NFC Championship Game, it was McNabb's seventh postseason win.

PASSING

Year	Team	Lg	G	Att	Comp	Pct	Yds	TD	Int
1999	Eagles	NFL	12	216	106	49.1	948	8	7
2000	Eagles	NFL	16	569	330	58.0	3365	21	13
2001	Eagles	NFL	16	493	285	57.8	3233	25	12
2002	Eagles	NFL	10	361	211	58.4	2289	17	6
2003	Eagles	NFL	16	478	275	57.5	3216	16	11
2004	Eagles	NFL	15	469	300	64.0	3875	31	8
2005	Eagles	NFL	9	357	211	59.1	2507	16	9
2006	Eagles	NFL	10	316	180	57.0	2647	18	6
	Eagles Totals		104	3259	1898	58.2	22080	152	72
	Career Totals		104	3259	1898	58.2	22080	152	72

RUSHING

Year	Team	Lg	Att	Yds	Avg	TD
1999	Eagles	NFL	47	313	6.7	0
2000	Eagles	NFL	86	629	7.3	6
2001	Eagles	NFL	82	482	5.9	2
2002	Eagles	NFL	63	460	7.3	6
2003	Eagles	NFL	71	355	5.0	3
2004	Eagles	NFL	41	220	5.4	3
2005	Eagles	NFL	25	55	2.2	1
2006	Eagles	NFL	32	212	6.6	3
	Eagles Totals		447	2726	6.1	24
	Career Totals		447	2726	6.1	24

NFL Pro Bowl (2000–04)

Billy Cunningham

RANK	POINTS	VOTES RECEIVED		RANK	POINTS	VOTES RECEIVED
1st	50	0		31st	20	3
2nd	49	0		32nd	19	1
3rd	48	0		33rd	18	3
4th	47	0		34th	17	1
5th	46	0		35th	16	0
6th	45	0		36th	15	0
7th	44	4		37th	14	1
8th	43	2		38th	13	4
9th	42	2		39th	12	0
10th	41	5		40th	11	0
11th	40	3		41st	10	0
12th	39	2		42nd	9	1
13th	38	8		43rd	8	1
14th	37	4.5		44th	7	2
15th	36	2.5		45th	6	0
16th	35	5		46th	5	1
17th	34	3		47th	4	0
18th	33	8		48th	3	0
19th	32	3		49th	2	0
20th	31	1		50th	1	0
21st	30	4		Not on List	0	10
22nd	29	4				
23rd	28	3				
24th	27	2				
25th	26	0				
26th	25	2				
27th	24	2				
28th	23	1				
29th	22	1				
30th	21	0				

TOP 10 VOTES	13
2ND 10 VOTES	40
3RD 10 VOTES	19
4TH 10 VOTES	13
5TH 10 VOTES	5
TOTAL VOTES	90
TOTAL POINTS	2746.5

▼ **TEAM**
Sixers

▼ **YEARS PLAYED**
1966–1972, 1975–1976

▼ **POSITION**
Forward

In 1983, when the Sixers won their second world championship, Billy Cunningham coached an outstanding sixth man, Bobby Jones. Sixteen years earlier, Billy was an exemplary sixth man himself, helping the Sixers capture their first title. In ranking Cunningham in their top 10, Doug Brown and Ned Hark pointed to Cunningham's integral role on the Sixers' phenomenal 1967 championship team. Coming off the bench to spell Chet Walker and Luke Jackson, Cunningham was fourth on the team in scoring and rebounds. Doug summed up Billy's game: "He could drive, shoot, rebound and play defense. He was a great team player." Ned also rated Cunningham high because he was a clutch player. "He would give the team a lift by hitting jumpers from the corner and grabbing rebounds." Paul Lightkep also remembered Cunningham's clutch play, while Dan McCarthy loved Billy's hustle. Harvey Feldman thought highly of Cunningham's ability to pass and rebound, as well as his sophistication as a player. "He had the same understanding of the game that [New York Knicks Hall of Famer] Bill Bradley had."

No voter lavished Cunningham with more praise, especially with regard to the way he played the game, than Ray Didinger. "He was exciting and colorful. He brought energy when he came off the bench in 1967, then became a starter and better player. He competed so hard; he played every game as if it were a playoff game. He had tremendous pride. He always gave his best; he was extremely competitive."

If people were asked to rate Joe Torre as a player, inevitably he would lose points in some voters' eyes because of his highly successful track record as manager of the Yankees. Yet Joe was quite a player in his own right, compiling more than 2300 hits. In the same vein, Billy Cunningham was so successful as a coach that some people, including Adam Kimelman, Paul Troy and Rod Smith, thought his coaching accomplishments overshadowed what he achieved as a player. "As great a player as he was," said Adam, "he was more remembered as a coach." In his eight years as Sixers coach (1978-85), the team played phenomenal .698 ball. In addition to guiding them to the world championship in 1983, Cunningham led them to the NBA finals two other seasons (1980 and 1982). While acknowledging that Cunningham was a "smart, competitive, beat you anyway I can" type of player, Rod didn't think that Billy stood out from the point of view of stats. He makes a good point. Cunningham finished in the top 10 in the NBA in scoring three times (third in 1969, fourth in 1970, and ninth in 1971): good but not exactly Allen Iverson. He also finished in the top 10 in rebounds twice (tenth in 1969 and sixth in 1970): impressive in view of Billy's height (6'6"), but not Barkley-like. On the other hand, he is one of six Sixers to average 20 or more points in four straight seasons, and one of just three Sixers to rack up 1000 rebounds in a season twice. Billy's jumping ability earned him the nickname of "the Kangaroo Kid."

Year	Team	Lg	G	Min	FGM	FGA	FGP	FTM	FTA	FTP	AST	REB	Pts	PPG
1965–66	Sixers	NBA	80	2134	431	1011	.426	281	443	.634	207	599	1143	14.3
1966–67	Sixers	NBA	81	2168	556	1211	.459	383	558	.686	205	589	1495	18.5
1967–68	Sixers	NBA	74	2076	516	1178	.438	368	509	.723	187	562	1400	18.9
1968–69	Sixers	NBA	82	3345	739	1736	.426	556	754	.737	287	1050	2034	24.8
1969–70	Sixers	NBA	81	3194	802	1710	.469	510	700	.729	352	1101	2114	26.1
1970–71	Sixers	NBA	81	3090	702	1519	.462	455	620	.734	395	946	1859	23.0
1971–72	Sixers	NBA	75	2900	658	1428	.461	428	601	.712	443	918	1744	23.3
1972–73	Carolina	ABA	84	3248	771	1583	.487	472	598	.789	530	1012	2028	24.1
1973–74	Carolina	ABA	32	1190	253	537	.471	149	187	.797	150	331	656	20.5
1974–75	Sixers	NBA	80	2859	609	1423	.428	345	444	.777	442	726	1563	19.5
1975–76	Sixers	NBA	20	640	103	251	.410	68	88	.773	107	147	274	13.7
Sixers Totals			654	22406	5116	11467	.446	3394	4717	.720	2625	6638	13626	20.8
Career Totals			770	26844	6140	13587	.451	4015	5502	.730	3305	7981	16310	21.2

Member of NBA Champions (1967)
NBA All-Star (1969–72)
ABA MVP (1973)
ABA All-Star (1973)
Number 32 retired by Sixers
Basketball Hall of Fame (1986)

16 Pete Rose

RANK	POINTS	VOTES RECEIVED
1st	50	1
2nd	49	0
3rd	48	1
4th	47	2
5th	46	5
6th	45	0
7th	44	1
8th	43	5
9th	42	6
10th	41	4
11th	40	3
12th	39	3
13th	38	2
14th	37	1
15th	36	4
16th	35	4
17th	34	4
18th	33	3
19th	32	5
20th	31	3
21st	30	0
22nd	29	2
23rd	28	1
24th	27	0
25th	26	2
26th	25	1
27th	24	1
28th	23	3
29th	22	0
30th	21	1

RANK	POINTS	VOTES RECEIVED
31st	20	0
32nd	19	1
33rd	18	2
34th	17	1
35th	16	1
36th	15	2
37th	14	2
38th	13	2
39th	12	1
40th	11	0
41st	10	1
42nd	9	1
43rd	8	1
44th	7	1
45th	6	0
46th	5	0
47th	4	0
48th	3	0
49th	2	0
50th	1	1
Not on List	0	15

TOP 10 VOTES	25
2ND 10 VOTES	32
3RD 10 VOTES	11
4TH 10 VOTES	12
5TH 10 VOTES	5
TOTAL VOTES	85
TOTAL POINTS	2715

▼ TEAM
Phillies

▼ YEARS PLAYED
1979–1983

▼ POSITION
First Baseman

Chris Wheeler recalls the caravan in which several Phillies, including recently signed free-agent Pete Rose, participated in the winter of 1979. The Phillies had won the National League Eastern Division title the previous three seasons, but each year they were quickly eliminated in the playoffs. Many of the team's veterans, including Larry Bowa, Greg Luzinski and Garry Maddox, who had endured the tough postseason losses, would good-naturedly rib their new teammate on the caravan. When it was Rose's turn to speak to the crowd, he would rib them back. Holding up his right hand, prominently displaying the World Series rings that he earned with the Reds and grinning broadly, Rose would cackle, "Check out my fingers, boys! How many of these do you have?" Two seasons later, Bowa, Luzinski, Maddox and the rest of the Phillies had rings on their fingers after beating the Astros in the playoffs and the Royals in the World Series. Many people think that Rose was the key to the Phils' breaking their lengthy drought and finally winning a Series. "He was the missing piece of the puzzle," said Wheels, who voted Rose eighth. "He got the Phillies over the hump. He made everybody better. He told Schmidt he was the best player he ever saw. [Schmidt responded by winning MVPs in 1980 and 1981, Rose's second and third years with the Phils.] He made Bowa more competitive than he already was."

Numerous others shared Wheels' sentiments, most notably Dave Bristowe, who voted the hit king first. "To me, whether you liked him or didn't, Pete Rose brought hustle, intensity and focus to the game of baseball and in doing so, also raised all those levels among his teammates. His grit, rawness and edge aligned with the Rocky spirit which the city had grown accustomed to at the time." Wayne Smith explained why he ranked Rose fifth: "He took a team that was always second best and turned them around with his attitude. He taught them how to win."

Ed Brittingham, who declined to include Rose on his list, strongly disagrees with the notion that Pete taught the Phillies how to win. "That's a dubious assertion and ignores the spectacular years of Carlton, McGraw and Schmidt. With the league's best starting pitcher, closer and position player on their roster, it's questionable how much the Phillies needed to 'learn' from Rose. The assertion also conveniently ignores the fact that the Phillies went from first place to fourth place the first year (1979) Rose was on the team."

Harvey Feldman also didn't think Rose was worthy of top 50 inclusion. "Ninety percent of the credit for the Phillies' success in 1980 belongs to manager Dallas Green, principally because he used the September call-ups [such as Marty Bystrom, who went 5-0 down the stretch] to embarrass the vets, including Rose, into playing better."

Gordie Jones had other reasons for passing on Pistol Pete. "I think of Rose more as a Red than a Phillie. Also, he was not much of a factor in 1983 when the Phillies made it back to the World Series." Rose was 42 in 1983 and showed his age by hitting .245 with little power; late in the season, manager Paul Owens was giving Len Matuszek some starts at first base. But Pete was the starter in the '83 playoffs and World Series, and showed he still had it by hitting .344 in the postseason. The Phillies released him after the season.

Year	Team	Lg	G	AB	R	H	HR	RBI	SB	Avg	SLG
1963	Cincinnati	N.L.	157	623	101	170	6	41	13	.273	.371
1964	Cincinnati	N.L.	136	516	64	139	4	34	4	.269	.326
1965	Cincinnati	N.L.	162	670	117	209	11	81	8	.312	.446
1966	Cincinnati	N.L.	156	654	97	205	16	70	4	.313	.460
1967	Cincinnati	N.L.	148	585	86	176	12	76	11	.301	.444
1968	Cincinnati	N.L.	149	626	94	210	10	49	3	.335	.470
1969	Cincinnati	N.L.	156	627	120	218	16	82	7	.348	.512
1970	Cincinnati	N.L.	159	649	120	205	15	52	12	.316	.470
1971	Cincinnati	N.L.	160	632	86	192	13	44	13	.304	.421
1972	Cincinnati	N.L.	154	645	107	198	6	57	10	.307	.417
1973	Cincinnati	N.L.	160	680	115	230	5	64	10	.338	.437
1974	Cincinnati	N.L.	163	652	110	185	3	51	2	.284	.388
1975	Cincinnati	N.L.	162	662	112	210	7	74	0	.317	.432
1976	Cincinnati	N.L.	162	665	130	215	10	63	9	.323	.450
1977	Cincinnati	N.L.	162	655	95	204	9	64	16	.311	.432
1978	Cincinnati	N.L.	159	655	103	198	7	52	13	.302	.421
1979	Phillies	N.L.	163	628	90	208	4	59	20	.331	.430
1980	Phillies	N.L.	162	655	95	185	1	64	12	.282	.354
1981	Phillies	N.L.	107	431	73	140	0	33	4	.325	.390
1982	Phillies	N.L.	162	634	80	172	3	54	8	.271	.338
1983	Phillies	N.L.	151	493	52	121	0	45	7	.245	.286
1984	Cin.-Mon.	N.L.	121	374	43	107	0	34	1	.286	.337
1985	Cincinnati	N.L.	119	405	60	107	2	46	8	.264	.319
1986	Cincinnati	N.L.	72	237	15	52	0	25	3	.219	.270
	Phillies Totals		745	2841	390	826	8	255	51	.291	.361
	Career Totals		3562	14053	2165	4256	160	1314	198	.303	.409

National League Rookie of the Year (1963)
National League All-Star (1965, 1967–71, 1973–82, 1985)
National League MVP (1973)
World Series MVP (1975)
Member of World Champions (1975–76, 1980)

17 Bill Barber

RANK	POINTS	VOTES RECEIVED
1st	50	0
2nd	49	0
3rd	48	0
4th	47	0
5th	46	1
6th	45	0
7th	44	0
8th	43	0
9th	42	1
10th	41	3
11th	40	8
12th	39	5
13th	38	4
14th	37	5
15th	36	4
16th	35	4
17th	34	2
18th	33	3
19th	32	2
20th	31	1
21st	30	2
22nd	29	6
23rd	28	2
24th	27	3
25th	26	5
26th	25	1
27th	24	2
28th	23	2
29th	22	2
30th	21	2

RANK	POINTS	VOTES RECEIVED
31st	20	1
32nd	19	1
33rd	18	2
34th	17	3
35th	16	1
36th	15	0
37th	14	3
38th	13	1
39th	12	0
40th	11	0
41st	10	1
42nd	9	0
43rd	8	0
44th	7	0
45th	6	1
46th	5	0
47th	4	1
48th	3	0
49th	2	1
50th	1	1
Not on List	0	13

TOP 10 VOTES	5
2ND 10 VOTES	38
3RD 10 VOTES	27
4TH 10 VOTES	12
5TH 10 VOTES	5
TOTAL VOTES	87
TOTAL POINTS	2535

▼ TEAM
Flyers

▼ YEARS PLAYED
1973–1984

▼ POSITION
Left Wing

Pitcher Don Sutton won 324 major league games, a feat accomplished by less than 20 hurlers, but some baseball fans think that the sportswriters made a mistake by electing him to the Baseball Hall of Fame. Their argument is that he was not a dominant pitcher, did not win a Cy Young Award, and rarely was a league leader in a category. Some hockey fans similarly have questioned the wisdom of the writers in electing Bill Barber to the Hockey Hall of Fame. Fred Warren is one of them. "He was just another left wing. He wasn't dominant. How significant of a contribution did he make to the Flyers?" Much like Sutton, who accumulated a lot of victories over the years by usually winning 16 to18 games per season, Barber totaled more than 400 goals and 875 points in his career by steadily producing good but not exceptional numbers. Barber only finished in the top five in goals and points once (1976), and never finished in the top five in assists, which lends credence to Fred's argument that Barber was not a dominant player. Half-seriously, Fred added: "Was Barber really any better than 'Cowboy' Bill Flett [the Flyers' right wing on the first Cup-winning team]?"

While nobody was as emphatic as Fred, other voters, including Andy Dziedzic and Lee Fiederer, were not that impressed with Barber and didn't include him in their top 50. Andy: "There were better players on the Stanley Cup team: Bernie (the main reason the Flyers won the Cups), Clarke, MacLeish and Leach." Lee thought that Barber benefited greatly from being on the same line as Bobby Clarke. "I'm not sure if Barber's success was attributable to Barber or Clarke."

Many voters disagreed with Fred and thought that Barber made a significant contribution to the Flyers' success. Ken and David Berky thought that Barber was a steady force and timely scorer on the Cup-winning teams. "Without Barber, the Flyers were not a great team." Jim Robinson emphasized that the Flyers from the Stanley Cup years had great chemistry and Barber was a big part of that chemistry. Joe Brown sized up Barber's contribution the same way: "He was part of a real good group of players. A lot of people in Philadelphia didn't follow hockey until the Stanley Cup years." Dan McCarthy and Mike Rad didn't think that Barber got the credit he deserved. "He was the 'glue' on the line with Clarke and Leach," said Mike.

Michael Beirne considered Barber the third best Flyer ever—behind Clarke and Parent. Jeff Skow listed many reasons why Barber finished high on his list: "He had all of the qualifications I was looking for. He had longevity, consistency, multi-time All-Star, good reputation in the city and was a standout on two Cup teams. Add to that his Hall of Fame status." But did he deserve that status?

Year	Team	Lg	Gm	G	A	Pts	PM
1972–73	Flyers	NHL	69	30	34	64	46
1973–74	Flyers	NHL	75	34	35	69	54
1974–75	Flyers	NHL	79	34	37	71	66
1975–76	Flyers	NHL	80	50	62	112	104
1976–77	Flyers	NHL	73	20	35	55	62
1977–78	Flyers	NHL	80	41	31	72	34
1978–79	Flyers	NHL	79	34	46	80	22
1979–80	Flyers	NHL	79	40	32	72	17
1980–81	Flyers	NHL	80	43	42	85	69
1981–82	Flyers	NHL	80	45	44	89	85
1982–83	Flyers	NHL	66	27	33	60	28
1983–84	Flyers	NHL	63	22	32	54	36
Flyers Totals			903	420	463	883	623
Career Totals			903	420	463	883	623

NHL All-Star (1975–76, 1978–82)
Member of Stanley Cup Champions (1974–75)
Number 7 retired by Flyers
Hockey Hall of Fame (1990)

RANK	POINTS	VOTES RECEIVED		RANK	POINTS	VOTES RECEIVED
1st	50	0		31st	20	1
2nd	49	1		32nd	19	4
3rd	48	0		33rd	18	1
4th	47	2		34th	17	1
5th	46	0		35th	16	2
6th	45	1		36th	15	1
7th	44	1		37th	14	0
8th	43	3		38th	13	1
9th	42	4		39th	12	1
10th	41	2		40th	11	3
11th	40	1		41st	10	0
12th	39	5		42nd	9	4
13th	38	0		43rd	8	0
14th	37	2		44th	7	1
15th	36	3		45th	6	1
16th	35	3		46th	5	0
17th	34	5		47th	4	1
18th	33	4		48th	3	0
19th	32	2.5		49th	2	0
20th	31	1.5		50th	1	1
21st	30	2		Not on List	0	10
22nd	29	5				
23rd	28	1				
24th	27	7		TOP 10 VOTES		14
25th	26	1		2ND 10 VOTES		27
26th	25	2		3RD 10 VOTES		26
27th	24	0		4TH 10 VOTES		15
28th	23	3		5TH 10 VOTES		8
29th	22	4		TOTAL VOTES		90
30th	21	1		TOTAL POINTS		2527.5

▼ TEAM
Eagles

▼ YEARS PLAYED
1977–1984

▼ POSITION
Running Back

Vince Papale may have been invincible back in the Dick Vermeil era, but according to Ray Didinger, Wilbert Montgomery was indispensable to the Eagles. "You can't minimize what he did for the Vermeil Eagles," said Ray. Vermeil coached the team from 1976 to 1982, leading them to the playoffs four times, including the unforgettable ride to the Super Bowl after the '80 season. Ray pointed out that while Brian Westbrook is on the small side for an NFL running back (205 lbs.), Wilbert was even smaller (195 lbs.). Wilbert's effort in the NFC Championship Game victory over the Cowboys—194 yards against a Dallas defense that had not allowed 100 yards rushing in a game in years—especially impressed Ray, considering that Montgomery was so banged up that there was uncertainty in the days before whether he would play. "What a courageous performance."

Cliff Patterson insisted that Montgomery carried the Eagles in their big moments and that the Eagles would not have gone to the Super Bowl without him, while Andy Salayda named Wilbert as the player whom the Raiders most needed to stop in the Super Bowl. (And they did.) Mike Koob added that as good as Brian Westbrook is, he can't run between tackles the way that Montgomery could.

Dave Myers said that in Montgomery's prime, he was one of the best running backs in the NFL—in the same class as Tony Dorsett and Walter Payton. Joe Fee cited Wilbert's feat of gaining 2000 yards from scrimmage in one season (in 1979, when his rushing and receiving yardage totaled 2006), and almost doing it another year (in 1981, when he rolled up 1923 total yards).

The hangup with some voters, including Adam Kimelman, Brent Saunders and Dennis Brady, is that Wilbert was not a standout running back for long enough, and that too much hoopla was made out of his heroics in the January '81 NFC Championship Game. "A lot of people remember the touchdown run against Dallas," said Brent Saunders, "but he didn't do enough over the long haul." Let's see what the numbers reveal. Between 1978 and 1981, when Montgomery was at the top of his game, he averaged more than 1200 yards per season on the ground, and finished in the top five in rushing in the NFL three times. However, in Wilbert's four other seasons with the Eagles, mainly because of injuries, his production was limited as he averaged only 400 yards per season on the ground. To Bill Jakavick, Wilbert wasn't as memorable as other Eagles from the 1980s like Randall Cunningham, Harold Carmichael and Mike Quick.

It was one of the coldest days I ever remember. The wind chill was minus 17, but by the time the game was over our hearts were so warm we didn't even notice. The scoreboard at the Vet after the game even read the temperature of the Superdome, the site of the Super Bowl: 72 degrees.

It had finally happened—the Eagles had beaten the hated Cowboys, 20-7, to advance to their first Super Bowl. The Eagles made the Cowboys wear their unlucky blue uniforms. The Vet was the loudest I can ever remember and the chants of "E-A-G-L-E-S—EAGLES!!!" were deafening from the opening kickoff until the final whistle. The thought of being one of 70,000 fanatical Eagles fans was unbelievable. All week leading up to the game, Dick Vermeil, their beloved coach, had said that Wilbert Montgomery might not be able to play due to injury. On the Eagles' second play of the game, he ran 42 yards untouched for a touchdown and everyone knew the game was ours. He ended the game by rushing for 194 yards which at the time was an NFC Championship Game record. The Eagles' defense held Dallas running back Tony Dorsett to 41 yards and pressured quarterback Danny White all day long.

The best part of the day was knowing that 10 of my best friends and I had already rented a Winnebago to drive down to New Orleans for the Super Bowl. Seeing each other in the parking lot, knowing the Eagles were finally NFC champs and we were going to be at the Super Bowl was like every Christmas morning of my life rolled into one moment and will be remembered until the day I die.

—JIM KENT

| Year | Team | Lg | G | Rushing | | | | Receiving | | | |
				Att	Yds	Avg	TD	Rec	Yds	Avg	TD
1977	Eagles	NFL	14	45	183	4.1	2	3	18	6.0	0
1978	Eagles	NFL	14	259	1220	4.7	9	34	195	5.7	1
1979	Eagles	NFL	16	338	1512	4.5	9	41	494	12.0	5
1980	Eagles	NFL	12	193	778	4.0	8	50	407	8.1	2
1981	Eagles	NFL	15	286	1402	4.9	8	49	521	10.6	2
1982	Eagles	NFL	8	114	515	4.5	7	20	258	12.9	2
1983	Eagles	NFL	5	29	139	4.8	0	9	53	5.9	0
1984	Eagles	NFL	16	201	789	3.9	2	60	501	8.4	0
1985	Detroit	NFL	7	75	251	3.3	0	7	55	7.9	0
	Eagles Totals		100	1465	6538	4.5	45	266	2447	9.2	12
	Career Totals		107	1540	6789	4.4	45	273	2502	9.2	12

NFL Pro Bowl (1978–79)

19 Tug McGraw

RANK	POINTS	VOTES RECEIVED	RANK	POINTS	VOTES RECEIVED
1st	50	0	31st	20	1
2nd	49	0	32nd	19	6
3rd	48	1	33rd	18	1
4th	47	0	34th	17	1
5th	46	0	35th	16	2
6th	45	0	36th	15	0
7th	44	0	37th	14	1
8th	43	2	38th	13	1
9th	42	2	39th	12	1
10th	41	7	40th	11	0
11th	40	1	41st	10	2
12th	39	3	42nd	9	1
13th	38	2	43rd	8	0
14th	37	2	44th	7	0
15th	36	6	45th	6	3
16th	35	4	46th	5	0
17th	34	2	47th	4	2
18th	33	3	48th	3	1
19th	32	2	49th	2	0
20th	31	4	50th	1	1
21st	30	3	Not on List	0	11
22nd	29	4			
23rd	28	1			
24th	27	4	TOP 10 VOTES		12
25th	26	4	2ND 10 VOTES		29
26th	25	1	3RD 10 VOTES		24
27th	24	2	4TH 10 VOTES		14
28th	23	2	5TH 10 VOTES		10
29th	22	1	TOTAL VOTES		89
30th	21	2	TOTAL POINTS		2451

▼ **TEAM**
Phillies

▼ **YEARS PLAYED**
1975–1984

▼ **POSITION**
Pitcher

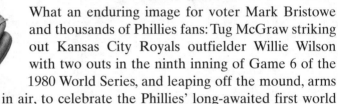

What an enduring image for voter Mark Bristowe and thousands of Phillies fans: Tug McGraw striking out Kansas City Royals outfielder Willie Wilson with two outs in the ninth inning of Game 6 of the 1980 World Series, and leaping off the mound, arms in air, to celebrate the Phillies' long-awaited first world championship. "He was a pressure pitcher who rose to the occasion," said Dan McCarthy. "He was always willing to take the ball." To say the least, Tug proved that in the memorable 1980 season. In the second half of the year, he allowed three earned runs in 52 innings, helping the Phillies erase a six-game deficit and edge the Expos for the division title. He kept up the great work in the postseason, saving two games in the Phils' nail-biting victory over the Astros in the League Championship Series and picked up a win and two saves in the World Series triumph over the Royals.

Dennis Brady also rated McGraw high for his clutch World Series performance and his status as the "Phillies' best relief pitcher ever." Most voters, in recalling the left-hander, focused on the intangibles that Tug brought to the table. "Phillies fans appreciated Schmidt; they loved Tug," said Terry Bickhart. "He captured the hearts of the fans. He was passionate. He wasn't the best reliever, but he was the reliever the Phillies needed." Jim Robinson: "He was all heart. He will always be a Philadelphia sports hero. He loved Philly fans, and we loved him."

Despite the Tugger's longevity, charisma and World Series heroics, some of our learned voters declined to put the screwball specialist on their lists. Steve Kennedy: "I just don't feel that he was one of the best at his position in the league, and did it long enough in Philadelphia. I think of him as a Met before I do a Phillie." Bob Cinalli: "He was a good finesse pitcher, but not one of the great relievers of all time. His numbers were not outstanding. Billy Wagner was phenomenal when he was in Philadelphia, better than Tug." Steve's and Bob's points have merit. As good as McGraw was, he never led the National League in saves and was not a dominant reliever like other pitchers of his era, such as Bruce Sutter, Rich Gossage and Lee Smith. Also, during his 10 seasons in Philly, he only led the team in saves three times (1979, 1980 and 1981); he and Gene Garber tied for co-leader in saves in 1975.

Tom Walter didn't include Tug because he thinks the importance of relievers is overrated. "They don't have the same value as starters. They are not worthy of the Cy Young Award."

Year	Team	Lg	G	W	L	SV	IP	H	BB	SO	ER	ERA
1965	N.Y. Mets	N.L.	37	2	7	1	97.2	88	48	57	36	3.32
1966	N.Y. Mets	N.L.	15	2	9	0	62.1	72	25	34	37	5.34
1967	N.Y. Mets	N.L.	4	0	3	0	17.1	13	13	18	15	7.79
1969	N.Y. Mets	N.L.	42	9	3	12	100.1	89	47	92	25	2.24
1970	N.Y. Mets	N.L.	57	4	6	10	90.2	77	49	81	33	3.28
1971	N.Y. Mets	N.L.	51	11	4	8	111	73	41	109	21	1.70
1972	N.Y. Mets	N.L.	54	8	6	27	106	71	40	92	20	1.70
1973	N.Y. Mets	N.L.	60	5	6	25	118.2	106	55	81	51	3.87
1974	N.Y. Mets	N.L.	41	6	11	3	88.2	96	32	54	41	4.16
1975	Phillies	N.L.	56	9	6	14	102.2	84	36	55	34	2.98
1976	Phillies	N.L.	58	7	6	11	97.1	81	42	76	27	2.50
1977	Phillies	N.L.	45	7	3	9	79	62	24	58	23	2.62
1978	Phillies	N.L.	55	8	7	9	89.2	82	23	63	32	3.21
1979	Phillies	N.L.	65	4	3	16	83.2	83	29	57	48	5.16
1980	Phillies	N.L.	57	5	4	20	92.1	62	23	75	15	1.46
1981	Phillies	N.L.	34	2	4	10	44	35	14	26	13	2.66
1982	Phillies	N.L.	34	3	3	5	39.2	50	12	25	19	4.31
1983	Phillies	N.L.	34	2	1	0	55.2	58	19	30	22	3.56
1984	Phillies	N.L.	25	2	0	0	38	36	10	26	16	3.79
Phillies Totals			463	49	37	94	722	633	232	491	249	3.10
Career Totals			824	96	92	180	1514.2	1318	582	1109	528	3.14

National League All-Star (1972, 1975)
Member of World Champions (1969, 1980)

20 Ron Jaworski

RANK	POINTS	VOTES RECEIVED		RANK	POINTS	VOTES RECEIVED
1st	50	0		31st	20	2
2nd	49	0		32nd	19	3
3rd	48	0		33rd	18	0
4th	47	0		34th	17	5
5th	46	0		35th	16	1
6th	45	1		36th	15	1
7th	44	1		37th	14	7
8th	43	3		38th	13	2
9th	42	1		39th	12	0
10th	41	1		40th	11	0
11th	40	4		41st	10	0
12th	39	4		42nd	9	0
13th	38	3		43rd	8	0
14th	37	5		44th	7	1
15th	36	0		45th	6	1
16th	35	1		46th	5	1
17th	34	5		47th	4	1
18th	33	3		48th	3	0
19th	32	2		49th	2	1
20th	31	6		50th	1	0
21st	30	4		Not on List	0	12
22nd	29	2				
23rd	28	1				
24th	27	1				
25th	26	2				
26th	25	2				
27th	24	4				
28th	23	0				
29th	22	4				
30th	21	2				

TOP 10 VOTES	7
2ND 10 VOTES	33
3RD 10 VOTES	22
4TH 10 VOTES	21
5TH 10 VOTES	5
TOTAL VOTES	88
TOTAL POINTS	2392

▼ TEAM
Eagles

▼ YEARS PLAYED
1977–1986

▼ POSITION
Quarterback

When Ron Jaworski arrived in Philadelphia in 1977 through a trade with the Los Angeles Rams, the Eagles were coming off a last-place, 4-10 season. In previous years, the Eagles had run through several starting quarterbacks, including John Reaves, Pete Liske, Roman Gabriel and Mike Boryla, who for the most part were ineffective. Jaworski brought stability to the position—he held the quarterback job until 1986—and also helped transform the Birds into winners. In Jaws' second season, the Eagles made the playoffs; in his third season, the Eagles picked up their first postseason win in 19 years by beating the Bears in the wild card game; and in 1980, Jaworski led his team to their inaugural Super Bowl appearance. Does Ron Jaworski deserve to be on the list? Absolutely no, according to some voters; absolutely yes, according to others.

Steve Kennedy, Paul Troy and Fred Schumacher were not in Jaworski's corner. Steve: "He's very popular in his role as an NFL analyst. That doesn't make him part of the Philly Top 50." Paul: "I don't remember thinking that he was one of the better players on the Eagles. Most of my memories of Jaworski are of him lying flat on his back." Fred: "I gave him kudos for takin' a lickin' and keepin' on tickin'. But a great quarterback? Hardly. But his legend grows with each passing day. People forget the boos." Andy Salayda described "the Polish Rifle" as a "serviceable" quarterback, noting that unlike Randall and Donovan, he was not the main force on the Eagles.

Jaworski, though, had his share of supporters. Mike Sielski was among his biggest: "He was a good drop-back passer. He was a big influence on the Eagles' turning things around in the late 1970s. He didn't get the credit he deserved; he was underrated. He had an MVP-type season in '80. He was the first Eagles quarterback to take them to the Super Bowl." Jaws' playoff success and affinity with Vermeil kept him high on Michael Brophy's list. Michael also liked Ron's work ethic, desire and commitment. Jody McDonald, John Surbeck, Dave Beck and Andy Dziedzic gave Jaworski points for his leadership ability. Jody: "He was a better leader than Donovan or Randall." Jody also cited Jaworski's toughness, which Rod Smith elaborated on: "I remember a player named Hartenstein putting a vicious hit from the back on Jaworski. Jaws was down for 30 seconds. Shook it off, took one play off, and came back in." Jaworski was also a smart player and unsung hero in Rod's book. Dick Streeter felt Jaworski was a great role model, while Joe Geier gave Jaws high marks for his popularity, good arm and longevity with the Birds.

Year	Team	Lg	G	Att	Comp	Pct	Yds	TD	Int
1974	L.A. Rams	NFL	5	24	10	41.7	144	0	1
1975	L.A. Rams	NFL	14	48	24	50.0	302	0	2
1976	L.A. Rams	NFL	5	52	20	38.5	273	1	5
1977	Eagles	NFL	14	346	166	48.0	2183	18	21
1978	Eagles	NFL	16	398	206	51.8	2487	16	16
1979	Eagles	NFL	16	374	190	50.8	2669	18	12
1980	Eagles	NFL	16	451	257	57.0	3529	27	12
1981	Eagles	NFL	16	461	250	54.2	3095	23	20
1982	Eagles	NFL	9	286	167	58.4	2076	12	12
1983	Eagles	NFL	16	446	235	52.7	3315	20	18
1984	Eagles	NFL	13	427	234	54.8	2754	16	14
1985	Eagles	NFL	16	484	255	52.7	3450	17	20
1986	Eagles	NFL	10	245	128	52.2	1405	8	6
1988	Miami	NFL	16	14	9	64.3	123	1	0
1989	Kansas City	NFL	6	61	36	59.0	385	2	5
	Eagles Totals		142	3918	2088	53.3	26963	175	151
	Career Totals		188	4117	2187	53.1	28190	179	164

NFL Pro Bowl (1980)
NFL co-MVP (1980)

21 Mo Cheeks

RANK	POINTS	VOTES RECEIVED		RANK	POINTS	VOTES RECEIVED
1st	50	0		31st	20	1
2nd	49	0		32nd	19	4
3rd	48	0		33rd	18	1
4th	47	0		34th	17	1
5th	46	0		35th	16	2
6th	45	0		36th	15	2
7th	44	1		37th	14	2
8th	43	0		38th	13	4
9th	42	1		39th	12	3
10th	41	1		40th	11	2
11th	40	1		41st	10	0
12th	39	3		42nd	9	2
13th	38	2		43rd	8	1
14th	37	2		44th	7	1
15th	36	1		45th	6	1
16th	35	2		46th	5	1
17th	34	9		47th	4	2
18th	33	5		48th	3	1
19th	32	5		49th	2	0
20th	31	5		50th	1	0
21st	30	3		Not on List	0	9
22nd	29	2				
23rd	28	2				
24th	27	3				
25th	26	4				
26th	25	1				
27th	24	3				
28th	23	1				
29th	22	0				
30th	21	3				

TOP 10 VOTES	3
2ND 10 VOTES	35
3RD 10 VOTES	22
4TH 10 VOTES	22
5TH 10 VOTES	9
TOTAL VOTES	91
TOTAL POINTS	2284

▼ TEAM
Sixers

▼ YEARS PLAYED
1979–1989

▼ POSITION
Guard

How important was Mo Cheeks to the Sixers in the 1980s, notably the 1983 championship team? Was he "the quarterback" of the team, as Jody McDonald said, and "the heart and soul of the Sixers," as Neil Goldstein described him? Or was he just a "cog in the wheel" as Mike Koob put it, a player who was adequate, did his job, but was not a premier guard like Isiah Thomas or Magic Johnson? Most people sided with Jody and Neil.

John Clark was one of Mo's biggest supporters: "He was the point guard and floor leader on the team that might have won many more titles if they didn't run into some of the greatest teams of all time in the Celtics and Lakers. His stats compare to some of the best point guards ever, and if Philly fans were to choose their favorite player in the history of Philadelphia sports, Mo Cheeks might be it." Steve Danawitz, a retired teacher and basketball coach, provided the coach's perspective: "If you are a coach teaching a kid to be a point guard at any level, Mo is the model: He directed the team, was unselfish, handled the ball well, played defense, passed the ball, and took mid-range shots. He ran the Sixers. He was the epitome of a point guard."

Greg Geier and Jason Garber pointed out that when Cheeks retired from the NBA in 1993, he was the NBA's leader in steals, and ranked second in assists. (He has not maintained those rankings, but is still in the top 10 in both categories.) Greg compared Cheeks to Steve Nash, who won the MVP for the Phoenix Suns in 2005 and 2006. Jason added, "Cheeks was the guy who didn't have the flash or the big name, but gave everything he had and more."

But Mike Koob had some voters in his camp. Mark Voigt didn't think that Cheeks was as good a guard as his teammate Andrew Toney. Bob Anderson also used other Sixers as a benchmark in assessing Cheeks: "Was he a better point guard than Doug Collins? *Maybe.* He was not that much better than Lionel Hollins. Wilt, Barkley and Doc were dominating players; Mo was not."

Year	Team	Lg	G	Min	FGM	FGA	FGP	FTM	FTA	FTP	AST	REB	Pts	PPG
1978–79	Sixers	NBA	82	2409	292	572	.510	101	140	.721	431	254	685	8.4
1979–80	Sixers	NBA	79	2623	357	661	.540	180	231	.779	556	274	898	11.4
1980–81	Sixers	NBA	81	2415	310	581	.534	140	178	.787	560	245	763	9.4
1981–82	Sixers	NBA	79	2498	352	676	.521	171	220	.777	667	248	881	11.2
1982–83	Sixers	NBA	79	2465	404	745	.542	181	240	.754	543	209	990	12.5
1983–84	Sixers	NBA	75	2494	386	702	.550	170	232	.733	478	205	950	12.7
1984–85	Sixers	NBA	78	2616	422	741	.570	175	199	.879	497	217	1025	13.1
1985–86	Sixers	NBA	82	3270	490	913	.537	282	335	.842	753	235	1266	15.4
1986–87	Sixers	NBA	68	2624	415	788	.527	227	292	.777	538	215	1061	15.6
1987–88	Sixers	NBA	79	2871	428	865	.495	227	275	.825	635	253	1086	13.7
1988–89	Sixers	NBA	71	2298	336	696	.483	151	195	.774	554	183	824	11.6
1989–90	Sac.-N.Y.	NBA	81	2519	307	609	.504	171	202	.847	453	240	789	18.8
1990–91	New York	NBA	76	2147	241	483	.499	105	129	.814	435	173	592	7.8
1991–92	Atlanta	NBA	56	1086	115	249	.462	26	43	.605	185	95	259	4.6
1992–93	New Jersey	NBA	35	510	51	93	.548	24	27	.889	107	42	126	3.6
	Sixers Totals		853	28583	4192	7940	.528	2005	2537	.790	6212	2538	10429	12.2
	Career Totals		1101	34845	4906	9374	.523	2331	2938	.793	7392	3088	12195	11.1

NBA All-Star (1983, 1986–88)
Member of NBA Champions (1983)
Number 10 retired by Sixers

Randall Cunningham

RANK	POINTS	VOTES RECEIVED
1st	50	0
2nd	49	0
3rd	48	0
4th	47	1
5th	46	1
6th	45	2
7th	44	1
8th	43	2
9th	42	2
10th	41	0
11th	40	1
12th	39	5
13th	38	3
14th	37	4
15th	36	3
16th	35	0
17th	34	4
18th	33	3
19th	32	3
20th	31	2
21st	30	3
22nd	29	3
23rd	28	2
24th	27	2
25th	26	2
26th	25	3
27th	24	2
28th	23	3
29th	22	0
30th	21	4

RANK	POINTS	VOTES RECEIVED
31st	20	1
32nd	19	0
33rd	18	0
34th	17	1
35th	16	1
36th	15	1
37th	14	0
38th	13	1
39th	12	1
40th	11	4
41st	10	2
42nd	9	0
43rd	8	4
44th	7	0
45th	6	2
46th	5	2
47th	4	0
48th	3	0
49th	2	1
50th	1	1
Not on List	0	17

TOP 10 VOTES	9
2ND 10 VOTES	28
3RD 10 VOTES	24
4TH 10 VOTES	10
5TH 10 VOTES	12
TOTAL VOTES	83
TOTAL POINTS	2224

▼ **TEAM**
Eagles

▼ **YEARS PLAYED**
1985–1995

▼ **POSITION**
Quarterback

In sizing up Randall Cunningham, the colorful and controversial Eagles starting quarterback for the better part of 10 years, voters' comments ran the gamut from glowing praise to scathing criticism.

Adam Kimelman and Jody McDonald were among the many people who were wowed by Randall's skills, especially his uncanny ability to run. "He was a revolutionary player," said Adam. "He paved the way for Steve Young and Michael Vick by changing what a quarterback did." Jody summed up Cunningham as follows: "He was a phenomenal talent. Steve Young is the best running quarterback of all time, but Randall was the most dangerous." In the opinion of Rod Smith, Randall was a better overall athlete and more accurate passer than Donovan McNabb.

Joe Fee paid Randall the highest compliment by comparing him to two of the all-time greats in other sports. "He changed the quarterback position. I liken what he did to what Babe Ruth and Wayne Gretzky did, only on a much smaller scale. The game changed because of them. Nowadays, having a quarterback who can run is pretty much of a necessity instead of an anomaly."

Some of our voters think the Babe would be rolling over in his grave after being compared to Randall Cunningham. John Surbeck is one of them. "He was inconsistent. He wasn't a great leader. He wasn't one of the five best quarterbacks in the league." Michael Barkann commended Randall on his "rocket arm" and ability to "run like a gazelle," but said that Randall's football acumen and ability to assimilate the offense were poor. Rob Betts had similar thoughts: "He had fantastic skills, but he never flourished in Philadelphia. He could dominate a game with his running and passing, but often showed up unprepared and befuddled by the complexities of the game. And all the playoff losses were a big negative." Randall's postseason record with the Eagles was a dismal 1-4, and included lackluster, first-round defeats in 1988, 1989 and 1990.

Jim Kent felt that after returning from his '91 knee surgery, Randall was too "Hollywood," and wasn't the same player. Glenn Young thought that Randall's legacy suffered because there was not more leadership to go with his ability.

I thought about my most memorable moment at a Philly sports event. It was '95, Randall's last year with the Eagles, Dallas at Philadelphia.

It was freezing that day. I mean Frigid! I met my buds in the lot as we always did prior for a few cold ones and some steaks. I'd attended many Birds games over the years, including the playoffs as well as the recent championship games. Never did I hear the place erupt as it did that day. The Vet was just louder than the Linc will ever be. Throw Dallas in the mix with the weather and the table was set.

What made this game particularly memorable for me was that I saw it from both a fan's and a player's point of view. I had been doing business with the club for a couple of years and the man that I met with regularly was none other than the legendary trainer, Otho Davis. The week prior to the game as I sat across from him in his office, which was in the locker room, he asked me if I had plans for the upcoming game. He then asked what size I was. He got up, walked into a closet and pulled out a brand-new sideline player's coat and told me to be at the park no later than 12. He also handed me a bench pass. Not to be confused with a field pass, which restricts visitors to the 30-yard line only. Watching Emmitt Smith try to gain one yard on two separate tries and failing was nothing less than electric. As I stood between Randall Cunningham and Rodney Peete on the sideline, their expression said it all. They both looked up in the sky with gaping grins as if Christ himself had come down and made the stop. The whole bench was feeding off the crowd like a lion that hadn't eaten for weeks. I thought the whole building was going to crumble.

I submit this because of my love and respect for the late Otho Davis. Not only was he well accomplished at his profession, he had a true feel for the game and especially the passion of Philadelphia Eagle football. He gave me a gift that day that I will never forget. On that day I also remember meeting a guy about my age who had also been the recipient of Otho's kindness. He was a toll collector. Apparently, Otho had developed a friendship with him and made his dream come true as well.

Just a tribute to a great human being.

—STEVE VAN ALLEN

PASSING

Year	Team	Lg	G	Att	Comp	Pct	Yds	TD	Int
1985	Eagles	NFL	6	81	34	42.0	548	1	8
1986	Eagles	NFL	15	209	111	53.1	1391	8	7
1987	Eagles	NFL	12	406	223	54.9	2786	23	12
1988	Eagles	NFL	16	560	301	53.8	3808	24	16
1989	Eagles	NFL	16	532	290	54.5	3400	21	15
1990	Eagles	NFL	16	465	271	58.3	3466	30	13
1991	Eagles	NFL	1	4	1	25.0	19	0	0
1992	Eagles	NFL	15	384	233	60.7	2775	19	11
1993	Eagles	NFL	4	110	76	69.1	850	5	5
1994	Eagles	NFL	14	490	265	54.1	3229	16	13
1995	Eagles	NFL	7	121	69	57.0	605	3	5
1997	Minnesota	NFL	6	88	44	50.0	501	6	4
1998	Minnesota	NFL	15	425	259	60.9	3704	34	10
1999	Minnesota	NFL	6	200	124	62.0	1475	8	9
2000	Dallas	NFL	6	125	74	59.2	849	6	4
2001	Baltimore	NFL	6	89	54	60.7	573	3	2
2002	Baltimore	NFL	0	0	0	0	0	0	0
	Eagles Totals		122	3362	1874	55.7	22877	150	105
	Career Totals		161	4289	2429	56.6	29979	207	134

RUSHING

Year	Team	Lg	Att	Yds	Avg	TD
1985	Eagles	NFL	29	205	7.1	0
1986	Eagles	NFL	66	540	8.2	5
1987	Eagles	NFL	76	505	6.6	3
1988	Eagles	NFL	93	624	6.7	6
1989	Eagles	NFL	104	621	6.0	4
1990	Eagles	NFL	118	942	8.0	5
1991	Eagles	NFL	0	0	0	0
1992	Eagles	NFL	87	549	6.3	5
1993	Eagles	NFL	18	110	6.1	1
1994	Eagles	NFL	65	288	4.4	3
1995	Eagles	NFL	21	98	4.7	0
1997	Minnesota	NFL	19	127	6.7	0
1998	Minnesota	NFL	32	132	4.1	1
1999	Minnesota	NFL	10	58	5.8	0
2000	Dallas	NFL	23	89	3.9	1
2001	Baltimore	NFL	14	40	2.9	1
2002	Baltimore	NFL	0	0	0	0
	Eagles Totals		677	4482	6.6	32
	Career Totals		775	4928	6.4	35

NFL Pro Bowl (1988–90, 1998)   NFL co-MVP (1990, 1998)

Harold Carmichael

RANK	POINTS	VOTES RECEIVED
1st	50	0
2nd	49	0
3rd	48	0
4th	47	1
5th	46	0
6th	45	0
7th	44	0
8th	43	0
9th	42	1
10th	41	0
11th	40	3
12th	39	0
13th	38	1
14th	37	1
15th	36	3
16th	35	3
17th	34	3
18th	33	1
19th	32	3.5
20th	31	1.5
21st	30	5
22nd	29	1
23rd	28	1
24th	27	3
25th	26	6
26th	25	3
27th	24	0
28th	23	3
29th	22	5
30th	21	3

RANK	POINTS	VOTES RECEIVED
31st	20	6
32nd	19	0
33rd	18	4
34th	17	2
35th	16	1
36th	15	4
37th	14	4
38th	13	0
39th	12	1
40th	11	1
41st	10	2
42nd	9	0
43rd	8	2
44th	7	1
45th	6	2
46th	5	1
47th	4	2
48th	3	1
49th	2	0
50th	1	0
Not on List	0	14

TOP 10 VOTES	2
2ND 10 VOTES	20
3RD 10 VOTES	30
4TH 10 VOTES	23
5TH 10 VOTES	11
TOTAL VOTES	86
TOTAL POINTS	2003.5

▼ TEAM
Eagles

▼ YEARS PLAYED
1971–1983

▼ POSITION
Wide Receiver

If statistics were the sole criterion in determining the Eagles' all-time best wide receiver, then Harold Carmichael, as Mark Voigt insisted, is the hands-down winner. He ranks first on the Birds' all-time list in the three key statistical categories for receivers: receptions, yards and touchdowns. Mark put Harold in his top 15, as did a few other voters, including Merrill Reese, Rob Neducsin and Dick Streeter. Rob: "If he wanted to catch the ball and the quarterback could get it to him, it was a complete pass. He was tough, and not afraid to block or go over the middle. He flourished with some pretty bad teams and was exciting." Dick: "He was an outstanding player, and a quiet unassuming leader. He was much more of a role model than T.O." Ralph Antonelli described Carmichael as "Mr. Dependable." "He had great hands. Jaws [and Roman Gabriel] were lucky to have him." Harold's height—he was 6'8"—made him one of the NFL's tallest receivers ever, which Cliff Patterson and Bob Bookbinder commented on. "I never saw a receiver that tall play the position that well," said Cliff, "and make it look that easy." Bob paid Harold these compliments: "I like that as a big man he had pretty good hands and was a 'go to' guy in tough situations. I don't remember him dropping many passes."

Jack Guziewicz remembered some drops by Harold, at least early in his career. "He was 'butterfingers,' but he developed good hands." Jon Grisdale thought Carmichael should have been a better receiver. "Carmichael didn't use his height to his advantage. [Redskins cornerback] Pat Fischer, who was much shorter [by almost a foot], used to eat him for lunch. He was easy to tackle for as big as he was." Despite Carmichael's place on the Eagles' leader board, Steve Kennedy, Ned Hark and Jim Rosen also declined to put him on their lists. "He was good, but not great," said Ned. "When he left the Eagles, he was not missed." Ned was also quite annoyed that Carmichael signed with the Cowboys after 13 years in Philadelphia.

"I didn't regard Carmichael as the most gifted receiver the Eagles had," said Jim Rosen. "He was just a physically imposing, good player. For example, I thought Mike Quick was a better receiver."

Year	Team	Lg	G	Rec	Yds	Avg	TD
1971	Eagles	NFL	9	20	288	14.4	0
1972	Eagles	NFL	13	20	276	13.8	2
1973	Eagles	NFL	14	67	1116	16.7	9
1974	Eagles	NFL	14	56	649	11.6	8
1975	Eagles	NFL	14	49	639	13.0	7
1976	Eagles	NFL	14	42	503	12.0	5
1977	Eagles	NFL	14	46	665	14.5	7
1978	Eagles	NFL	16	55	1072	19.5	8
1979	Eagles	NFL	16	52	872	16.8	11
1980	Eagles	NFL	16	48	815	17.0	9
1981	Eagles	NFL	16	61	1028	16.9	6
1982	Eagles	NFL	9	35	540	15.4	4
1983	Eagles	NFL	15	38	515	13.6	3
1984	Dallas	NFL	2	1	7	7.0	0
	Eagles Totals		180	589	8978	15.2	79
	Career Totals		182	590	8985	15.2	79

NFL Pro Bowl (1973, 1978–80)

Tommy McDonald

RANK	POINTS	VOTES RECEIVED
1st	50	0
2nd	49	0
3rd	48	0
4th	47	0
5th	46	0
6th	45	0
7th	44	1
8th	43	3
9th	42	1
10th	41	2
11th	40	2
12th	39	2
13th	38	3
14th	37	2
15th	36	7
16th	35	2
17th	34	2
18th	33	1
19th	32	2
20th	31	5
21st	30	2
22nd	29	1
23rd	28	0
24th	27	2
25th	26	2
26th	25	3
27th	24	1
28th	23	2
29th	22	0
30th	21	1
31st	20	3
32nd	19	1
33rd	18	3
34th	17	4
35th	16	2
36th	15	1
37th	14	1
38th	13	2
39th	12	0
40th	11	0
41st	10	1
42nd	9	3
43rd	8	0
44th	7	1
45th	6	1
46th	5	0
47th	4	0
48th	3	0
49th	2	1
50th	1	0
Not on List	0	27

TOP 10 VOTES	7
2ND 10 VOTES	28
3RD 10 VOTES	14
4TH 10 VOTES	17
5TH 10 VOTES	7
TOTAL VOTES	73
TOTAL POINTS	1986

▼ TEAM
Eagles

▼ YEARS PLAYED
1957–1963

▼ POSITION
Wide Receiver

If Tommy McDonald ever dropped a pass for the Eagles, Ray Didinger doesn't remember it. And if an opponent ever intimidated Tommy, Ray doesn't remember that, either. Tommy's great hands and mental toughness were two of the reasons why Ray ranked him tenth. Ray rattled off some more reasons: "He is the smallest player [5'9", 175 lbs.] in the Hall of Fame. He should not have waited as long as he did. [He wasn't elected until 30 years after he retired.] He was one of the dominant players in the NFL, the definition of a big-play receiver. He had high touchdown totals. When he retired, there was only one player with more touchdowns than Tommy, Don Hutson [the Hall of Fame receiver for the Packers who played in the 1930s and 1940s]."

Merrill Reese, who voted McDonald 11th, had the same adulation for the University of Oklahoma star. "He believed no defender could stay with him. The harder you hit him, the quicker he jumped up. His competitive fires burned every second. He had incredible moves." Tommy was also a top 20 pick of Bob Cinalli and John Mitchell. Bob: "He was unbelievable at getting open. No matter how hard a defensive player hit him, he would bounce back. He was the ultimate receiver. Modern-day receivers are not as good; they drop too many balls." John: "He has a championship [1960]; Carmichael and Quick do not. Tommy was an earlier version of Lance Alworth. He was the best receiver I ever saw pre–Jerry Rice." Jerry McDonough described McDonald as "worth the price of admission." So much that when the Eagles traded McDonald to Dallas after the 1963 season, Jerry's friend chose not to renew his season tickets.

In ranking McDonald high, Bob Anderson made a statement about him which has merit but also is debatable: "He was the best receiver in the history of Philadelphia pro football." Terry Bickhart didn't agree with Bob. "Harold Carmichael always seemed to have a bigger impact on the game." Ned Hark was one of the voters who did not choose McDonald. "He didn't stand out as much as Van Brocklin or Bednarik who were the guts of the team without whom they would not have won the 1960 championship."

In November 1962, I was 15, and in my second year of being an Eagles season ticket holder. (I think the price for the seven home games that year was $28.00.) The Cuban Missile Crisis had recently ended and my biggest concern during it was that if the world ended, there would be no game next Sunday.

In any event, the first home game at Franklin Field after the end of the Cuban Missile Crisis was against the Packers with Vince Lombardi, Paul Hornung, Bart Starr and others. They were undefeated at the time, and the Eagles were struggling so far, but they were basically the same team that won in 1960 (although Van Brocklin had retired). This was the first rematch since the 1960 title game, and we all knew the Birds would turn their season around with a big win back at Franklin Field where glory was captured two years before.

The Eagles won the toss and got a good kickoff return to midfield. On the first play from scrimmage, Sonny Jurgensen executed a perfect play fake and froze the defense. Tommy McDonald streaked down the sideline, wide open. Jurgensen threw a perfectly gorgeous rainbow and 60,671 voices rose in anticipation of a stunning strike to open the game against the champions. When McDonald crossed the five-yard line, there was no doubt. Between the five-yard line and the goal line, the screaming was intense. As the ball was about to reach his fingertips, out of nowhere materialized either Willie Wood or Herb Adderly (from northeast Philadelphia), who flicked the ball away. The sound of 60,000 screams changing to utter silence was very memorable. In fact, that was my main recollection of the game; I remember that as much as the fans pleading, in the third quarter, "We don't want a touchdown, we just want a first down." You see, as of the third quarter of the game, the Eagles had not yet achieved a first down. The final score that day was 49-0. Needless to say, the Packers went on to repeat as champs, and the Birds finished in last place.

—JIM ROSEN

Year	Team	Lg	G	Rec	Yds	Avg	TD
1957	Eagles	NFL	12	9	228	25.3	3
1958	Eagles	NFL	10	29	603	20.8	9
1959	Eagles	NFL	12	47	846	18.0	10
1960	Eagles	NFL	12	39	801	20.5	13
1961	Eagles	NFL	14	64	1144	17.9	13
1962	Eagles	NFL	14	58	1146	19.8	10
1963	Eagles	NFL	14	41	731	17.8	8
1964	Dallas	NFL	14	46	612	13.3	2
1965	Los Angeles	NFL	14	67	1036	15.5	9
1966	Los Angeles	NFL	13	55	714	13.0	2
1967	Atlanta	NFL	14	33	436	13.2	4
1968	Cleveland	NFL	9	7	113	16.1	1
	Eagles Totals		88	287	5499	19.2	66
	Career Totals		152	495	8410	17.0	84

NFL Pro Bowl (1958–62, 1965)
Member of NFL Champions (1960)
Pro Football Hall of Fame (1998)

25 Larry Bowa

RANK	POINTS	VOTES RECEIVED
1st	50	0
2nd	49	0
3rd	48	0
4th	47	0
5th	46	0
6th	45	0
7th	44	0
8th	43	0
9th	42	0
10th	41	1
11th	40	0
12th	39	0
13th	38	1
14th	37	0
15th	36	3
16th	35	2
17th	34	0
18th	33	1
19th	32	9
20th	31	5
21st	30	3
22nd	29	4
23rd	28	2
24th	27	4
25th	26	3
26th	25	2
27th	24	2
28th	23	1
29th	22	5
30th	21	2
31st	20	3
32nd	19	3
33rd	18	3
34th	17	2
35th	16	1
36th	15	1
37th	14	1
38th	13	1
39th	12	2
40th	11	1
41st	10	2
42nd	9	2
43rd	8	1
44th	7	2
45th	6	0
46th	5	1
47th	4	2
48th	3	3
49th	2	5
50th	1	0
Not on List	0	14

TOP 10 VOTES	1
2ND 10 VOTES	21
3RD 10 VOTES	28
4TH 10 VOTES	18
5TH 10 VOTES	18
TOTAL VOTES	86
TOTAL POINTS	1844

▼ TEAM
Phillies

▼ YEARS PLAYED
1970–1981

▼ POSITION
Shortstop

When Larry Bowa broke into the majors in 1970 for Frank Lucchesi's Phillies, expectations were not high. He was a skinny kid who had been cut from his high school baseball team for three straight years. Lucchesi stuck with him, though, and Bowa persevered and had a stellar, 12-year run with the Phillies.

Bowa's glove work at shortstop was his strong suit. Jody McDonald described Bowa as a "Hall of Fame defensive player." As a Phillie, he led National League shortstops in fielding percentage five times, and in 1972, he set a National League record by commiting just nine errors. John Mitchell had an insightful take on Bowa's D. "He played shortstop not to make errors. He was more interested in protecting his fielding percentage than risking an error to make a play." John recalled that Bowa used to complain about Reds shortstop Dave Concepcion winning the Gold Glove some years despite making more errors. (Concepcion won six Gold Gloves to Bowa's two.) Bowa used to rib his rival, "Your name must be Elmer. Every time I look in the paper, I see E-Concepcion."

Bowa's hitting drew some sharp criticism from the voters. "He was a marginal hitter," said Rod Smith. "His left-handed hitting was embarrassing, a joke." Greg Veith was even more caustic. "He was an absolutely terrible offensive player. He had a low lifetime on base percentage with no power." Greg shot down the notion, advanced by some voters, that Bowa was a spark plug. "How can you be a spark plug when you have trouble reaching base?"

But Jody Mac stressed the improvement in Bowa's hitting over the years. "His offense went from abysmal to productive." Indeed, in Bowa's first four years with the Phillies, he hit just .242, but in his last eight years, he stroked the ball at a respectable .274 clip, which included seasons of .305, .294 and .283.

But it wasn't Bowa's offense or defense that drew the most comments, but his intangibles. Dan Brown described him as "the heart and soul of the Phillies"; Dave Beck liked his "fiery persona and tenacity," while Dick Streeter praised Bowa's "hustle, enthusiasm and leadership." Andy Musser agreed that Bowa was one of the leaders of the '80 Phillies, a team which he thought was much better than the '93 squad.

Year	Team	Lg	G	AB	R	H	HR	RBI	SB	Avg	SLG
1970	Phillies	N.L.	145	547	50	137	0	34	24	.250	.303
1971	Phillies	N.L.	159	650	74	162	0	25	28	.249	.292
1972	Phillies	N.L.	152	579	67	145	1	31	17	.250	.320
1973	Phillies	N.L.	122	446	42	94	0	23	10	.211	.249
1974	Phillies	N.L.	162	669	97	184	1	36	39	.275	.338
1975	Phillies	N.L.	136	583	79	178	2	38	24	.305	.377
1976	Phillies	N.L.	156	624	71	155	0	49	30	.248	.301
1977	Phillies	N.L.	154	624	93	175	4	41	32	.280	.340
1978	Phillies	N.L.	156	654	78	192	3	43	27	.294	.370
1979	Phillies	N.L.	147	539	74	130	0	31	20	.241	.314
1980	Phillies	N.L.	147	540	57	144	2	39	21	.267	.322
1981	Phillies	N.L.	103	360	34	102	0	31	16	.283	.339
1982	Chi. Cubs	N.L.	142	499	50	123	0	29	8	.246	.305
1983	Chi. Cubs	N.L.	147	499	73	133	2	43	7	.267	.339
1984	Chi. Cubs	N.L.	133	391	33	87	0	17	10	.223	.269
1985	Cubs-Mets	N.L.	86	214	15	50	0	15	5	.234	.304
Phillies Totals			1739	6815	816	1798	13	421	288	.264	.324
Career Totals			2247	8418	987	2191	15	525	318	.260	.320

National League All-Star (1974–76, 1978–79)
National League Gold Glove (1972, 1978)
Member of World Champions (1980)

26 ▶ Bill Bergey

RANK	POINTS	VOTES RECEIVED		RANK	POINTS	VOTES RECEIVED
1st	50	0		31st	20	4
2nd	49	0		32nd	19	2
3rd	48	0		33rd	18	1
4th	47	0		34th	17	1
5th	46	0		35th	16	3
6th	45	0		36th	15	1
7th	44	0		37th	14	0
8th	43	0		38th	13	2
9th	42	0		39th	12	2
10th	41	1		40th	11	1
11th	40	2		41st	10	1
12th	39	1		42nd	9	1
13th	38	2		43rd	8	0
14th	37	1		44th	7	2
15th	36	3		45th	6	2
16th	35	4		46th	5	2
17th	34	6		47th	4	0
18th	33	1		48th	3	4
19th	32	2		49th	2	0
20th	31	2		50th	1	1
21st	30	2		Not on List	0	23
22nd	29	0				
23rd	28	4				
24th	27	3		**TOP 10 VOTES**	1	
25th	26	0		**2ND 10 VOTES**	24	
26th	25	3		**3RD 10 VOTES**	22	
27th	24	2		**4TH 10 VOTES**	17	
28th	23	2		**5TH 10 VOTES**	13	
29th	22	3		**TOTAL VOTES**	77	
30th	21	3		**TOTAL POINTS**	1780	

▼ **TEAM**
Eagles

▼ **YEARS PLAYED**
1974–1980

▼ **POSITION**
Linebacker

After the Eagles finished 5-8-1 in 1973, their 11th losing season in 12 years, they made a monumental trade. They gave up two first-round draft picks and a second-round pick to the Bengals in exchange for middle linebacker Bill Bergey. Ned Hark thought the Eagles got the short end of the deal. "Bergey was overrated. He was more of a mouthpiece than a dominant player." Gordie Jones passed on Bergey because he regarded the linebacker as just as much a Bengal as an Eagle; Bergey played almost half his career in Cincinnati. Dennis Brady didn't think Bergey was as good as other Eagles linebackers, notably Seth Joyner.

The majority of the voters, though, thought that the Eagles' trade with Cincinnati paid huge dividends. Glenn Young explained why he picked Bergey tenth: "To me, Bergey epitomized leadership. Perhaps my picks are biased, but Bergey symbolized the overachieving nature of the Eagles team that made the playoffs and the Super Bowl. I thought if the team could least afford to lose one player, it was him. He led that defense by his recklessness and guts." Michael Beirne thought that Bergey dominated the line of scrimmage, and since the days of Bednarik, other than Reggie White, no player has had as much of a presence on the Eagles' defense as Bergey. Both Joe Brown and Jim Robinson rated Bergey 15th because they strongly believed that the Arkansas State star was one of the best middle line-backers of his era. Joe put Bergey in the same category as Jack Lambert. Jim added that Bergey made his teammates play better, and commended him for staying active in the community after he retired.

"He stood out on bad teams," added Wayne Smith. And some good ones, including one very good one. It was in Bergey's final season that the Eagles reached the Super Bowl. A knee injury that Bergey had sustained the year before led to his retirement after the memorable season, in which the Raiders beat the Birds in Super Bowl XV.

Year	Team	Lg	G	Int	Yds	TD
1969	Cincinnati	NFL	14	2	62	0
1970	Cincinnati	NFL	14	3	35	0
1971	Cincinnati	NFL	14	1	16	0
1972	Cincinnati	NFL	12	0	0	0
1973	Cincinnati	NFL	14	3	50	0
1974	Eagles	NFL	14	5	57	0
1975	Eagles	NFL	14	3	48	0
1976	Eagles	NFL	14	2	48	0
1977	Eagles	NFL	14	2	4	0
1978	Eagles	NFL	16	4	70	0
1979	Eagles	NFL	3	1	0	0
1980	Eagles	NFL	16	1	7	0
	Eagles Totals		91	18	234	0
	Career Totals		159	27	397	0

NFL Pro Bowl (1969, 1974, 1976–78)

MICHAEL BEIRNE'S TOP 10

1. Wilt Chamberlain
2. Mike Schmidt
3. Julius Erving
4. Bobby Clarke
5. Steve Carlton
6. Allen Iverson
7. Richie Ashburn
8. Bernie Parent
9. Chuck Bednarik
10. Robin Roberts

Hal Greer

RANK	POINTS	VOTES RECEIVED
1st	50	0
2nd	49	0
3rd	48	0
4th	47	0
5th	46	0
6th	45	0
7th	44	0
8th	43	1
9th	42	0
10th	41	0
11th	40	0
12th	39	1
13th	38	3
14th	37	1
15th	36	2
16th	35	2
17th	34	3
18th	33	1
19th	32	6
20th	31	6
21st	30	2
22nd	29	3
23rd	28	0
24th	27	4
25th	26	1
26th	25	0
27th	24	2
28th	23	5
29th	22	3
30th	21	4

RANK	POINTS	VOTES RECEIVED
31st	20	0
32nd	19	3
33rd	18	1
34th	17	2
35th	16	1
36th	15	4
37th	14	0
38th	13	0
39th	12	3
40th	11	0
41st	10	1
42nd	9	1
43rd	8	0
44th	7	2
45th	6	1
46th	5	1
47th	4	2
48th	3	0
49th	2	0
50th	1	2
Not on List	0	26

TOP 10 VOTES	1
2ND 10 VOTES	25
3RD 10 VOTES	24
4TH 10 VOTES	14
5TH 10 VOTES	10
TOTAL VOTES	74
TOTAL POINTS	1757

▼ TEAM
Sixers

▼ YEARS PLAYED
1964–1973

▼ POSITION
Guard

What was the greatest single-season team in Philadelphia history? The 1983 Sixers with Doc and Moses? What about the 1960 Eagles starring Bednarik and Van Brocklin? Are the Cup-winning Flyers from 1974 to 1975 worthy?

There is a strong argument that the greatest of all the Philly teams was the 1967 Sixers, coached by Alex Hannum, who jumped out of the gate with a 46-4 record and finished at 68-13. While they didn't quite manhandle their opponents in the playoffs like the 1983 Sixers squad did, they still disposed of Cincinnati (3-1), Boston (4-1) and San Francisco (4-2) handily.

The guts of that team, said Andy Musser, was Hal Greer. "He had a great jump shot," said Andy. "He was good defensively and was a good assist man." Dan McCarthy, Cliff Patterson and Neil Goldstein also discussed Greer's fine jump shot. Michael Beirne: "He was the perfect piece for the perfect team." "He is one of the best guards ever," insisted Doug Brown. Some of Greer's accomplishments, cited by Doug and John Senkow, support that notion. When he retired, he was tenth on the NBA's all-time scoring list. Several players have passed him since, but he still accumulated more career points than outstanding guards Magic Johnson, Isiah Thomas and Reggie Theus. He was an All-Star for 10 consecutive seasons, and was elected to the Hall of Fame.

As good as Greer was, the Sixers have had better guards, according to some voters. Mark Voigt didn't think Greer was as good in the backcourt as Iverson or Toney. Jon Grisdale preferred Guy Rodgers from the Warriors days and Mo Cheeks over Greer. Jack Guziewicz agreed with Jon about Cheeks. "Mo was a better field general than Greer," said Jack. "Wilt was the 'Boss' of the 1967 Sixers." In downgrading Greer, Jerry McDonough noted that he spent a lot of years (five) outside of Philadelphia—in Syracuse. The franchise moved from Syracuse to Philadelphia after the 1962-63 season.

Year	Team	Lg	G	Min	FGM	FGA	FGP	FTM	FTA	FTP	AST	REB	Pts	PPG
1958–59	Syracuse	NBA	68	1625	308	679	.454	137	176	.778	101	196	753	11.1
1959–60	Syracuse	NBA	70	1979	388	815	.476	148	189	.783	188	303	924	13.2
1960–61	Syracuse	NBA	79	2763	623	1381	.451	305	394	.774	302	455	1551	19.6
1961–62	Syracuse	NBA	71	2705	644	1442	.447	331	404	.819	313	524	1619	22.8
1962–63	Syracuse	NBA	80	2631	600	1293	.464	362	434	.834	275	457	1562	19.5
1963–64	Sixers	NBA	80	3157	715	1611	.444	435	525	.829	374	484	1865	23.3
1964–65	Sixers	NBA	70	2600	539	1245	.433	335	413	.811	313	355	1413	20.2
1965–66	Sixers	NBA	80	3326	703	1580	.445	413	514	.804	384	473	1819	22.7
1966–67	Sixers	NBA	80	3086	699	1524	.459	367	466	.788	303	422	1765	22.1
1967–68	Sixers	NBA	82	3263	777	1626	.478	422	549	.769	372	444	1976	24.1
1968–69	Sixers	NBA	82	3311	732	1595	.459	432	543	.796	414	435	1896	23.1
1969–70	Sixers	NBA	80	3024	705	1551	.455	352	432	.815	405	376	1762	22.0
1970–71	Sixers	NBA	81	3060	591	1371	.431	326	405	.805	369	369	1508	18.6
1971–72	Sixers	NBA	81	2410	389	866	.449	181	234	.774	316	271	959	11.8
1972–73	Sixers	NBA	38	848	91	232	.392	32	39	.821	111	106	214	5.6
Sixers Totals			754	28085	5941	13201	.450	3295	4120	.800	3361	3730	15177	20.1
Career Totals			1122	39788	8504	18811	.452	4578	5717	.801	4540	5665	21586	19.2

NBA All-Star (1961–70)
Member of NBA Champions (1967)
Number 15 retired by Sixers
Basketball Hall of Fame (1982)

28 Mike Quick

RANK	POINTS	VOTES RECEIVED		RANK	POINTS	VOTES RECEIVED
1st	50	0		31st	20	5
2nd	49	0		32nd	19	2
3rd	48	0		33rd	18	1
4th	47	0		34th	17	2
5th	46	0		35th	16	5
6th	45	0		36th	15	1
7th	44	0		37th	14	4
8th	43	1		38th	13	2
9th	42	0		39th	12	2
10th	41	2		40th	11	2
11th	40	0		41st	10	1
12th	39	1		42nd	9	2
13th	38	1		43rd	8	1
14th	37	2		44th	7	1
15th	36	0		45th	6	5
16th	35	2		46th	5	2
17th	34	0		47th	4	0
18th	33	0		48th	3	1
19th	32	2		49th	2	2
20th	31	2		50th	1	1
21st	30	3		Not on List	0	19
22nd	29	0				
23rd	28	2				
24th	27	3		TOP 10 VOTES	3	
25th	26	2		2ND 10 VOTES	10	
26th	25	0		3RD 10 VOTES	27	
27th	24	5		4TH 10 VOTES	26	
28th	23	4		5TH 10 VOTES	15	
29th	22	3		TOTAL VOTES	81	
30th	21	5		TOTAL POINTS	1639	

▼ TEAM
Eagles

▼ YEARS PLAYED
1982–1990

▼ POSITION
Wide Receiver

It was vintage Mike Quick, and Mike Koob remembers it well. The Eagles and Falcons played to a 17-17 tie through regulation in November 1985. In overtime, following a punt, the Eagles started a possession buried on their own one-yard line. Ron Jaworski hit Quick with a strike across the middle, and the great receiver kicked it into high gear and raced 99 yards for a dramatic, game-winning touchdown.

It was that type of play that prompted a few voters to include Quick in their top 20. Merrill Reese was one of them. "He had sheer talent in the class of T.O." Rob Neducsin said about Quick: "In his prime, he was dominating and undefendable. He was an exciting, first-class athlete." Joe Brown described Quick as "one of the best all-time Eagles." Joe added, "He was dominant, consistent, a hard worker, and had good character." Rob Betts: "He had great hands and speed, ran great routes, and was a smart player." Rob thought Quick ranked right up there with Steve Largent and James Lofton as one of the great receivers of his time.

From 1983 to 1987, Quick averaged 62 catches and 1087 yards per year. He was voted to the Pro Bowl all five years; in two of those seasons, he was the Eagles' only selection. How vital was he to the Eagles during those five years? He scored 53 touchdowns, while no other Eagle crashed the end zone more than nine times.

Sadly, however, injuries cut short Quick's career and he caught just 44 passes after 1987. He fractured his fibula in 1988 and sustained a serious knee injury in 1989; by 1990, his career was over. "If he didn't blow out his knee," said Rob Betts, "he might have gone to the Hall of Fame."

The problem with Quick, some voters felt, including Frank Minch, Bob Bookbinder and Ned Hark, was that his heyday was during a time when the Eagles were mediocre. "[When Quick established himself as a star player], the Eagles were sinking into 'the Swamp Fox' period [1983-85, when Marion Campbell was coach]."

Quick's last two stellar seasons were at the beginning of Buddy Ryan's tenure, when the Birds also had losing records. "When the Eagles got good, starting in 1988, Quick did not contribute much," said Ned. Bob Cinalli thought that Quick, even at his best, was not in the same class as Tommy McDonald.

Year	Team	Lg	G	Rec	Yds	Avg	TD
1982	Eagles	NFL	9	10	156	15.6	1
1983	Eagles	NFL	16	69	1409	20.4	13
1984	Eagles	NFL	14	61	1052	17.2	9
1985	Eagles	NFL	16	73	1247	17.1	11
1986	Eagles	NFL	16	60	939	15.7	9
1987	Eagles	NFL	12	46	790	17.2	11
1988	Eagles	NFL	8	22	508	23.1	4
1989	Eagles	NFL	6	13	228	17.5	2
1990	Eagles	NFL	4	9	135	15.0	1
	Eagles Totals		101	363	6464	17.8	61
	Career Totals		101	363	6464	17.8	61

NFL Pro Bowl (1983–87)

29 Jim Bunning

RANK	POINTS	VOTES RECEIVED
1st	50	0
2nd	49	0
3rd	48	1
4th	47	0
5th	46	0
6th	45	0
7th	44	0
8th	43	0
9th	42	2
10th	41	1
11th	40	0
12th	39	3
13th	38	0
14th	37	3
15th	36	2
16th	35	1
17th	34	3
18th	33	3
19th	32	2
20th	31	4
21st	30	4
22nd	29	1
23rd	28	3
24th	27	2
25th	26	0
26th	25	0
27th	24	2
28th	23	2
29th	22	1
30th	21	1
31st	20	1
32nd	19	5
33rd	18	0
34th	17	2
35th	16	2
36th	15	1
37th	14	1
38th	13	4
39th	12	0
40th	11	0
41st	10	0
42nd	9	2
43rd	8	0
44th	7	0
45th	6	0
46th	5	2
47th	4	3
48th	3	0
49th	2	1
50th	1	0
Not on List	0	35

TOP 10 VOTES	4
2ND 10 VOTES	21
3RD 10 VOTES	16
4TH 10 VOTES	16
5TH 10 VOTES	8
TOTAL VOTES	65
TOTAL POINTS	1625

100

▼ **TEAM**
Phillies

▼ **YEARS PLAYED**
1964–1967, 1970–1971

▼ **POSITION**
Pitcher

Dennis Brady was eight years old when he watched Jim Bunning on television pitch against the Mets in the first game of a doubleheader at Shea Stadium on Fathers' Day in June 1964. Bunning retired all 27 Mets he faced, becoming the first pitcher since 1922 to throw a regular-season perfect game. That incredible performance carried a lot of weight in Dennis' decision to rank Bunning near the top. Steve Bucci cited the perfect game and Bunning's plaque in Cooperstown as important in ranking the right-hander high.

Jeff Skow recognized that Bunning's gem against the Mets was an awesome performance, but said he had to look beyond one regular-season game in deciding whether Bunning deserved to be on his top 50 list. "I really have no love for Jim Bunning. He's really not a Philadelphia star. He was here for two stints totaling just six seasons. He was never on a championship team. So then I have to focus on the stats. His last two seasons were both garbage, so my focus is on the four seasons covering 1964-67. They were all 17 wins or more which is great, but just not dominant enough to make my list. They would have needed to be 20-plus win seasons, with some Cy Youngs and a World Series appearance in that short of a period."

Even though Bunning never was a 20-game winner for the Phillies (although he did win 20 for the Tigers once), did not capture a Cy Young Award, nor pitch in a World Series, several voters thought Jim was so good during those four years in Philadelphia that he belonged close to the top. "He was a fierce competitor," said Chris Wheeler. "He could melt you with a look. He was tough, had a great arm, and commanded great respect." Bob Anderson and John Mitchell were on the same page in assessing Bunning; they each ranked the right-hander 14th, and mentioned his name in the same breath as several all-time great pitchers. John: "Those four years with the Phillies, he was just a half-tick behind Koufax, Marichal and Gibson." Bob: "He was not quite in the same category as Carlton or

Roberts, but he was tremendous those four years. He had great control, and was smart, dignified and classy."

Lee Fiederer didn't feel Bunning had enough longevity to make his list, while Patrick Dooley downgraded Bunning because he didn't bring a championship to town. Ken Berky didn't think that Bunning quite compared to Gibson, Koufax, or Drysdale. While Gibson and Koufax were first-ballot Hall of Famers and Drysdale was elected in his tenth year of eligibility, Bunning was passed up by the Baseball Writers Association of America and elected by the Veterans' Committee, 24 years after he retired.

MIKE SIELSKI'S TOP 10

1. Wilt Chamberlain
2. Chuck Bednarik
3. Mike Schmidt
4. Julius Erving
5. Bobby Clarke
6. Steve Carlton
7. Reggie White
8. Donovan McNabb
9. Allen Iverson
10. Richie Ashburn

Year	Team	Lg	G	W	L	CG	SH	IP	H	BB	SO	ER	ERA
1955	Detroit	A.L.	15	3	5	0	0	51	59	32	37	36	6.35
1956	Detroit	A.L.	15	5	1	0	0	53.1	55	28	34	22	3.71
1957	Detroit	A.L.	45	20	8	14	1	267.1	214	72	182	80	2.69
1958	Detroit	A.L.	35	14	12	10	3	219.2	188	79	177	86	3.52
1959	Detroit	A.L.	40	17	13	14	1	249.2	220	75	201	108	3.89
1960	Detroit	A.L.	36	11	14	10	3	252	217	64	201	78	2.79
1961	Detroit	A.L.	38	17	11	12	4	268	232	71	194	95	3.19
1962	Detroit	A.L.	41	19	10	12	2	258	262	74	184	103	3.59
1963	Detroit	A.L.	39	12	13	6	2	248.1	245	69	196	107	3.88
1964	Phillies	N.L.	41	19	8	13	5	284.1	248	46	219	83	2.63
1965	Phillies	N.L.	39	19	9	15	7	291	253	62	268	84	2.60
1966	Phillies	N.L.	43	19	14	16	5	314	260	55	252	84	2.41
1967	Phillies	N.L.	40	17	15	16	6	302.1	241	73	253	77	2.29
1968	Pittsburgh	N.L.	27	4	14	3	1	160	168	48	95	69	3.88
1969	Pitt.-L.A.	N.L.	34	13	10	5	0	212.1	212	49	124	87	3.49
1970	Phillies	N.L.	34	10	15	4	0	219	233	56	147	100	4.11
1971	Phillies	N.L.	29	5	12	1	0	110	126	37	58	67	5.48
	Phillies Totals		226	89	73	65	23	1520.2	1361	329	1197	495	2.93
	Career Totals		591	224	184	151	40	3760.10	3433	1000	2855	1366	3.27

American League All-Star (1957, 1959, 1961–63)
National League All-Star (1964, 1966)
Number 14 retired by Phillies
Baseball Hall of Fame (1996)

30 Eric Lindros

RANK	POINTS	VOTES RECEIVED
1st	50	0
2nd	49	0
3rd	48	0
4th	47	0
5th	46	0
6th	45	0
7th	44	0
8th	43	0
9th	42	1
10th	41	0
11th	40	3
12th	39	3
13th	38	3
14th	37	0
15th	36	2
16th	35	1
17th	34	4
18th	33	5
19th	32	1
20th	31	0
21st	30	0
22nd	29	3
23rd	28	2
24th	27	1
25th	26	2
26th	25	4
27th	24	0
28th	23	1
29th	22	3
30th	21	3

RANK	POINTS	VOTES RECEIVED
31st	20	4
32nd	19	1
33rd	18	2
34th	17	1
35th	16	0
36th	15	2
37th	14	1
38th	13	0
39th	12	1
40th	11	0
41st	10	1
42nd	9	1
43rd	8	1
44th	7	2
45th	6	1
46th	5	1
47th	4	0
48th	3	0
49th	2	0
50th	1	2
Not on List	0	37

TOP 10 VOTES	1
2ND 10 VOTES	22
3RD 10 VOTES	19
4TH 10 VOTES	12
5TH 10 VOTES	9
TOTAL VOTES	63
TOTAL POINTS	1569

▼ **TEAM**
Flyers

▼ **YEARS PLAYED**
1993–2000

▼ **POSITION**
Center

When a Philadelphia team trades six players, two number one draft picks, plus 15 million dollars to acquire the rights to you and you are only 19 years old, there is absolutely no question about it: Philly fans will never let you live it down if you don't produce. Eric Lindros felt that type of pressure when the Flyers were awarded Lindros' rights by an arbitrator in a convoluted transaction with the Quebec Nordiques in 1992. In passing on the question of whether Lindros was worth all the hype, voters steered clear of the middle of the road: Either they fervently supported Lindros or scathingly criticized him.

John Mitchell, Jim Robinson and Bill McClain were unequivocal: Lindros didn't live up to his potential. "The Next One became The Never One," said John. Jim disliked Lindros' attitude: "He complained and blamed everything on everybody else."

Lindros had a series of injuries during his years with the Flyers, and the way in which he responded to those injuries drew some ire and sarcasm from the voters. Bob Anderson ripped into Lindros: "He was a fraud. He didn't care about winning the Stanley Cup; he cared about himself. When he said he couldn't play because he was hurt, sometimes it was because his feelings were hurt." Paul Troy mentioned complaints that Bobby Clarke had voiced: "If LeClair or Desjardins are injured, I don't have to see their parents in the dressing room."

If Lindros were a selfish, whining, underachieving baby, you wouldn't have known it from the comments of many of the voters. Steve Bucci rated big Eric 18th: "He was one of the best players in the league for a few years. He was a league MVP. [He became the first Flyer since his nemesis Bobby Clarke to win the Hart Trophy.] The Flyers went to the finals [in 1997] with him. People remember the end." "Had it not been for Lindros' concussions, he would be a certain Hall of Famer," opined Joe Fee. Andy Dziedzic said that before Lindros' concussions dampened his aggressiveness, he was "an absolute stud, a dominant force in the NHL."

Joe Gribb, Paul Lightkep and David Berky were also big Lindros fans. Joe: "He and Hextall were the heart of the Flyers' teams from the 1990s. He was a force on the ice; he may not have won the Cup, but the Flyers were always in the hunt and they were a much better team with him on the ice than when he was out." Paul: "He set a new standard for a different type of hockey player. He had incredible skills and he had a combination of size, speed and athleticism in one. Clarke and the Flyers put pressure on him to be a leader, which he wasn't meant to be." David: "He was a hockey player built like a linebacker who could skate, pass and demolish his opponent. I remember John LeClair having three consecutive 50-goal seasons on the Lindros line. When Clarke challenged him to play like the best, Lindros was relentless until his untimely injury led to the Primeau trade [in 2000]."

Season	Team	Lg	Gm	G	A	Pts	PM
1992–93	Flyers	NHL	61	41	34	75	147
1993–94	Flyers	NHL	65	44	53	97	103
1994–95	Flyers	NHL	46	29	41	70	60
1995–96	Flyers	NHL	73	47	68	115	163
1996–97	Flyers	NHL	52	32	47	79	136
1997–98	Flyers	NHL	63	30	41	71	134
1998–99	Flyers	NHL	71	40	53	93	120
1999–00	Flyers	NHL	55	27	32	59	83
2001–02	N.Y. Rangers	NHL	72	37	36	73	138
2002–03	N.Y. Rangers	NHL	81	19	34	53	141
2003–04	N.Y. Rangers	NHL	39	10	22	32	60
2005–06	Toronto	NHL	33	11	11	22	43
	Flyers Totals		486	290	369	659	946
	Career Totals		711	367	472	839	1328

NHL MVP (1995)
NHL All-Star (1994, 1996–00)

31 ▶ Dick Allen

RANK	POINTS	VOTES RECEIVED
1st	50	0
2nd	49	1
3rd	48	0
4th	47	1
5th	46	0
6th	45	0
7th	44	0
8th	43	0
9th	42	0
10th	41	0
11th	40	1
12th	39	2
13th	38	1
14th	37	1
15th	36	0
16th	35	4
17th	34	3
18th	33	0
19th	32	2
20th	31	4
21st	30	2
22nd	29	1
23rd	28	3
24th	27	1
25th	26	1
26th	25	1
27th	24	4
28th	23	0
29th	22	1
30th	21	1

RANK	POINTS	VOTES RECEIVED
31st	20	3
32nd	19	2
33rd	18	4
34th	17	4
35th	16	2
36th	15	1
37th	14	2
38th	13	3
39th	12	1
40th	11	1
41st	10	2
42nd	9	1
43rd	8	2
44th	7	2
45th	6	0
46th	5	1
47th	4	2
48th	3	1
49th	2	0
50th	1	1
Not on List	0	30

TOP 10 VOTES	2
2ND 10 VOTES	18
3RD 10 VOTES	15
4TH 10 VOTES	23
5TH 10 VOTES	12
TOTAL VOTES	70
TOTAL POINTS	1560

▼ TEAM
Phillies

▼ YEARS PLAYED
1963–1969, 1975–1976

▼ POSITION
Third and First Baseman

Fred Schumacher has been watching baseball since the 1940s and the best power hitter he has ever seen was not Willie Mays, not Mickey Mantle and not Mark McGwire, but Richie "Dick" Allen. "If he played longer in Philadelphia, we'd be saying, 'Mike who?' I would have paid money to see Allen play, but not Schmidt." Neil Goldstein sized up Allen the same way. "He had tremendous raw talent—he was built like a goddess. He would hit 70 home runs in a season at Citizens Bank Park." He just might have. Fred and Neil were so awed by Allen's prodigious home runs that they rated him in their top five—second and fourth, respectively. Mike Koob felt that Allen was a victim of the prejudice of the times, which put a damper on his production. "If he came up in 1994 instead of 1964, he would be Albert Pujols-like—he would be a stone-cold Hall of Famer." Other voters, including Gordie Jones, Michael Beirne and John Mitchell, raved about Allen's enormous talent at hitting a baseball.

Jerry McDonough extolled Allen's strength and power, but also mentioned an underrated aspect of his game that Richie Ashburn used to discuss often: his base running. "He was not a prolific base stealer, but he had great instincts," said Jerry. "He never got thrown out on the bases."

Bob Kelly and Rob Betts passed on "Crash," pointing out that he had his best years, not in Philadelphia, but in Chicago. Playing for his favorite manager, Chuck Tanner, Allen won the MVP for the White Sox in 1972, and was on his way to another in 1973 when he broke his leg mid-season. He led the American League in home runs in 1974 despite retiring from baseball with a few weeks left in the season. He reconsidered and returned to Philadelphia to play for two more seasons, but by then, as Rob emphasized, his best days were behind him.

The biggest gripe that voters voiced about Allen was his propensity to stir up controversy off the field. "He didn't have his head screwed on straight" (John Mitchell). "He had a lousy reputation"

(Bill McElroy). "Too many off-the-field problems kept him off my list" (Jim Kent). While Allen had some potent offensive seasons in his first tour of duty with the Phillies, he clashed with Phillies management sometimes because of his rebellious behavior. Like the time Allen skipped a game in New York to attend a Joe Frazier fight. Those problems eventually culminated in his being traded to the Cardinals after the 1969 season in a multi-player deal which included Curt Flood.

August 3, 1969. Reds at Phils, and it's Helmet Day. Dad had made the mistake of saying he would take me to the game; I think it was probably a 1 p.m. start in those days. Anyway, he must have had a good night the night before because he was sleeping very late; I wake him to tell him we have to leave soon for the game; my sister Hilaire comes along as well for some reason. Dad picks up his friend Denny Flanagan on the way to the game.

Final score: Reds 19, Phils 17; Tony Taylor hits a grand slam; Richie Allen homers. The thing I remember most, though, is my father doubled over laughing in the inning in which the Reds scored 10 or 11; I don't think it took much to rekindle the previous night's party, and I think in all the excitement my father and his pal forgot there were little ears nearby. In that inning my father and his pal were howling at Phils pitcher Dick Farrell to "hang in there" or some such thing, but I think it included a few unmentionables.

Anyway, Hilaire and I got our helmets, watched a slugfest, and got a rare glimpse at how fathers watched games with their pals before they had kids; that game is seared into my mind. Billy Champion was the Phils' starting pitcher and he was also the starting pitcher at a doubleheader I attended earlier that year (July 20, 1969) when the Phils played the Cubbies who were about to fall out of first place to the amazins [the Mets who went on to win the World Series]. Billy Champion and Grant Jackson went for the Phils against Fergie Jenkins and Ken Holzman, I think. How I wish Connie Mack were still around and being talked about in the same tones as Wrigley and Fenway.

—GREG VEITH

Year	Team	Lg	G	AB	R	H	HR	RBI	SB	Avg	SLG
1963	Phillies	N.L.	10	24	6	7	0	2	0	.292	.458
1964	Phillies	N.L.	162	632	125	201	29	91	3	.318	.557
1965	Phillies	N.L.	161	619	93	187	20	85	15	.302	.494
1966	Phillies	N.L.	141	524	112	166	40	110	10	.317	.632
1967	Phillies	N.L.	122	463	89	142	23	77	20	.307	.566
1968	Phillies	N.L.	152	521	87	137	33	90	7	.263	.520
1969	Phillies	N.L.	118	438	79	126	32	89	9	.288	.573
1970	St. Louis	N.L.	122	459	88	128	34	101	5	.279	.560
1971	Los Angeles	N.L.	155	549	82	162	23	90	8	.295	.468
1972	Chisox	A.L.	148	506	90	156	37	113	19	.308	.603
1973	Chisox	A.L.	72	250	39	79	16	41	7	.316	.612
1974	Chisox	A.L.	128	462	84	139	32	88	7	.301	.563
1975	Phillies	N.L.	119	416	54	97	12	62	11	.233	.385
1976	Phillies	N.L.	85	298	52	80	15	49	11	.268	.480
1977	Oakland	A.L.	54	171	19	41	5	31	1	.240	.351
Phillies Totals			1070	3935	697	1143	204	655	86	.290	.530
Career Totals			1749	6332	1099	1848	351	1119	133	.292	.534

National League Rookie of the Year (1964)
National League All-Star (1965–67, 1970)
American League MVP (1972)
American League All-Star (1972–74)

32 Rick MacLeish

RANK	POINTS	VOTES RECEIVED		RANK	POINTS	VOTES RECEIVED
1st	50	0		31st	20	1
2nd	49	0		32nd	19	2
3rd	48	0		33rd	18	1
4th	47	0		34th	17	1
5th	46	0		35th	16	3
6th	45	0		36th	15	6
7th	44	0		37th	14	1
8th	43	0		38th	13	0
9th	42	0		39th	12	4
10th	41	0		40th	11	1
11th	40	0		41st	10	2
12th	39	2		42nd	9	2
13th	38	1		43rd	8	4
14th	37	1		44th	7	0
15th	36	3		45th	6	0
16th	35	1		46th	5	3
17th	34	2		47th	4	0
18th	33	0		48th	3	3
19th	32	2		49th	2	1
20th	31	3		50th	1	1
21st	30	0		Not on List	0	29
22nd	29	2				
23rd	28	7				
24th	27	1		TOP 10 VOTES		0
25th	26	2		2ND 10 VOTES		15
26th	25	1		3RD 10 VOTES		20
27th	24	3		4TH 10 VOTES		20
28th	23	2		5TH 10 VOTES		16
29th	22	2		TOTAL VOTES		71
30th	21	0		TOTAL POINTS		1442

▼ **TEAM**
Flyers

▼ **YEARS PLAYED**
1971–1981, 1984

▼ **POSITION**
Center

Jim Schloth thought Rick MacLeish's ability to score game-winning goals was awesome. There was one goal in particular that stood out in Jim's memory. "He gave the Flyers their first championship by scoring the only goal by both teams in a 1-0 victory." Jim, of course, is referring to Game 6 of the 1974 Stanley Cup Finals against the Bruins, in which MacLeish netted a goal late in the first period, and then Bernie and the defense shut down the high-powered Boston offense to preserve the historic win. That goal capped a postseason in which MacLeish led the Flyers in both goals and points.

John Mitchell and Bob Anderson both thought MacLeish was the most talented player on the Flyers' Stanley Cup teams. John felt that MacLeish held this distinction by far. In Bob Anderson's opinion, MacLeish's accomplishments with the Flyers should have earned him a place in the Hockey Hall of Fame. "Nobody could stop his wrist shot. He scored key third-period goals, killed penalties, was great at winning faceoffs. He made [the wings on his line] Ross Lonsberry and Gary Dornhoefer better." MacLeish had the best wrist shot that Mike Rad ever saw. "When 'Rick the Stick' was coming up the ice, you could tell when he was going to score."

Bob Chazin and Paul Lightkep both marveled at MacLeish's skating ability, and in so doing, compared him to some hockey legends. Bob said MacLeish skated very effortlessly, likening him to Guy LaFleur. Paul said that MacLeish's moves on the ice were comparable to those of "the Great Gretzky."

As impressed as Bob Anderson was with MacLeish's skill, he acknowledged that Rick was laconic and laid-back. That rubbed some people the wrong way because it sometimes gave the impression that MacLeish was not doing his best. "It appeared as if he did not hustle all the time on a team which included Bobby Clarke and Bob Kelly who were always hustling," said Jim Kent. "He had so much talent," said Frank Minch, "but he didn't show it all the time." Rob Betts likes hockey players who are strong at both ends of the ice and nixed MacLeish for that reason. "He was a one-way player, just offense. He didn't play defense." Mike Koob didn't think that MacLeish, on the whole, contributed to the Flyers' success as much as the "LCB line" of Leach, Clarke and Barber.

Year	Team	Lg	Gm	G	A	Pts	PM
1970–71	Flyers	NHL	26	2	4	6	19
1971–72	Flyers	NHL	17	1	2	3	9
1972–73	Flyers	NHL	78	50	50	100	69
1973–74	Flyers	NHL	78	32	45	77	42
1974–75	Flyers	NHL	80	38	41	79	50
1975–76	Flyers	NHL	51	22	23	45	16
1976–77	Flyers	NHL	79	49	48	97	42
1977–78	Flyers	NHL	76	31	39	70	33
1978–79	Flyers	NHL	71	26	32	58	47
1979–80	Flyers	NHL	78	31	35	66	28
1980–81	Flyers	NHL	78	38	36	74	25
1981–82	Hart.-Pitt.	NHL	74	19	28	47	44
1982–83	Pittsburgh	NHL	6	0	5	5	2
1983–84	Flyers	NHL	29	8	14	22	4
1983–84	Detroit	NHL	25	2	8	10	4
	Flyers Totals		741	328	369	697	384
	Career Totals		846	349	410	759	434

NHL All-Star Game (1976–77, 1980)
Member of Stanley Cup Champions (1974–75)

Curt Schilling

RANK	POINTS	VOTES RECEIVED		RANK	POINTS	VOTES RECEIVED
1st	50	0		31st	20	2
2nd	49	0		32nd	19	2
3rd	48	0		33rd	18	2
4th	47	0		34th	17	1
5th	46	0		35th	16	4
6th	45	0		36th	15	2
7th	44	0		37th	14	0
8th	43	0		38th	13	4
9th	42	1		39th	12	0
10th	41	1		40th	11	2
11th	40	1		41st	10	2
12th	39	2		42nd	9	1
13th	38	2		43rd	8	0
14th	37	1		44th	7	3
15th	36	1		45th	6	1
16th	35	0		46th	5	1
17th	34	4		47th	4	2
18th	33	2		48th	3	0
19th	32	2		49th	2	1
20th	31	2		50th	1	1
21st	30	1		Not on List	0	34
22nd	29	2				
23rd	28	0				
24th	27	2		TOP 10 VOTES		2
25th	26	0		2ND 10 VOTES		17
26th	25	1		3RD 10 VOTES		16
27th	24	3		4TH 10 VOTES		19
28th	23	2		5TH 10 VOTES		12
29th	22	2		TOTAL VOTES		66
30th	21	3		TOTAL POINTS		1441

▼ TEAM
Phillies

▼ YEARS PLAYED
1992–2000

▼ POSITION
Pitcher

Brothers Kevin and Ryan Kent like to debate sports and while they agree on some things, on the question of whether Curt Schilling, the hard-throwing, outspoken Phillies pitcher for years, is a great Philadelphia athlete, they don't see eye-to-eye. Ryan is in Schill's corner: "Undoubtedly, he will be heading for Cooperstown when he retires. He was the bright spot for the Phillies for years, and up until we made the *wonderful* deal (in July 2000) bringing Nelson Figueroa and Vicente Padilla [Ryan, let's not forget the Phillies also acquired Travis Lee and Omar Daal in that deal.], Schilling was the face of the team." Kevin saw it in another light. "When Schilling retires, he won't be remembered as a Phillie. He was in the World Series with two teams (Arizona and Boston), and I just don't feel he belongs on the same list as Daulton, Dykstra and Kruk, who forever will be three of the most beloved players in Phillies history."

In sizing up Schilling, Steve Bucci and Ray Didinger were in Ryan's camp. Steve said that his first consideration when making his list was whether the player was in his sport's Hall of Fame, or had the potential to be. In Steve's opinion, Curt has Hall of Fame credentials. Ray said that Schilling gave the Phillies great confidence when he was on the mound; he pitched with no fear, was a great competitor, and had a high level of focus and concentration. Ray also described Schilling as a big-game pitcher, a point mimicked by Jody McDonald. Jody thought Schilling's shutout against the Blue Jays in Game 5 of the 1993 World Series was the best single-game, postseason performance of any athlete on the list. The Phillies had squandered a five-run lead the night before, but Schilling gave the Phillies life by throwing a five-hit, complete-game shutout.

"He was dominating," added Rod Smith. "He made batters look foolish trying to catch up with his high fastball." Hitters had so much trouble catching up with Schilling's heater in 1997 and 1998 that he piled up 300 strikeouts each year, a point noted by Dave Sautter. In making his picks, Dave deemed as important how fans in other cities viewed the player. In ranking Schilling 17th, Dave thought that the big right-hander was regarded as an outstanding pitcher, not just in Philadelphia, but by baseball fans throughout the country.

Kevin, don't worry, though. A lot of other voters saw it your way and chose not to put Schilling on their lists. John Clark and Gordie Jones thought that his name will be associated more with the Diamondbacks and Red Sox than the Phillies. Other voters took exception to Schilling's constant whining that he wanted out of Philadelphia. "He deserted Philadelphia when he demanded to be traded" (Paul Lightkep). "He had a chip on his shoulder" (Dick Streeter).

On September 1,1997, I and 50,868 other baseball fans passed on Labor Day picnics and a final day at the Shore in order to witness the first visit by the New York Yankees to Philadelphia since the A's left town in 1954. It was already warm and sunny when my friend and I settled into our seats mid-way down the right field line. We wouldn't leave our seats until the final pitch. Interleague play was in its inaugural season and, along with this first-in-a-lifetime chance for many to experience firsthand the fabled Yankee mystique, we fans were also drawn by the prospect of seeing stars like Derek Jeter, Wade Boggs, Bernie Williams, Mariano Rivera and Paul O'Neil. The Yankees were defending World Series champs and were in the midst of a heated A.L. East race. The final bit of excitement the Yankees brought that day was their newest starting pitcher, highly touted Japanese import Hideki Irabu. The Phillies, on the other hand, were on their way to 94 losses that year, finishing 33 games out of first place.

One of the few bright spots that season was the continued development of that day's starter, Curt Schilling, into one of the game's premier pitchers. Hitting his stride for the first time since 1993, Schilling would finish the year at 17-11 with seven complete games and the first of two consecutive 300-strikeout seasons. Schilling dominated the game from the first batter, fanning Jeter and sending the already-enthusiastic crowd into a frenzy. The Phils nicked Irabu for two runs in the bottom of the first. Mickey Morandini stroked three hits, Mike Lieberthal had two RBIs, and Tony Barron knocked a home run, leading to Irabu's departure in the fourth. As the temperature creeped into the low 80s, Schilling breezed along, giving up only one run in eight innings. Jeter would be the victim on four of Schilling's then-career-high 16 strikeouts. Schilling yielded only seven hits—and did not walk a batter—before turning it over to Ricky Bottalico to close the game out. The 5-1 win was the first in a three-game sweep of the Bronx Bombers, setting the tone for one of the more memorable series in Veterans Stadium history. Schilling's performance would be a precursor to his many masterful performances in high-profile games over the next several seasons.

—ED BRITTINGHAM

Year	Team	Lg	G	W	L	CG	SH	IP	H	BB	SO	ER	ERA
1988	Baltimore	A.L.	4	0	3	0	0	15.2	22	10	4	16	9.82
1989	Baltimore	A.L.	5	0	1	0	0	9.2	10	3	6	6	6.23
1990	Baltimore	A.L.	35	1	2	0	0	46	38	19	32	13	2.54
1991	Houston	N.L.	56	3	5	0	0	76.2	79	39	71	32	3.81
1992	Phillies	N.L.	42	14	11	10	4	226.1	165	59	147	59	2.35
1993	Phillies	N.L.	34	16	7	7	2	235.1	234	57	186	105	4.02
1994	Phillies	N.L.	13	2	8	1	0	82.1	87	28	58	41	4.48
1995	Phillies	N.L.	17	7	5	1	0	116	96	26	114	46	3.57
1996	Phillies	N.L.	26	9	10	8	2	183.1	149	50	182	65	3.19
1997	Phillies	N.L.	35	17	11	7	2	254.1	208	58	319	84	2.97
1998	Phillies	N.L.	35	15	14	15	2	269.2	236	61	300	97	3.25
1999	Phillies	N.L.	24	15	6	8	1	180.1	159	44	152	71	3.54
2000	Phillies	N.L.	16	6	6	4	1	113.2	110	32	96	49	3.91
2000	Arizona	N.L.	13	5	6	4	1	98.2	94	13	72	40	3.69
2001	Arizona	N.L.	35	22	6	6	1	257.2	237	39	293	85	2.98
2002	Arizona	N.L.	36	23	7	5	1	259.1	218	33	316	93	3.23
2003	Arizona	N.L.	24	8	9	3	2	168	144	32	194	55	2.95
2004	Boston	A.L.	32	21	6	3	0	227.2	206	35	203	82	3.26
2005	Boston	A.L.	32	8	8	0	0	93.1	121	22	87	59	5.69
2006	Boston	A.L.	31	15	7	0	0	204	220	28	183	90	3.97
	Phillies Totals		242	101	78	61	14	1659	1444	415	1554	617	3.35
	Career Totals		545	207	138	82	19	3110	2833	688	3015	1188	3.44

National League Championship Series MVP (1993)
National League All-Star (1997–99, 2001–02)
American League All-Star (2004)
World Series co-MVP (2001)
Member of World Champions (2001, 2004)

34 ▸ Ron Hextall

RANK	POINTS	VOTES RECEIVED
1st	50	0
2nd	49	0
3rd	48	0
4th	47	0
5th	46	0
6th	45	0
7th	44	0
8th	43	0
9th	42	0
10th	41	1
11th	40	0
12th	39	0
13th	38	0
14th	37	0
15th	36	2
16th	35	2
17th	34	2
18th	33	3
19th	32	3
20th	31	0
21st	30	5
22nd	29	1
23rd	28	3
24th	27	4
25th	26	2
26th	25	4
27th	24	1
28th	23	0
29th	22	2
30th	21	2

RANK	POINTS	VOTES RECEIVED
31st	20	3
32nd	19	3
33rd	18	1
34th	17	1
35th	16	1
36th	15	1
37th	14	1
38th	13	0
39th	12	3
40th	11	2
41st	10	2
42nd	9	3
43rd	8	4
44th	7	2
45th	6	0
46th	5	0
47th	4	0
48th	3	1
49th	2	0
50th	1	0
Not on List	0	35

TOP 10 VOTES	1
2ND 10 VOTES	12
3RD 10 VOTES	24
4TH 10 VOTES	16
5TH 10 VOTES	12
TOTAL VOTES	65
TOTAL POINTS	1430

▼ TEAM
Flyers

▼ YEARS PLAYED
1987–1992, 1995–1999

▼ POSITION
Goalie

The Flyers came within an eyelash of winning their third Stanley Cup in 1987 when they beat the Rangers, Islanders and Canadians in the first three rounds of the playoffs, and forced a seventh game to Wayne Gretzky and Mark Messier's Oilers, losing 3-1. The hero for the Flyers throughout this valiant run was rookie goaltender Ron Hextall, who started all 26 postseason games, winning 15. Hextall was named the MVP of the playoffs and won the Vezina Trophy as the NHL's best goalie during the regular season.

Harvey Feldman put Hextall's amazing '87 season in perspective: "Winning the MVP of the playoffs while playing for a team that lost as a rookie—that alone would put him on the list somewhere. And he had a decent career with not much help." Paul Troy described Hextall as a "born leader" and "terrific goalie." John Mitchell and Gregg Asman also lauded Hextall for his postseason performance. Dave Myers and Mike Koob considered Hextall the Flyers' best goalie behind Parent in their history. Dave described Hextall as "supremely talented" and "very fast for his size."

Other words of praise for Hextall: "He brought a 'can win' attitude to the team that I feel brought them to the brink of winning the Stanley Cup in 1997" (Joe Gribb). "He was the toughest SOB ever to play goalie" (Joe Fee).

Hextall's tough-guy attitude did not sit well with Greg Veith. "Hextall made a big splash as a rookie, and then continued to garner unusually high fan support which in my opinion stemmed largely from his eagerness to fight. But he was able to sustain his support because of his feistiness, which frankly I saw as phony; how can a goalie fight?" Greg also thought that Hextall got more mileage than he deserved from the 1987 season. "I believe the books are filled with goalies who had miraculous runs and then leveled off." Greg put Hextall in that category. Greg's parting shot toward Hextall: "He was overrated! And a self-promoter."

Rod Smith and Mike Rad also thought that Hextall did not

maintain his high level of play after 1987. Rod: "His rookie season was the best. He could make some incredible saves, but let in some soft, back-breaking goals in big games." Mike said Hextall came up small in some postseasons (in '88, the Flyers went down to the Capitals in the first round of the playoffs), and when the Flyers' fans razzed him, he let it affect his play.

My cousin and I went to the sixth game of the 1987 Stanley Cup Finals at the Spectrum. I was annoyed with him for chirping in my ear about how the Oilers were a dynasty but he still hoped the Flyers would win. As we got to our seats, I remembered waiting in line all morning when the tickets went on sale. There was a two-ticket-per-person limit, so you had to decide what game to ask for. Everyone was grabbing up games three and four. They were a certainty and without Tim Kerr, I guess my cousin's opinion was the popular one. By the time I got to the window, they only had game six and they only had obstructed-view tickets. I bought 'em anyway and hoped for the best. These were the ones at the back of the second level right next to the stairs for the third level. One seat was completely blocked. The other seat gave you a decent view. We were behind the goal and you couldn't see the far end of the ice if you sat straight up. If you leaned forward just a hair it was fine. We were in the last row and there was a space behind the better seat. We took turns standing back there. We had to crouch down when the action was at the far end of the ice, but we did get to see everything, so it was worth it.

It was way louder than usual in there. There was some rough stuff early on, mostly matching minors, but we did get a power play. Grant Fuhr was on our end, so we were hoping to see him get burned, but the Oilers scored shorthanded. I don't even remember who, but it really took the wind out of our sails. Near the end of the first period something happened that I will never ever forget. The Flyers were killing a penalty on Dave Poulin and the Oilers were having target practice on Ron Hextall. The penalty expired but the Oilers were all over the place. They scored before the Flyers could get settled. During the following face off, Poulin tried to lift Mark Messier's stick, missed and clipped his face. The referee's hand went up right away. Hextall immediately turned and blasted the net of its pegs so hard it went flying into the end boards top first with a huge crash. It was as if he was saying, "I don't care what it takes! They're not getting any more!" There was no one else near Hextall, so the referee skated over to talk, but he didn't see any of it.

The Flyers scored early in the second period and that got the crowd back into it. Hextall was in front of us now and the Oilers got it going after that, so all the action was at our end. They peppered him but he stopped everything. He was so good that after one sequence the entire crowd was screaming the chant, "Ronnie! Ronnie!" for what seemed like a minute and a half. Did I mention how loud it was? We were exhausted at the second intermission, but we held hope for a goal at our end of the ice in the third.

Half way through the third we were starting to feel desperate. Hextall was still doing his thing but Fuhr was playing well, too. A couple minutes later the Oilers took a penalty. Everyone knew this was the best chance. When Brian Propp scored the desperation turned to inspiration. We were in for a fantastic finish. The crowd was still buzzing and so were the Flyers. A puck was heading out of the Oilers' zone and JJ Daigneault was racing to keep it from crossing the blue line. Everyone was yelling, "Keep it in! Just keep it in!" but he wound up and blasted one at Fuhr. When the net rippled that place erupted. The crowd really went nuts. Everyone was hugging people they didn't even know. Hextall got a lot of support after that and they held on to win. Streamers were flying all over the place. The noise was so loud I remember getting a headache. I've been to a few hundred sporting events and that's the only time it ever hurt. I've been to World Series games, the World Cup and the Olympics, but this was the best game I ever saw.

—JOE FEE

Year	Team	Lg	Gm	W	L	T	Sh	Avg
1986–87	Flyers	NHL	66	37	21	6	1	3.00
1987–88	Flyers	NHL	62	30	22	7	0	3.50
1988–89	Flyers	NHL	64	30	28	6	0	3.23
1989–90	Flyers	NHL	8	4	2	1	0	4.15
1990–91	Flyers	NHL	36	13	16	5	0	3.13
1991–92	Flyers	NHL	45	16	21	6	3	3.40
1992–93	Quebec	NHL	54	29	16	5	0	3.45
1993–94	N.Y. Islanders	NHL	65	27	26	6	5	3.08
1994–95	Flyers	NHL	31	17	9	4	1	2.89
1995–96	Flyers	NHL	53	31	13	7	4	2.17
1996–97	Flyers	NHL	55	31	16	5	5	2.56
1997–98	Flyers	NHL	46	21	17	7	4	2.17
1998–99	Flyers	NHL	23	10	7	4	0	2.53
	Flyers Totals		489	240	172	58	18	2.98
	Career Totals		608	296	214	69	23	2.97

Vezina Trophy (1987)
Conn Smythe Trophy (1987)
NHL All-Star (1987–88)

35 Norm Van Brocklin

RANK	POINTS	VOTES RECEIVED
1st	50	0
2nd	49	0
3rd	48	0
4th	47	0
5th	46	0
6th	45	1
7th	44	1
8th	43	2
9th	42	1
10th	41	2
11th	40	1
12th	39	3
13th	38	5
14th	37	0
15th	36	3
16th	35	3
17th	34	0
18th	33	1
19th	32	0
20th	31	2
21st	30	4
22nd	29	0
23rd	28	0
24th	27	0
25th	26	0
26th	25	1
27th	24	0
28th	23	2
29th	22	0
30th	21	2

RANK	POINTS	VOTES RECEIVED
31st	20	0
32nd	19	1
33rd	18	0
34th	17	1
35th	16	0
36th	15	1
37th	14	0
38th	13	1
39th	12	1
40th	11	1
41st	10	1
42nd	9	3
43rd	8	3
44th	7	0
45th	6	0
46th	5	0
47th	4	0
48th	3	2
49th	2	1
50th	1	1
Not on List	0	49

TOP 10 VOTES	7
2ND 10 VOTES	18
3RD 10 VOTES	9
4TH 10 VOTES	6
5TH 10 VOTES	11
TOTAL VOTES	51
TOTAL POINTS	1344

▼ TEAM
Eagles

▼ YEARS PLAYED
1958–1960

▼ POSITION
Quarterback

Many Eagles quarterbacks—Sonny Jurgensen, Norm Snead, Ron Jaworski, Randall Cunningham and Donovan McNabb—have had outstanding seasons, but if you ask Ray Didinger, Norm Van Brocklin's performance in 1960 was the best ever for a Birds signal-caller. "No other quarterback in football would have led them to the championship. The '60 Eagles weren't that talented a team. He was a leader, a difference-maker. When he stepped into the huddle, he gave the team a confidence level, and raised the confidence level of other players." Van Brocklin led the Eagles to a strong regular season—10-2—and a victory over the Packers for the NFL championship.

Like Ray, Neil Goldstein, Jon Grisdale and Frank Minch felt that Van Brocklin's critical role in helping the Eagles win the world championship, which has eluded the team in the decades since, warranted a high spot on their lists. Chris Wheeler admired Van Brocklin's toughness and the great respect that he commanded. Steve Danawitz commended "the Dutchman" for being a leader, a great drop-back passer, and because he didn't take guff from anybody. "If he were the quarterback on the Eagles, and T.O. treated him like he did Donovan, Van Brocklin would have told T.O. to screw himself."

The short stay of Van Brocklin in Philadelphia—just three years—was the sticking point for many voters, including Jody McDonald, Mike Rad and Tom Walter, in keeping him off their lists. Tom said that he struggled with ranking the short-tenured players; Moses Malone was one of the only such players whom he included. Jeff Skow really dissected the question of whether Van Brocklin belonged in the top 50 and concluded that he did not. "He didn't play long enough in Philly to make my list. While he was the 1960 league MVP and on the 1960 NFL championship team, he would have needed to put together three spectacular seasons to make up for his lack of longevity. His yardage totals in Philly represented the best three-season stretch of his career, but if you excluded his 1960 season, he had more interceptions than TDs while he was in town and that doesn't sit well with me as an Eagles fan, especially when there are so many other worthy candidates."

Year	Team	Lg	G	Att	Comp	Pct	Yds	TD	Int
1949	Los Angeles	NFL	8	58	32	55.1	601	6	2
1950	Los Angeles	NFL	12	233	127	54.5	2061	18	14
1951	Los Angeles	NFL	12	194	100	51.5	1725	13	11
1952	Los Angeles	NFL	12	205	113	55.1	1736	14	17
1953	Los Angeles	NFL	12	286	156	54.5	2393	19	14
1954	Los Angeles	NFL	12	260	139	53.5	2637	13	21
1955	Los Angeles	NFL	12	272	144	52.9	1890	8	15
1956	Los Angeles	NFL	12	124	68	54.8	966	7	12
1957	Los Angeles	NFL	12	265	132	49.8	2105	20	21
1958	Eagles	NFL	12	374	198	52.9	2409	15	20
1959	Eagles	NFL	12	340	191	56.1	2617	16	14
1960	Eagles	NFL	12	284	153	53.9	2471	24	17
	Eagles Totals		36	998	542	54.3	7497	55	51
	Career Totals		140	2895	1553	53.6	23611	173	178

NFL Pro Bowl (1950–55, 1958–60)
NFL MVP (1960)
Member of NFL Champions (1951, 1960)
Pro Football Hall of Fame (1971)

36 Brian Dawkins

RANK	POINTS	VOTES RECEIVED		RANK	POINTS	VOTES RECEIVED
1st	50	0		31st	20	2
2nd	49	0		32nd	19	2
3rd	48	0		33rd	18	2
4th	47	0		34th	17	1
5th	46	0		35th	16	2
6th	45	0		36th	15	2
7th	44	0		37th	14	2
8th	43	0		38th	13	0
9th	42	1		39th	12	4
10th	41	1		40th	11	3
11th	40	2		41st	10	5
12th	39	0		42nd	9	1
13th	38	2		43rd	8	0
14th	37	0		44th	7	2
15th	36	1		45th	6	1
16th	35	1		46th	5	2
17th	34	0		47th	4	0
18th	33	0		48th	3	1
19th	32	1		49th	2	1
20th	31	3		50th	1	0
21st	30	3		Not on List	0	35
22nd	29	0				
23rd	28	5				
24th	27	1				
25th	26	2				
26th	25	0				
27th	24	2				
28th	23	2				
29th	22	1				
30th	21	4				

TOP 10 VOTES	2
2ND 10 VOTES	10
3RD 10 VOTES	20
4TH 10 VOTES	20
5TH 10 VOTES	13
TOTAL VOTES	65
TOTAL POINTS	1340

▼ TEAM
Eagles

▼ YEARS PLAYED
1996-Present

▼ POSITION
Safety

Joe Fee asked a question which is certain to stir up controversy among Birds diehards: "I may be showing my bias toward past Eagles, but is Brian Dawkins that good?"

According to many voters, Dawkins is definitely that good. Steve Kennedy and Mike Sielski are among them. They both gave Dawkins high marks for being the best—or close to the best—free safety in football over a several-year period. Dennis Brady and John Mitchell had similar opinions about the Eagles' second-round pick from Clemson in 1996. Dennis hailed him as the best Eagles safety ever, while John predicted that Dawkins' status as best free safety in the NFL for years will one day earn him a place in the Pro Football Hall of Fame.

Other voters raved about Dawkins' reputation as a legendary hitter. "He's an intimidator," commented Merrill Reese. "He creates an atmosphere for receivers coming over the middle." Ken Miller and Andy Dziedzic couldn't have agreed more. Ken: "I love his game. He can flat out hit. He hits hard and punishes players." Andy: "B. Dawk is an absolute animal. He's one of the most feared defensive backs in the league." Dave Myers didn't focus on Brian's ability to hit, but summed up what makes him such an outstanding safety: "He can cover, sack and intercept."

But Dawkins had other detractors besides Joe Fee. Mike Koob characterized Dawkins as overrated. "He's not as big a hitter or as good a cover man as everybody says." Dan McCarthy and Ned Hark both thought Dawkins is very good; he's just not in the category of a dominant player. Ned added, "In 50 years, people won't put Dawkins on the list of all-time Eagles."

Or will they?

Year	Team	Lg	Games	Int	Yds	TD	Sacks
1996	Eagles	NFL	14	3	41	0	1
1997	Eagles	NFL	15	3	76	1	0
1998	Eagles	NFL	14	2	39	0	1
1999	Eagles	NFL	16	4	127	1	1.5
2000	Eagles	NFL	13	4	62	0	2
2001	Eagles	NFL	15	2	15	0	1.5
2002	Eagles	NFL	16	2	27	0	3
2003	Eagles	NFL	7	1	0	0	0.5
2004	Eagles	NFL	15	4	40	0	3
2005	Eagles	NFL	16	3	24	0	3.5
2006	Eagles	NFL	16	4	38	0	1
	Eagles Totals		157	32	489	2	18
	Career Totals		157	32	489	2	18

NFL Pro Bowl (1999, 2001–02, 2004–06)

37 Bobby Jones

RANK	POINTS	VOTES RECEIVED
1st	50	0
2nd	49	0
3rd	48	0
4th	47	0
5th	46	0
6th	45	0
7th	44	0
8th	43	1
9th	42	1
10th	41	0
11th	40	0
12th	39	0
13th	38	0
14th	37	0
15th	36	0
16th	35	1
17th	34	0
18th	33	1
19th	32	1
20th	31	0
21st	30	2
22nd	29	3
23rd	28	3
24th	27	0
25th	26	3
26th	25	1
27th	24	2
28th	23	4
29th	22	2
30th	21	4

RANK	POINTS	VOTES RECEIVED
31st	20	3
32nd	19	5
33rd	18	4
34th	17	3
35th	16	1
36th	15	3
37th	14	1
38th	13	1
39th	12	3
40th	11	3
41st	10	0
42nd	9	2
43rd	8	0
44th	7	1
45th	6	2
46th	5	3
47th	4	2
48th	3	2
49th	2	1
50th	1	2
Not on List	0	29

TOP 10 VOTES	2
2ND 10 VOTES	3
3RD 10 VOTES	24
4TH 10 VOTES	27
5TH 10 VOTES	15
TOTAL VOTES	71
TOTAL POINTS	1292

▼ TEAM
Sixers

▼ YEARS PLAYED
1979–1986

▼ POSITION
Forward

In explaining his decision to rank Bobby Jones high on his list, Fran Garvin quoted George Gervin. "Gervin said Jones was the best defensive player that he ever opposed." That's quite a compliment from a guy who won four NBA scoring titles in a five-year stretch (1978-82) for the Spurs. Jones was named to the NBA's All-Defensive team his first five years with the Sixers. Ken Miller, Ralph Antonelli, Cliff Patterson and Ned Hark raved about Jones' defense as well as his team play. "He was a totally unselfish team player," said Ned. "He was a great off-the-ball defensive player. He was a great player without the numbers. He did the intangibles—he cut off passes, shut down passing lanes." Chuck Cutshall liked Jones because he was a contrast to the stars who surrounded him on the Sixers. "He was a low-key, low-maintenance, stay-out-of-the-limelight teammate who knew how to get the job done. That personifies a true hero."

Jones, indeed, was one of the unsung heroes on the Sixers' 1983 championship team. He won the NBA's Sixth Man Award, which voters Andy Paul and Jim Robinson considered important in deciding that Jones cracked their top 25. Andy likened Jones to Jim Eisenreich, outfielder on the Phillies' 1993 World Series team. "Jones was a critical component on the last pro team in Philadelphia to win a championship," said Andy. Jim said that Jones defined the role of a sixth man.

Ray Didinger agreed that Jones was a very valuable member of the '83 Sixers—a selfless teammate who played great defense and didn't care about statistics. But Jones didn't quite warrant a place on Ray's list. Mike Sielski also thought Jones was an outstanding defensive player, but didn't think the 6'9" North Carolina product was a "difference-maker" on the Sixers like Erving, Malone, Cheeks and Toney.

Bob Anderson and Mike Koob thought that Jones wasn't top 50 material because he was not a starter. "He was a good sixth man," said Mike, "but that's it."

Year	Team	Lg	G	Min	FGM	FGA	FGP	FTM	FTA	FTP	AST	REB	Pts	PPG
1974–75	Denver	ABA	84	2706	529	876	.604	187	269	.695	303	692	1245	14.8
1975–76	Denver	ABA	83	2845	510	878	.581	215	308	.698	331	791	1235	14.9
1976–77	Denver	NBA	82	2419	501	879	.570	236	329	.717	264	678	1238	15.1
1977–78	Denver	NBA	75	2440	440	761	.578	208	277	.751	252	636	1088	14.5
1978–79	Sixers	NBA	80	2304	378	704	.537	209	277	.755	201	531	965	12.1
1979–80	Sixers	NBA	81	2125	398	748	.532	257	329	.781	146	450	1053	13.0
1980–81	Sixers	NBA	81	2046	407	755	.539	282	347	.813	226	435	1096	13.5
1981–82	Sixers	NBA	76	2181	416	737	.564	263	333	.790	189	393	1095	14.4
1982–83	Sixers	NBA	74	1749	250	460	.543	165	208	.793	142	344	665	9.0
1983–84	Sixers	NBA	75	1761	226	432	.523	167	213	.784	187	323	619	8.3
1984–85	Sixers	NBA	80	1633	207	385	.538	186	216	.861	155	297	600	7.5
1985–86	Sixers	NBA	70	1519	189	338	.559	114	145	.786	126	169	492	7.0
Sixers Totals			617	15318	2471	4559	.542	1643	2068	.794	1372	2942	6585	10.7
Career Totals			774	20177	3412	6199	.550	2087	2674	.780	1888	4256	8911	11.5

ABA All-Star (1976)
NBA All-Star (1977–78, 1981–82)
Member of NBA Champions (1983)
Number 24 retired by Sixers

38 Reggie Leach

RANK	POINTS	VOTES RECEIVED
1st	50	0
2nd	49	0
3rd	48	0
4th	47	0
5th	46	0
6th	45	0
7th	44	0
8th	43	0
9th	42	0
10th	41	0
11th	40	0
12th	39	0
13th	38	1
14th	37	1
15th	36	2
16th	35	1
17th	34	0
18th	33	2
19th	32	1
20th	31	2
21st	30	3
22nd	29	4
23rd	28	1
24th	27	4
25th	26	3
26th	25	2
27th	24	1
28th	23	2
29th	22	0
30th	21	2

RANK	POINTS	VOTES RECEIVED
31st	20	0
32nd	19	1
33rd	18	1
34th	17	1
35th	16	1
36th	15	2
37th	14	3
38th	13	3
39th	12	2
40th	11	3
41st	10	1
42nd	9	0
43rd	8	2
44th	7	4
45th	6	1
46th	5	2
47th	4	2
48th	3	1
49th	2	0
50th	1	1
Not on List	0	36

TOP 10 VOTES	0
2ND 10 VOTES	10
3RD 10 VOTES	22
4TH 10 VOTES	17
5TH 10 VOTES	15
TOTAL VOTES	64
TOTAL POINTS	1261

▼ **TEAM**
Flyers

▼ **YEARS PLAYED**
1975–1982

▼ **POSITION**
Right Wing

After they won their first Stanley Cup in 1974, the Flyers had another strong season as they won the division and headed into the playoffs with high hopes. About that time, the marketing department circulated a bumper sticker to help fuel the passion of Flyers fans for a repeat performance. It contained a simple message: Again? Jody McDonald believed that if the Flyers had not acquired Reggie Leach from the California Golden Seals in the off-season, they probably would not have won the Cup again. "He gave the Flyers that little extra. He brought something different to the team. He was a great goal scorer and could also bang the boards." Jody thought so highly of Leach that he ranked "the Rifle" 14th. Bob Anderson was on the same page as Jody Mac, ranking Reggie 15th. "He changed the dimension of the team; he made Barber and Clarke better. He's the best offensive wing the Flyers have ever had."

A slew of other voters—Lee Fiederer, Ralph Antonelli and Joe Brown among them—put Leach in their top 25 because of his penchant for generating excitement and scoring goals. "What a wrist shot," said Michael Brophy, "and a move he had to the center before letting it fly." Leach's performance in 1975-76 was especially unforgettable for the voters, as Reggie scored 80 goals—61 in the regular season and 19 more in the postseason. The Flyers were denied a third straight Cup when they were swept in the finals by the Canadians, but nevertheless, as Joe Fee recalled, Leach was named MVP of the playoffs.

Bob Chazin made another good point about Leach: "He was not nearly as good with other teams as he was with the Flyers." Prior to joining the Flyers and after he left them, Leach played five seasons in Boston, California and Detroit and was mediocre; he never scored as many as 25 goals in a season. Fortunately, he saved all his great playing for the Flyers, for whom he averaged 38 goals in eight seasons in orange and black.

Leach took heat from some of the voters who thought that he did little else but score. "He was very one-dimensional," said Michael Beirne. "A trash can could have scored goals with Barber feeding him the puck." Rob Betts also hung the one-dimensional tag on Reggie. "He scored a lot, but he wasn't the team player that Gary Dornhoefer was." Jon Grisdale favored defensive players, and he thought Reggie was deficient in that area.

Year	Team	Lg	Gm	G	A	Pts	PM
1970–71	Boston	NHL	23	2	4	6	0
1971–72	Boston-Calif.	NHL	73	13	20	33	19
1972–73	California	NHL	76	23	12	35	45
1973–74	California	NHL	78	22	24	46	34
1974–75	Flyers	NHL	80	45	33	78	63
1975–76	Flyers	NHL	80	61	30	91	41
1976–77	Flyers	NHL	77	32	14	46	23
1977–78	Flyers	NHL	72	24	28	52	24
1978–79	Flyers	NHL	76	34	20	54	20
1979–80	Flyers	NHL	76	50	26	76	28
1980–81	Flyers	NHL	79	34	36	70	59
1981–82	Flyers	NHL	66	26	21	47	18
1982–83	Detroit	NHL	78	15	17	32	13
	Flyers Totals		684	321	225	546	289
	Career Totals		934	381	285	666	387

NHL All-Star (1976, 1980)
Conn Smythe Trophy (1976)
Member of Stanley Cup Champions (1975)

39

Andrew Toney

RANK	POINTS	VOTES RECEIVED
1st	50	1
2nd	49	0
3rd	48	0
4th	47	0
5th	46	0
6th	45	0
7th	44	0
8th	43	1
9th	42	1
10th	41	0
11th	40	0
12th	39	0
13th	38	0
14th	37	0
15th	36	0
16th	35	1
17th	34	2
18th	33	0
19th	32	2
20th	31	0
21st	30	0
22nd	29	3
23rd	28	2
24th	27	1
25th	26	1
26th	25	2
27th	24	2
28th	23	2
29th	22	5
30th	21	1

RANK	POINTS	VOTES RECEIVED
31st	20	1
32nd	19	0
33rd	18	2
34th	17	3
35th	16	1
36th	15	3
37th	14	4
38th	13	0
39th	12	2
40th	11	3
41st	10	3
42nd	9	1
43rd	8	0
44th	7	1
45th	6	3
46th	5	2
47th	4	2
48th	3	0
49th	2	0
50th	1	2
Not on List	0	40

TOP 10 VOTES	3
2ND 10 VOTES	5
3RD 10 VOTES	19
4TH 10 VOTES	19
5TH 10 VOTES	14
TOTAL VOTES	60
TOTAL POINTS	1138

▼ TEAM
Sixers

▼ YEARS PLAYED
1981–1988

▼ POSITION
Guard

There's no question about Andrew Toney's biggest fan among those surveyed: Narberth native Dan Brown. Basketball was Dan's favorite sport growing up and Toney was his favorite player. He was so wowed by Andrew's skills, he picked him first. "He didn't get the press that Dr. J. did, but he was a great all-around player. He was a clutch shooter—the bigger the game, the better he was, especially against Boston." To add credibility to his first-place selection of Toney, Dan quoted a man who once described Andrew as the best player he ever played with: Charles Barkley.

John Mitchell followed up on Dan's comment about Toney's propensity to bring his game to another level in big games against the Celtics. In the 1980-81 season, the Sixers suffered a gut-wrenching loss to the Celtics in the Eastern Conference Finals. They were up 3-1, but the Celtics won three straight games by a total of five points to knock off the Sixers. The following season was *déjà vu*—almost. Once again, they squared off against Boston in the Eastern Conference Finals and jumped out to a 3-1 lead. The Celtics won Games 5 and 6 to force Game 7 at the Boston Garden. But then, thanks largely to the heroics of "the Boston Strangler" who played "out of his mind," the Sixers thumped the Celtics to advance to the finals.

Andy Paul and Jason Garber both thought highly of Toney, ranking him 19th. "If he hadn't gotten hurt," wondered Andy, "who knows what he would have done?" Jason answered Andy's question by making this prediction: "If injuries did not derail his career, he probably would have been one of the 50 best players in the NBA." As Jason pointed out, Toney started to have foot problems in only his sixth year in the league and then played only two more partial seasons.

It was because Toney's career was shortened by his foot injury that many voters decided to pass on him. Jim Kent and Greg Geier both thought that Toney didn't have enough good years to make the list. Their point has merit. The record reflects that Toney was only a starter for the Sixers in four seasons: his rookie year in '81, the glorious '83 season, '84 and '85. (In '82, he averaged about 25 minutes a game, but only started one contest.) And as Jason mentioned, Toney's foot injury then led to his early retirement; he started just 27 games after the '85 season.

Joe Brown felt that Toney didn't belong on his top 50 list, not only because he was a starter for just four years, but also because he was not that much of an impact player. "I would have rated Fred Carter higher than Toney."

Other criticisms of Toney: "He was a one-dimensional player— he could only shoot. He wasn't close to the player that Hal Greer was" (Michael Beirne). "His commitment to winning and to playing defense was suspect" (Rod Smith).

ADAM KIMELMAN'S TOP 10

1. Wilt Chamberlain
2. Mike Schmidt
3. Julius Erving
4. Chuck Bednarik
5. Bobby Clarke
6. Steve Carlton
7. Reggie White
8. Richie Ashburn
9. Bernie Parent
10. Robin Roberts

Year	Team	Lg	G	Min	FGM	FGA	FGP	FTM	FTA	FTP	AST	REB	Pts	PPG
1980–81	Sixers	NBA	75	1768	399	806	.495	161	226	.712	273	143	968	12.9
1981–82	Sixers	NBA	77	1909	511	979	.522	227	306	.742	283	134	1274	16.5
1982–83	Sixers	NBA	81	2474	626	1250	.501	324	411	.788	365	225	1598	19.7
1983–84	Sixers	NBA	78	2556	593	1125	.527	390	465	.839	373	193	1588	20.4
1984–85	Sixers	NBA	70	2237	450	914	.492	306	355	.862	363	177	1245	17.8
1985–86	Sixers	NBA	6	84	11	36	.306	3	8	.375	12	5	25	4.2
1986–87	Sixers	NBA	52	1058	197	437	.451	133	167	.796	188	85	549	10.6
1987–88	Sixers	NBA	29	522	72	171	.421	58	72	.806	108	47	211	7.3
Sixers Totals			468	12608	2859	5718	.500	1602	2010	.797	1965	1009	7458	15.9
Career Totals			468	12608	2859	5718	.500	1602	2010	.797	1965	1009	7458	15.9

NBA All-Star (1983–84)
Member of NBA Champions (1983)

40

Greg Luzinski

RANK	POINTS	VOTES RECEIVED
1st	50	0
2nd	49	0
3rd	48	0
4th	47	0
5th	46	0
6th	45	0
7th	44	0
8th	43	0
9th	42	0
10th	41	0
11th	40	0
12th	39	0
13th	38	1
14th	37	1
15th	36	0
16th	35	2
17th	34	0
18th	33	0
19th	32	0
20th	31	0
21st	30	0
22nd	29	2
23rd	28	1
24th	27	3
25th	26	7
26th	25	2
27th	24	1
28th	23	3
29th	22	3
30th	21	1

RANK	POINTS	VOTES RECEIVED
31st	20	3
32nd	19	1
33rd	18	4
34th	17	0
35th	16	2
36th	15	1
37th	14	2
38th	13	1
39th	12	2
40th	11	1
41st	10	3
42nd	9	2
43rd	8	3
44th	7	3
45th	6	2
46th	5	1
47th	4	1
48th	3	2
49th	2	1
50th	1	2
Not on List	0	36

TOP 10 VOTES	0
2ND 10 VOTES	4
3RD 10 VOTES	23
4TH 10 VOTES	17
5TH 10 VOTES	20
TOTAL VOTES	64
TOTAL POINTS	1122

▼ TEAM
Phillies

▼ YEARS PLAYED
1970–1980

▼ POSITION
Outfielder

Chuck Cutshall has fond childhood memories of sitting among the "bull's-eyes" in the left field seats at Veterans Stadium. "I always felt like there was a chance for a game-changing home run whenever 'the Bull' stepped to the plate." Greg Luzinski pleased Chuck and the Veterans Stadium crowds by delivering many a home run during his decade in Philly.

"He was a valuable part of the nucleus that made the Phillies into contenders and into the playoffs after decades of ineptitude," said Doug Brown. Not years, folks—*decades*. From 1918 to 1974, a span of 57 seasons, the Phillies had a winning record just 11 times. But in 1975, the tide began to turn as the Phillies finished second to the Pirates in the National League Eastern Division. Luzinski had a league-leading 120 RBIs and finished second in the MVP vote. The Phillies then won three divisions in a row, and as Mike Koob said, during those three years, Mike Schmidt and Greg Luzinski were a great one-two punch. Dan Brown and John Mitchell gave Luzinski the upper hand over Schmidt during the division-winning years of 1976-78. Dan said that "the Bull" carried the Phillies, while John said Luzinski was more clutch than Schmidt during those three years. "He was the Phillies' main horse, the 'go to' guy." Luzinski drove in more runs than Schmidt over the three-year period (326 vs. 286) and, in 1977, Greg again finished runner-up in the MVP vote.

But then Schmidt brought his game to a higher level, hitting 45 and 48 home runs in '79 and '80. But Luzinski, as Lee Fiederer pointed out, suffered a rapid decline in productivity, hitting less than 20 home runs both years. He was then sold to the White Sox for whom he finished his career.

Luzinski had some other flaws, even during his banner years with the Phillies, which many voters were quick to point out. Fred Warren remembered Luzinski's propensity to strike out (Greg had eight 100-strikeout seasons for the Phils), while Rod Smith and Joe Fee recalled his shaky defense in left field. Rod also criticized Luzinski for being one-dimensional (he just hit home runs) and because he was incredibly slow. (He swiped just 29 bases during his decade in Philadelphia.) Joe added, "I think his persona was bigger than his performance."

Year	Team	Lg	G	AB	R	H	HR	RBI	SB	Avg	SLG
1970	Phillies	N.L.	8	12	0	2	0	0	0	.167	.167
1971	Phillies	N.L.	28	100	13	30	3	15	2	.300	.470
1972	Phillies	N.L.	150	563	66	158	18	68	0	.281	.453
1973	Phillies	N.L.	161	610	76	174	29	97	3	.285	.484
1974	Phillies	N.L.	85	302	29	82	7	48	3	.272	.394
1975	Phillies	N.L.	161	596	85	179	34	120	3	.300	.540
1976	Phillies	N.L.	149	533	74	162	21	95	1	.304	.478
1977	Phillies	N.L.	149	554	99	171	39	130	3	.309	.594
1978	Phillies	N.L.	155	540	85	143	35	101	8	.265	.526
1979	Phillies	N.L.	137	452	47	114	18	81	3	.252	.427
1980	Phillies	N.L.	106	368	44	84	19	56	3	.228	.440
1981	Chisox	A.L.	104	378	55	100	21	62	0	.265	.476
1982	Chisox	A.L.	159	583	87	170	18	102	1	.292	.451
1983	Chisox	A.L.	144	502	73	128	32	95	2	.255	.502
1984	Chisox	A.L.	125	412	47	98	13	58	5	.238	.364
Phillies Totals			1289	4630	618	1299	223	811	29	.281	.489
Career Totals			1821	6505	880	1795	307	1128	37	.276	.478

National League All-Star (1975–78)
Member of World Champions (1980)

41 Tim Kerr

RANK	POINTS	VOTES RECEIVED
1st	50	0
2nd	49	0
3rd	48	0
4th	47	0
5th	46	0
6th	45	0
7th	44	0
8th	43	0
9th	42	0
10th	41	0
11th	40	0
12th	39	1
13th	38	1
14th	37	3
15th	36	0
16th	35	1
17th	34	0
18th	33	1
19th	32	2
20th	31	0
21st	30	2
22nd	29	0
23rd	28	0
24th	27	2
25th	26	1
26th	25	4
27th	24	1
28th	23	1
29th	22	2
30th	21	0

RANK	POINTS	VOTES RECEIVED
31st	20	4
32nd	19	0
33rd	18	0
34th	17	1
35th	16	3
36th	15	1
37th	14	5
38th	13	2
39th	12	0
40th	11	5
41st	10	4
42nd	9	0
43rd	8	1
44th	7	1
45th	6	1
46th	5	3
47th	4	4
48th	3	3
49th	2	1
50th	1	0
Not on List	0	39

TOP 10 VOTES	0
2ND 10 VOTES	9
3RD 10 VOTES	13
4TH 10 VOTES	21
5TH 10 VOTES	18
TOTAL VOTES	61
TOTAL POINTS	1065

▼ **TEAM**
Flyers

▼ **YEARS PLAYED**
1981–1991

▼ **POSITION**
Center/Right Wing

It is an image from the mid-to-late 1980s that many voters recall vividly: 6'3", 230-pound Tim Kerr planted in front of the net, taking a pass or fielding a rebound, and ripping a shot past the goalie. "He was a statue of steel between the circles," said Paul Troy. "He would post up and unleash a great shot. He is one of the best offensive players the Flyers have ever had." No question about that. Kerr's 363 goals put him third on the all-time Flyers list, and his 145 power play goals are first by far. Dan McCarthy, Joe Fee and Bob Anderson shared Paul's sentiments about Kerr's superior ability as a scorer. Dan: "He was tough. He stood in front of the net, took punishment, and scored goals." Joe: "He had a pure wrist shot; he couldn't be moved from the crease." Bob: "He was gutsy, strong, and had a great shot." John Clark was so impressed with Kerr's contributions to the Flyers over several years that he ranked him 24th.

For Jon Grisdale, Kerr's string of four 50-goal seasons wasn't enough. "Scoring goals is the easy part of hockey," said Jon. When John Surbeck was deciding which Flyers wings to include in his top 50 list, he went with Reggie Leach and Gary Dornhoefer, who played on Stanley Cup winners, over Kerr, who did not. Kerr came close, as he played on the 1985 and 1987 Flyers teams which lost to the Oilers in the finals. Kerr pulled his weight in the playoffs of those years, scoring 10 goals in 12 games in the 1985 postseason and eight goals in 12 games in the 1987 playoffs. But he lost points for John because the Flyers failed to win the prized Cup. Gregg Asman also passed on Kerr for that reason. Gregg also pointed out that Kerr was injury-prone. Kerr missed almost the entire 1988 season due to a shoulder injury and parts of the 1990 and 1991 seasons, his final two years in Philadelphia, with assorted injuries.

Year	Team	Lg	Gm	G	A	Pts	PM
1980–81	Flyers	NHL	68	22	23	45	84
1981–82	Flyers	NHL	61	21	30	51	138
1982–83	Flyers	NHL	24	11	8	19	6
1983–84	Flyers	NHL	79	54	39	93	29
1984–85	Flyers	NHL	74	54	44	98	57
1985–86	Flyers	NHL	76	58	26	84	79
1986–87	Flyers	NHL	75	58	37	95	57
1987–88	Flyers	NHL	8	3	2	5	12
1988–89	Flyers	NHL	69	48	40	88	73
1989–90	Flyers	NHL	40	24	24	48	34
1990–91	Flyers	NHL	27	10	14	24	8
1991–92	N.Y. Rangers	NHL	32	7	11	18	12
1992–93	Hartford	NHL	22	0	6	6	7
	Flyers Totals		601	363	287	650	577
	Career Totals		655	370	304	674	596

NHL All-Star (1984–87)

Tom Gola

RANK	POINTS	VOTES RECEIVED
1st	50	0
2nd	49	0
3rd	48	0
4th	47	0
5th	46	0
6th	45	0
7th	44	0
8th	43	1
9th	42	1
10th	41	0
11th	40	2
12th	39	2
13th	38	3
14th	37	4
15th	36	1
16th	35	0
17th	34	1
18th	33	1
19th	32	0
20th	31	0
21st	30	0
22nd	29	3
23rd	28	1
24th	27	0
25th	26	1
26th	25	2
27th	24	0
28th	23	2
29th	22	1
30th	21	0

RANK	POINTS	VOTES RECEIVED
31st	20	2
32nd	19	1
33rd	18	1
34th	17	0
35th	16	0
36th	15	0
37th	14	2
38th	13	1
39th	12	0
40th	11	1
41st	10	0
42nd	9	0
43rd	8	1
44th	7	4
45th	6	2
46th	5	0
47th	4	1
48th	3	1
49th	2	1
50th	1	1
Not on List	0	55

TOP 10 VOTES	2
2ND 10 VOTES	14
3RD 10 VOTES	10
4TH 10 VOTES	8
5TH 10 VOTES	11
TOTAL VOTES	45
TOTAL POINTS	1054

▼ **TEAM**
Warriors

▼ **YEARS PLAYED**
1956, 1958–1962

▼ **POSITION**
Forward

How great a college player was Tom Gola? Consider this: he was inducted into the Basketball Hall of Fame after his 10-year NBA career with the Warriors and Knicks, but was viewed by some to be a disappointment at the pro level. After all, at La Salle College, he was a four-time All-American and led the Explorers to an NCAA title. Despite his Hall of Fame induction, Steve Danawitz and Harvey Feldman didn't consider Gola a dominant pro player and left him off their top 50 lists. "He was dominant in college—one of the best college players of his era," said Steve. "He was a good solid player in the pros—mostly defense—but he wasn't taking over games. He wasn't nearly as good as [Celtics great Bob] Cousy."

Jerry McDonough and Neil Goldstein agreed that Gola wasn't as good in the pros as he was in college, but still thought he was a strong NBA player, and included him on their lists. Jerry: "He did all phases of the game well. He would defend the other team's best scorer. He saw the whole floor, could break the press, and was a good ball handler. He wouldn't make stupid mistakes." Neil: "He had a good head for the game—he was very smart. He knew how to set up guys; he was a tremendous passer, great rebounder, good scorer and good leader." Bob Cinalli liked Gola's versatility. "He could play point guard, shooting guard, and forward; he could rebound and pass the ball beautifully."

Joe Geier was so impressed with Gola's play as a Warrior that he ranked him in his top 20, at 18th. "He was a very good all-round player. He was more of a playmaker than [his Warriors teammate Paul] Arizin. He could rebound." Michael Barkann and Andy Musser rated Gola even higher; Michael placed Gola ninth, while Andy put him 13th. Michael cited Gola's Hall of Fame status and passion for the game. Andy noted, "He was a total team player who carried himself very well."

Year	Team	Lg	G	Min	FGM	FGA	FGP	FTM	FTA	FTP	AST	REB	Pts	PPG
1955–56	Warriors	NBA	68	2346	244	592	.412	244	333	.733	404	616	732	10.8
1957–58	Warriors	NBA	59	2126	295	711	.415	223	299	.746	327	639	813	13.8
1958–59	Warriors	NBA	64	2333	310	773	.401	281	357	.787	269	710	901	14.1
1959–60	Warriors	NBA	75	2870	426	983	.433	270	340	.794	409	779	1122	15.0
1960–61	Warriors	NBA	74	2712	420	940	.447	210	281	.747	292	692	1050	14.2
1961–62	Warriors	NBA	60	2462	322	765	.421	176	230	.765	295	587	820	13.7
1962–63	San Fran.-N.Y.	NBA	73	2670	363	791	.459	170	219	.776	298	517	896	12.3
1963–64	New York	NBA	74	2156	258	602	.429	154	212	.726	257	469	670	9.1
1964–65	New York	NBA	77	1727	204	455	.448	133	180	.739	220	319	541	7.0
1965–66	New York	NBA	74	1127	122	271	.450	82	105	.781	191	289	326	4.4
Warriors Totals			400	14849	2017	4764	.423	1404	1840	.763	1996	4023	5438	13.6
Career Totals			698	22529	2964	6883	.431	1943	2556	.760	2962	5617	7871	11.3

NBA All-Star (1960–64)
Member of NBA Champions (1956)
Basketball Hall of Fame (1976)

43 John LeClair

RANK	POINTS	VOTES RECEIVED		RANK	POINTS	VOTES RECEIVED
1st	50	0		31st	20	1
2nd	49	0		32nd	19	5
3rd	48	0		33rd	18	1
4th	47	0		34th	17	1
5th	46	0		35th	16	3
6th	45	0		36th	15	2
7th	44	0		37th	14	1
8th	43	0		38th	13	2
9th	42	1		39th	12	1
10th	41	0		40th	11	0
11th	40	0		41st	10	2
12th	39	0		42nd	9	2
13th	38	0		43rd	8	8
14th	37	0		44th	7	2
15th	36	0		45th	6	2
16th	35	1		46th	5	0
17th	34	2		47th	4	0
18th	33	1		48th	3	2
19th	32	0		49th	2	1
20th	31	2		50th	1	1
21st	30	0		Not on List	0	40
22nd	29	3				
23rd	28	2				
24th	27	1		TOP 10 VOTES	1	
25th	26	0		2ND 10 VOTES	6	
26th	25	1		3RD 10 VOTES	16	
27th	24	2		4TH 10 VOTES	17	
28th	23	1		5TH 10 VOTES	20	
29th	22	4		TOTAL VOTES	60	
30th	21	2		TOTAL POINTS	1053	

▼ TEAM
Flyers

▼ YEARS PLAYED
1995–2005

▼ POSITION
Left Wing

If you were a big hockey fan in the 1990s, you saw a lot of low-scoring (2-1, 3-2) games. During that time when goals were hard to come by, John LeClair became the first Flyer to fire off five straight 40-goal seasons; three of those five years, he reached the 50 mark. Mike Sielski felt that LeClair's goal-scoring prowess was especially impressive given the style of hockey at the time. "In the history of big-time scorers for the Flyers, there have not been many better than LeClair. He played in the era of the neutral zone trap, 'the dead puck era,' when goal-scoring was down. He was spectacular when Eric Lindros was there and good even after he left." LeClair, who was joined by Lindros and Mikael Renberg on the Flyers' Legion of Doom line, is fifth on the team's all-time goals list with 308. During his five-year binge, he was tied for third in goals in the NHL twice, and ranked fifth two other years.

The Kent brothers thought that LeClair and Lindros were an incredible scoring tandem. Ryan: "The Legion of Doom and the rest of the Flyers in the 1995-99 era were extremely exciting to watch. LeClair was a goal-scoring machine. Hockey is quite the team sport, yet [LeClair and Lindros] were the superstars, which made watching hockey enjoyable for years." Kevin: "In his prime, he was an absolute dominant force in front of the net and when paired with Lindros, the two were nearly unstoppable at times."

There was a big debate as to how much Lindros' presence affected LeClair's production. Bob Anderson thought that LeClair was good enough that he could have scored with anybody playing center—Lindros or Terry Crisp, for God's sake. Brent Saunders made the point more emphatically: "LeClair made Lindros, not the other way around." Bryan Davis definitely did not see it Brent's way. "He would have been pedestrian if it weren't for number 88 feeding him in front. Lindros could have banked half of LeClair's goals in off a trash can wearing a number 10 jersey."

Like Bryan, Steve Kennedy did not vote for LeClair, although it didn't have anything to do with Lindros. "LeClair was a great regular season tough guy and scorer. Come playoff time, that was another story." The numbers are clear that LeClair did not shine in many postseasons. In 1998, after his third straight 50-goal season, LeClair managed just one goal as the Flyers were bumped in the first round by Buffalo. The next year, the Flyers went down in the opening round to Toronto, and LeClair contributed just three points in the six-game series. LeClair was also ineffective in the Flyers' first-round defeats by Buffalo and Ottawa in the 2001 and 2002 playoffs; he scored just one goal in 11 games over those two series.

Year	Team	Lg	Gm	G	A	Pts	PM
1990–91	Montreal	NHL	10	2	5	7	2
1991–92	Montreal	NHL	59	8	11	19	14
1992–93	Montreal	NHL	72	19	25	44	33
1993–94	Montreal	NHL	74	19	24	43	32
1994–95	Montreal	NHL	9	1	4	5	10
1994–95	Flyers	NHL	37	25	24	49	20
1995–96	Flyers	NHL	82	51	46	97	64
1996–97	Flyers	NHL	82	50	47	97	58
1997–98	Flyers	NHL	82	51	36	87	32
1998–99	Flyers	NHL	76	43	47	90	30
1999–00	Flyers	NHL	82	40	37	77	36
2000–01	Flyers	NHL	16	7	5	12	0
2001–02	Flyers	NHL	82	25	26	51	30
2002–03	Flyers	NHL	35	18	10	28	16
2003–04	Flyers	NHL	75	23	32	55	51
2005–06	Pittsburgh	NHL	73	22	29	51	61
Flyers Totals			649	333	310	643	337
Career Totals			946	404	408	812	489

Member of Stanley Cup Champions (1993)
NHL All-Star (1996-00)

Garry Maddox

RANK	POINTS	VOTES RECEIVED
1st	50	0
2nd	49	0
3rd	48	0
4th	47	0
5th	46	0
6th	45	0
7th	44	0
8th	43	0
9th	42	0
10th	41	0
11th	40	0
12th	39	1
13th	38	0
14th	37	0
15th	36	0
16th	35	0
17th	34	0
18th	33	2
19th	32	0
20th	31	0
21st	30	0
22nd	29	2
23rd	28	0
24th	27	2
25th	26	0
26th	25	3
27th	24	1
28th	23	4
29th	22	2
30th	21	1
31st	20	3
32nd	19	2
33rd	18	4
34th	17	4
35th	16	2
36th	15	2
37th	14	1
38th	13	2
39th	12	2
40th	11	2
41st	10	3
42nd	9	1
43rd	8	4
44th	7	2
45th	6	1
46th	5	2
47th	4	1
48th	3	1
49th	2	3
50th	1	1
Not on List	0	39

TOP 10 VOTES	0
2ND 10 VOTES	3
3RD 10 VOTES	15
4TH 10 VOTES	24
5TH 10 VOTES	19
TOTAL VOTES	61
TOTAL POINTS	974

▼ TEAM
Phillies

▼ YEARS PLAYED
1975–1986

▼ POSITION
Outfielder

In May 1975, the Phillies traded popular first base-man Willie Montanez to the San Francisco Giants to open up a spot for Dick Allen, whom they signed soon after. In return for Montanez, the Phillies acquired young center fielder Garry Maddox. Allen only held the Phillies' first base job for two years; Montanez turned into a journeyman, but Maddox was a fixture in center field for more than 10 years.

The voters, even those who did not include him, gushed about Garry's defense, which earned him eight straight Gold Gloves and the nickname, "the Secretary of Defense." "He was the best defensive center fielder I've ever seen" (Brent Saunders). "He was great at tracking down fly balls" (Bob Chazin). "He was the best defensive outfielder the Phillies have ever had—he had to cover a lot of left field because Luzinski was so bad" (Dennis Brady). Chuck Cutshall commended Maddox on his great attitude, while Dave Beck said that Maddox was one of the leaders of the 1980 world championship team.

Despite Maddox's slew of Gold Gloves, there were pollsters who didn't think he was worthy. "While he was a great defensive center fielder who caught everything in sight, he was only okay offensively," said Mike Sielski. "He didn't make as much of a difference on the Phillies as Greg Luzinski or Larry Bowa." Andy Musser was quick to praise Maddox for his impeccable defense, but sometimes was frustrated with Garry's performance at the plate. "He was more of a swinger than a hitter." (Maddox had seven straight seasons with the Phillies in which he walked less than 20 times.) Others were not impressed with the lack of pop in Garry's bat. Bill Jakavick didn't like his numbers offensively when compared to others like Luzinski, while Mike Koob didn't think Maddox had enough power. While Gregg Asman pointed out that Maddox had a .330 season for the Phillies in 1976 (third in the National League that year), it was his only .300 season for the Phillies, and his season highs in home runs and RBIs for the Phils were 14 and 74, very modest numbers for an outfielder.

While Bob Kelly said Maddox exhibited "quiet class," Bryan Davis said that Maddox's low profile cost him a place on his list. "You have to remember that he was on a team of great personalities—Bowa, Rose, Luzinski. Even Bake McBride had more personality than Garry." Wow, that's harsh.

Year	Team	Lg	G	AB	R	H	HR	RBI	SB	Avg	SLG
1972	San Francisco	N.L.	125	458	62	122	12	58	13	.266	.432
1973	San Francisco	N.L.	144	587	81	187	11	76	24	.319	.460
1974	San Francisco	N.L.	135	538	74	153	8	50	21	.284	.398
1975	San Francisco	N.L.	17	52	4	7	1	4	1	.135	.212
1975	Phillies	N.L.	99	374	50	109	4	46	24	.291	.433
1976	Phillies	N.L.	146	531	75	175	6	68	29	.330	.456
1977	Phillies	N.L.	139	571	85	167	14	74	22	.292	.448
1978	Phillies	N.L.	155	598	62	172	11	68	33	.288	.410
1979	Phillies	N.L.	148	548	70	154	13	61	26	.281	.425
1980	Phillies	N.L.	143	549	59	142	11	73	25	.259	.386
1981	Phillies	N.L.	94	323	37	85	5	40	9	.263	.337
1982	Phillies	N.L.	119	412	39	117	8	61	7	.284	.417
1983	Phillies	N.L.	97	324	27	89	4	32	7	.275	.367
1984	Phillies	N.L.	77	241	29	68	5	19	3	.282	.390
1985	Phillies	N.L.	105	218	22	52	4	23	4	.239	.339
1986	Phillies	N.L.	6	7	1	3	0	1	0	.429	.429
	Phillies Totals		1328	4696	556	1333	85	566	189	.284	.409
	Career Totals		1749	6331	777	1802	117	754	248	.285	.413

National League Gold Glove (1975–82)
Member of World Champions (1980)

Jerome Brown

RANK	POINTS	VOTES RECEIVED
1st	50	0
2nd	49	0
3rd	48	0
4th	47	0
5th	46	0
6th	45	0
7th	44	0
8th	43	0
9th	42	0
10th	41	1
11th	40	0
12th	39	0
13th	38	2
14th	37	1
15th	36	0
16th	35	0
17th	34	1
18th	33	1
19th	32	2
20th	31	1
21st	30	2
22nd	29	3
23rd	28	3
24th	27	2
25th	26	2
26th	25	0
27th	24	0
28th	23	1
29th	22	2
30th	21	0

RANK	POINTS	VOTES RECEIVED
31st	20	2
32nd	19	1
33rd	18	0
34th	17	1
35th	16	2
36th	15	1
37th	14	1
38th	13	1
39th	12	3
40th	11	0
41st	10	0
42nd	9	2
43rd	8	1
44th	7	1
45th	6	2
46th	5	2
47th	4	2
48th	3	1
49th	2	1
50th	1	0
Not on List	0	52

TOP 10 VOTES	1
2ND 10 VOTES	8
3RD 10 VOTES	15
4TH 10 VOTES	12
5TH 10 VOTES	12
TOTAL VOTES	48
TOTAL POINTS	974

▼ TEAM
Eagles

▼ YEARS PLAYED
1987–1991

▼ POSITION
Defensive Tackle

Mark Bristowe remembered longtime sports anchor Al Meltzer interviewing Jerome Brown after a game in which J.B. had injured his shoulder. Meltzer concluded the interview by thanking Brown and then unwittingly slapped him on the shoulder. The 300-pound Jerome gave Al a mean look. Jerome directed most of his meanness toward running backs and quarterbacks, not sportscasters. "He was a missile when he set his sights on a quarterback," said Mark.

Although Brown's career was limited to five seasons because a car accident in 1992 claimed his life, Michael Barkann and Mark Eckel included Brown in their top 25. "He was a very dominating, nasty defensive player," said Michael, who ranked Brown 19th. "He was a possible Hall of Famer if he hadn't died." Mark rated Brown 24th, describing him as a tremendous defensive tackle. Jerome's dominance and incredible speed and agility earned him many other votes. "He was a heart on the Eagles' defense, a perfect example of how to shut down the run game of the other team. He was large, but still quick and athletic" (Bob Bookbinder). "He was a couple steps behind White in dominance" (Jeff Skow). "He was so strong and quick, still on the upside and had not peaked when he died" (Rob Betts). "He was emotionally important to the Eagles' defense" (Sean Bergin).

Ray Didinger was in a quandary as to whether to include Brown on his top 50 list. On the one hand, Ray pointed out that in 1991 Brown was MVP of the great Eagles defense, and the best defensive tackle in football that year. On the other hand, Ray noted: "As good as he was in 1991, he had a couple so-so seasons earlier in his career. His conditioning was not as good as it could have been." Ray decided to pass on Jerome, as did Joe Brown. He mimicked Ray by saying that Jerome did not have the best work ethic. Joe added, "He wouldn't have been as good if Reggie and Clyde Simmons weren't there." Other voters, including John Surbeck and Dennis Brady, thought Jerome's career was too short to warrant inclusion on their lists.

Year	Team	Lg	G	Int	Yds	TD	Sacks
1987	Eagles	NFL	12	2	7	0	4
1988	Eagles	NFL	16	1	-5	0	5
1989	Eagles	NFL	16	0	0	0	10.5
1990	Eagles	NFL	16	0	0	0	1
1991	Eagles	NFL	16	0	0	0	9
	Eagles Totals		76	3	2	0	29.5
	Career Totals		76	3	2	0	29.5

NFL Pro Bowl (1990–91)
Number 99 retired by Eagles

GORDIE JONES' TOP 10

1. Wilt Chamberlain
2. Mike Schmidt
3. Chuck Bednarik
4. Julius Erving
5. Bobby Clarke
6. Steve Carlton
7. Charles Barkley
8. Reggie White
9. Bernie Parent
10. Richie Ashburn

46 Mark Howe

RANK	POINTS	VOTES RECEIVED
1st	50	0
2nd	49	0
3rd	48	0
4th	47	1
5th	46	0
6th	45	0
7th	44	0
8th	43	0
9th	42	1
10th	41	0
11th	40	2
12th	39	1
13th	38	0
14th	37	0
15th	36	0
16th	35	0
17th	34	1
18th	33	2
19th	32	2
20th	31	0
21st	30	1
22nd	29	2
23rd	28	2
24th	27	0
25th	26	2
26th	25	1
27th	24	0
28th	23	1
29th	22	1
30th	21	1
31st	20	1
32nd	19	1
33rd	18	2
34th	17	1
35th	16	1
36th	15	3
37th	14	0
38th	13	3
39th	12	1
40th	11	0
41st	10	1
42nd	9	3
43rd	8	1
44th	7	1
45th	6	2
46th	5	1
47th	4	1
48th	3	1
49th	2	2
50th	1	2
Not on List	0	51

TOP 10 VOTES	2
2ND 10 VOTES	8
3RD 10 VOTES	11
4TH 10 VOTES	13
5TH 10 VOTES	15
TOTAL VOTES	49
TOTAL POINTS	945

TEAM
Flyers

YEARS PLAYED
1983–1992

POSITION
Defenseman

Mark Howe's father, Gordie, was regarded as one of hockey's best players of all time. He won six NHL MVPs and held many scoring records until Wayne Gretzky came along. What impressed Jim Robinson most about Mark was that he didn't rest on his father's name; he proved his greatness on his own. "He wasn't as good as his father," said Jim, "but he's still the Flyers' best defenseman ever."

Many other voters took it a step further: not only was Howe the best defenseman for the *Flyers*, he was one of the best defensemen in the *NHL* during his decade in Philadelphia. Steve Bucci: "Teammates and opponents put him on a pedestal." Andy Salayda: "With Paul Coffey and Ray Bourque, he was one of the best defensemen in the league. He did it more with savvy than brute strength." Bob Anderson: "He was so smart, so skilled. He could kill penalties, get the puck out of the zone, and run the power play." Mike DiColla was also impressed with the way Howe brought the puck up from the Flyers' zone. "He was a wing playing defense. If he played in the new [wide-open] NHL, he would score 70 goals in a season." Wait a minute, Mike. Maybe not 70. Possibly 40, though. Frank Minch and Mike Rad ranked Howe high on their lists because unlike Flyers defensemen from the Stanley Cup years, he was good at both ends. "He was an offensive defenseman, like Bobby Orr," said Frank.

Greg Geier and Bill Jakavick, respectively, disagreed with their peers on Howe. According to Greg, there are two types of hockey players: stars and everybody else. "Howe wasn't in the star category. He was really good, but not good enough to make my top 50." Bill said that there were too many other hockey players that he liked better for him to squeeze Howe in. "He would have been there if it were a top 150." Bryan Davis, like many Philadelphia fans, is fond of athletes with passion and personality. Howe didn't cut the mustard for that reason. "He was very nondescript. We like some emotion in this town, some pizzazz."

Year	Team	Lg	Gm	G	A	Pts	PM
1979–80	Hartford	NHL	74	24	56	80	20
1980–81	Hartford	NHL	63	19	46	65	54
1981–82	Hartford	NHL	76	8	45	53	18
1982–83	Flyers	NHL	76	20	47	67	18
1983–84	Flyers	NHL	71	19	34	53	44
1984–85	Flyers	NHL	73	18	39	57	31
1985–86	Flyers	NHL	77	24	58	82	36
1986–87	Flyers	NHL	69	15	43	58	37
1987–88	Flyers	NHL	75	19	43	62	62
1988–89	Flyers	NHL	52	9	29	38	45
1989–90	Flyers	NHL	40	7	21	28	24
1990–91	Flyers	NHL	19	0	10	10	8
1991–92	Flyers	NHL	42	7	18	25	18
1992–93	Detroit	NHL	60	3	31	34	22
1993–94	Detroit	NHL	44	4	20	24	8
1994–95	Detroit	NHL	18	1	5	6	10
		Flyers Totals	594	138	342	480	323
		Career Totals	929	197	545	742	455

NHL All-Star (1981, 1983, 1986–88)

Lenny Dykstra

RANK	POINTS	VOTES RECEIVED
1st	50	0
2nd	49	0
3rd	48	0
4th	47	0
5th	46	0
6th	45	0
7th	44	0
8th	43	0
9th	42	0
10th	41	0
11th	40	1
12th	39	0
13th	38	1
14th	37	0
15th	36	0
16th	35	0
17th	34	0
18th	33	3
19th	32	0
20th	31	1
21st	30	1
22nd	29	1
23rd	28	3
24th	27	1
25th	26	1
26th	25	1
27th	24	0
28th	23	3
29th	22	2
30th	21	1

RANK	POINTS	VOTES RECEIVED
31st	20	2
32nd	19	1
33rd	18	1
34th	17	1
35th	16	0
36th	15	1
37th	14	3
38th	13	4
39th	12	3
40th	11	0
41st	10	4
42nd	9	1
43rd	8	4
44th	7	0
45th	6	0
46th	5	2
47th	4	1
48th	3	2
49th	2	1
50th	1	1
Not on List	0	48

TOP 10 VOTES	0
2ND 10 VOTES	6
3RD 10 VOTES	14
4TH 10 VOTES	16
5TH 10 VOTES	16
TOTAL VOTES	52
TOTAL POINTS	906

▼ TEAM
Phillies

▼ YEARS PLAYED
1989–1996

▼ POSITION
Outfielder

Lenny Dykstra didn't take crap from anybody. Legend has it that Lenny was at a restaurant in suburban Philadelphia one time, using language which a stuffy politician sitting at a nearby table didn't think was appropriate. The politician had the effrontery to go over and ask Dykstra to tone it down. Lenny's matter-of-fact response: "Dude, I'll deck you."

Dykstra had the same disdain for opposing pitchers that he did for meddlesome restaurant patrons. Rob Elias described Dykstra's intensity well: "I still remember the tension when he stepped into the batter's box. He approached each at-bat like he was defusing a bomb." That was especially the case in the memorable 1993 season when, as Randy Axelrod noted, Lenny had an MVP-caliber year. (Lenny finished second in the National League MVP vote that year, behind Barry Bonds.) Dykstra received many other accolades for his play with the Phillies, primarily the 1993 season: "He was the catalyst. He set the table; he was a smart hitter who knew how to work pitchers" (Ray Didinger). "He was the best player on the '93 Phillies" (Jody McDonald). "He was a great motivator and very exciting" (Paul Lalley). "He was a great athlete—he could hit, run and field" (Michael Barkann). "He was the igniter" (Andy Paul). "He was the fire plug of the team, a mini-version of Pete Rose" (Andy Salayda). "He was hard-working, had a lot of clutch hits in 1993, and was the city's darling" (Joe Geier).

Dykstra was at his very best in the 1993 postseason when, as Fran Garvin put it, he was "unconscious"—he stroked six home runs against the Braves and Blue Jays. It was Dykstra's play in 1993 that was the impetus for Greg Veith's description of him as the greatest clutch player in any sport in Philadelphia history.

Greg Geier didn't dispute Lenny's outstanding 1993 season; he just felt that other than that magical year, Dykstra didn't do much else of note for the Phillies. Lee Fiederer called Lenny "a one-year wonder." A two-year wonder might be more appropriate. Aside from

1990, when Lenny finished second in the National League in hitting, and 1993, he never played more than 100 games in a season for the Phils. His much-publicized car accident in 1991 and various other injuries landed Dykstra on the disabled list several times. It was Dykstra's back condition that forced his early retirement.

Gregg Asman acknowledged that "the Dude" was a hero on the 1993 team that captured the fans' hearts but that was not enough to make Gregg's list. "I just don't see him as someone who stands out in Philadelphia sports history." Steve Bucci didn't include Dykstra on his list because he was about as impressed with Lenny's personality as the politician at the restaurant.

Year	Team	Lg	G	AB	R	H	HR	RBI	SB	Avg	SLG
1985	N.Y. Mets	N.L.	83	236	40	60	1	19	15	.254	.331
1986	N.Y. Mets	N.L.	147	431	77	127	8	45	31	.295	.445
1987	N.Y. Mets	N.L.	132	431	86	123	10	43	27	.285	.455
1988	N.Y. Mets	N.L.	126	429	57	116	8	33	30	.270	.385
1989	N.Y. Mets	N.L.	56	159	27	43	3	13	13	.270	.415
1989	Phillies	N.L.	90	352	39	78	4	19	17	.222	.330
1990	Phillies	N.L.	149	590	106	192	9	60	33	.325	.441
1991	Phillies	N.L.	63	246	48	73	3	12	24	.297	.427
1992	Phillies	N.L.	85	345	53	104	6	39	30	.301	.406
1993	Phillies	N.L.	161	637	143	194	19	66	37	.305	.482
1994	Phillies	N.L.	84	315	68	86	5	24	15	.273	.435
1995	Phillies	N.L.	62	254	37	67	2	18	10	.264	.354
1996	Phillies	N.L.	40	134	21	35	3	13	3	.261	.418
	Phillies Totals		734	2873	515	829	51	251	169	.289	.422
	Career Totals		1278	4559	802	1298	81	404	285	.285	.419

Member of World Champions (1986)
National League All-Star (1990, 1994–95)

Paul Arizin

RANK	POINTS	VOTES RECEIVED
1st	50	0
2nd	49	0
3rd	48	0
4th	47	0
5th	46	0
6th	45	0
7th	44	0
8th	43	0
9th	42	0
10th	41	0
11th	40	1
12th	39	0
13th	38	1
14th	37	3
15th	36	1
16th	35	3
17th	34	0
18th	33	0
19th	32	0
20th	31	1
21st	30	1
22nd	29	2
23rd	28	2
24th	27	2
25th	26	1
26th	25	3
27th	24	1
28th	23	0
29th	22	1
30th	21	0
31st	20	1
32nd	19	1
33rd	18	0
34th	17	0
35th	16	2
36th	15	0
37th	14	1
38th	13	1
39th	12	3
40th	11	0
41st	10	0
42nd	9	0
43rd	8	0
44th	7	0
45th	6	0
46th	5	1
47th	4	0
48th	3	0
49th	2	2
50th	1	0
Not on List	0	65

TOP 10 VOTES	0
2ND 10 VOTES	10
3RD 10 VOTES	13
4TH 10 VOTES	9
5TH 10 VOTES	3
TOTAL VOTES	35
TOTAL POINTS	849

▼ TEAM
Warriors

▼ YEARS PLAYED
1951–1952, 1955–1962

▼ POSITION
Forward/Guard

Neil Goldstein and Steve Danawitz, basketball diehards since the 1950s, talked about how dramatically the pro game has changed over the decades. One of the most glaring differences, they agreed, is how much faster today's NBA players are than they were back in the '50s. Back when Paul Arizin was a perennial All-Star for the Warriors. "He was great in his day," said Neil, "but he wouldn't be great today. He couldn't keep up with the players. He was slow as molasses." Arizin had bad asthma, and Neil remembers hearing him wheezing up and down the court from the stands at the old Convention Hall. Steve pointed out that Arizin was the first player to become well-known for his jump shot, but "he couldn't step on a court today, he was too slow."

Joe Geier remembered Arizin's "flat" jump shot, which he learned playing basketball in a gymnasium with a low ceiling at the elementary school in South Philadelphia that he attended. Joe cited Arizin's well-deserved Hall of Fame status and great scoring record—he led the NBA in scoring twice and finished second in two other seasons. Like Joe, Ken Berky, Jack Guziewicz and Bob Cinalli ranked Arizin in their top 25 and spoke highly of the jump shot of "Pitchin' Paul." "He was the Allen Iverson of his day," said Bob. "He didn't play much defense, but he was a scorer."

Jerry McDonough recalled Arizin's penchant for hitting his patented jump shot from way outside. "He would have scored another thousand points if they had three-pointers back then." Jerry told the story that when the Celtics used to play the Warriors, their legendary coach Red Auerbach would stay awake the night before trying to figure out how to stop Arizin. "He was a great player," said Jerry. "Nobody in the league could stop him." Jerry also said, "Arizin could jump through the roof." Arizin, who stood 6'4", finished in the top 10 in rebounds twice.

Year	Team	Lg	G	Min	FGM	FGA	FGP	FTM	FTA	FTP	AST	REB	Pts	PPG
1950–51	Warriors	NBA	65		352	864	.407	417	526	.793	138	640	1121	17.2
1951–52	Warriors	NBA	66	2939	548	1222	.448	578	707	.818	170	745	1674	25.4
1952–53	Military service													
1953–54	Military service													
1954–55	Warriors	NBA	72	2953	529	1325	.399	454	585	.776	210	675	1512	21.0
1955–56	Warriors	NBA	72	2724	617	1378	.448	507	627	.810	189	539	1741	24.2
1956–57	Warriors	NBA	71	2767	613	1451	.422	591	713	.829	150	561	1817	25.6
1957–58	Warriors	NBA	68	2377	483	1229	.393	440	544	.809	135	503	1406	20.7
1958–59	Warriors	NBA	70	2799	632	1466	.431	587	722	.813	119	637	1851	26.4
1959–60	Warriors	NBA	72	2618	593	1400	.424	420	526	.798	165	621	1606	22.3
1960–61	Warriors	NBA	79	2935	650	1529	.425	532	639	.833	188	681	1832	23.2
1961–62	Warriors	NBA	78	2785	611	1490	.410	484	601	.805	201	527	1706	21.9
	Warriors Totals		713	24897	5628	13354	.421	5010	6190	.810	1665	6129	16266	22.8
	Career Totals		713	24897	5628	13354	.421	5010	6190	.810	1665	6129	16266	22.8

NBA All-Star (1951–52, 1955–62)
Member of NBA Champions (1956)
Basketball Hall of Fame (1978)

49 Del Ennis

RANK	POINTS	VOTES RECEIVED		RANK	POINTS	VOTES RECEIVED
1st	50	0		31st	20	2
2nd	49	0		32nd	19	2
3rd	48	0		33rd	18	1
4th	47	0		34th	17	2
5th	46	0		35th	16	0
6th	45	0		36th	15	0
7th	44	0		37th	14	3
8th	43	0		38th	13	1
9th	42	0		39th	12	1
10th	41	0		40th	11	1
11th	40	0		41st	10	0
12th	39	1		42nd	9	0
13th	38	0		43rd	8	1
14th	37	2		44th	7	1
15th	36	0		45th	6	0
16th	35	0		46th	5	1
17th	34	1		47th	4	0
18th	33	1		48th	3	1
19th	32	0		49th	2	1
20th	31	1		50th	1	1
21st	30	2		Not on List	0	64
22nd	29	0				
23rd	28	0				
24th	27	2		TOP 10 VOTES	0	
25th	26	1		2ND 10 VOTES	6	
26th	25	1		3RD 10 VOTES	11	
27th	24	1		4TH 10 VOTES	13	
28th	23	2		5TH 10 VOTES	6	
29th	22	1		TOTAL VOTES	36	
30th	21	1		TOTAL POINTS	723	

▼ TEAM
Phillies

▼ YEARS PLAYED
1946–1956

▼ POSITION
Outfielder

Richie Ashburn didn't understand it, nor did Ray Didinger. Del Ennis, a local boy from Olney High who shared the outfield for nine years with Whitey, was often a victim of the Philly boo birds. Ray, who rated Ennis 31st, aptly summed him up: "He was one of the best power hitters in baseball for a lot of years." He definitely was. Jerry McDonough had the pleasure of watching Ennis and pointed to an impressive accomplishment in explaining why he ranked this "Whiz Kid" in his top 20: he averaged 100 RBIs a season over a 10-year period. In fact, he did it for slightly longer, averaging 102 ribbies for the 11 seasons in his hometown. In every one of those seasons except one, he led the team in RBIs, and he paced the squad in long balls eight times. Only Mike Schmidt stands ahead of Ennis on the Phillies' all-time home run list, while Del is third on the team's all-time RBI list behind Schmidt and nineteenth-century great Ed Delahanty.

Jon Grisdale described Ennis the way many would describe a Phillies outfielder from a generation later, Greg Luzinski: "He was slow and built like a bull. He was a great hitter." As Bob Kelly said, "He was one of the premier players of his time who was overlooked by the Hall of Fame voters." And by All-Star Game voters. Despite all those 20-home run, 100-RBI seasons, Ennis was only a three-time All-Star. Even in 1950, when Ennis led the National League in RBIs and the Phillies were on their way to winning the pennant, he wasn't picked for the mid-season classic.

Why the lack of respect from the Philly fans and the baseball world? Jim Rosen offered one reason: "He wasn't regarded in the same stature as Duke Snider, Willie Mays and Hank Aaron." And it didn't help that Ted Williams, Joe DiMaggio and Mickey Mantle were going strong in the American League. Bob Cinalli felt that Ennis also took a back seat to two of his longtime teammates, Ashburn and Robin Roberts, who were the elite players for the Phillies during that time.

Year	Team	Lg	G	AB	R	H	HR	RBI	SB	Avg	SLG
1946	Phillies	N.L.	141	540	70	169	17	73	5	.313	.485
1947	Phillies	N.L.	139	541	71	149	12	81	9	.275	.410
1948	Phillies	N.L.	152	589	86	171	30	95	2	.290	.525
1949	Phillies	N.L.	154	610	92	184	25	110	2	.302	.525
1950	Phillies	N.L.	153	595	92	185	31	126	2	.311	.551
1951	Phillies	N.L.	144	532	76	142	15	73	4	.267	.408
1952	Phillies	N.L.	151	592	90	171	20	107	6	.289	.475
1953	Phillies	N.L.	152	578	79	165	29	125	1	.285	.484
1954	Phillies	N.L.	145	556	73	145	25	119	2	.261	.444
1955	Phillies	N.L.	146	564	82	167	29	120	4	.296	.518
1956	Phillies	N.L.	153	630	80	164	26	95	7	.260	.430
1957	St. Louis	N.L.	136	490	61	140	24	105	7	.286	.494
1958	St. Louis	N.L.	106	329	22	86	3	47	1	.261	.350
1959	Cincinnati	N.L.	5	12	1	4	0	1	0	.333	.333
1959	Chisox	A.L.	26	96	10	21	2	7	0	.219	.344
	Phillies Totals		1630	6327	891	1812	259	1124	37	.286	.479
	Career Totals		1903	7254	985	2063	288	1284	45	.284	.472

National League All-Star (1946, 1951, 1955)

Johnny Callison

RANK	POINTS	VOTES RECEIVED
1st	50	0
2nd	49	0
3rd	48	0
4th	47	0
5th	46	0
6th	45	0
7th	44	0
8th	43	0
9th	42	0
10th	41	1
11th	40	0
12th	39	0
13th	38	0
14th	37	0
15th	36	0
16th	35	2
17th	34	0
18th	33	3
19th	32	1
20th	31	0
21st	30	0
22nd	29	1
23rd	28	0
24th	27	0
25th	26	2
26th	25	1
27th	24	0
28th	23	1
29th	22	0
30th	21	0
31st	20	2
32nd	19	0
33rd	18	2
34th	17	0
35th	16	2
36th	15	2
37th	14	2
38th	13	1
39th	12	3
40th	11	3
41st	10	1
42nd	9	3
43rd	8	0
44th	7	0
45th	6	2
46th	5	3
47th	4	3
48th	3	1
49th	2	1
50th	1	1
Not on List	0	56

TOP 10 VOTES	1
2ND 10 VOTES	6
3RD 10 VOTES	5
4TH 10 VOTES	17
5TH 10 VOTES	15
TOTAL VOTES	44
TOTAL POINTS	701

▼ **TEAM**
Phillies

▼ **YEARS PLAYED**
1960–1969

▼ **POSITION**
Outfielder

1964 was an unforgettable—and forgettable—season for Johnny Callison. He hit a walk-off, three-run homer in the bottom of the ninth inning of the All-Star Game against Red Sox fire-baller Dick Radatz to give the National League a 7-4 win, and he finished second in the National League MVP vote on the strength of his 31 home runs and 104 RBIs. As longtime Phillies fans know so well, the Phillies were comfortably in first place with two weeks left in the season before collapsing and losing 10 straight games—and the pennant—to the Cardinals. Had the Phillies hung on to win, undoubtedly the MVP would have gone to Johnny C. instead of Cardinals third baseman Ken Boyer, and as Gregg Asman said, Callison would have been a folk hero.

Callison was at his peak then—1964 was his third year in a four-year stretch in which he averaged 28 home runs and 92 RBIs per season. He was, as John Mitchell said, tremendous for those few years. At the age of 26, Callison appeared on the verge of becoming a bona fide star. But then things unexpectedly went sour for him. Over the next four seasons (1966-69), he averaged just 14 home runs and 56 RBIs per season, and it was because of Callison's nosedive that many voters—including Jody McDonald, Michael Beirne, Harvey Feldman and Mark Voigt—chose not to write Callison's name on their lists. Mark viewed Johnny as "kind of a flash in the pan" because his success was relatively short-lived.

Many others overlooked the loss of zing in Callison's bat and rated him high because of his stellar defense and fan appeal. "He went after the ball in right field with reckless abandon, crashing into walls," said Doug Brown. "Bobby Abreu wouldn't do that." Probably not—at least when he was with the Phillies. Bob Chazin also commended Callison for his very good glove in right, as well as his great attitude. Paul Lightkep gave Johnny extra points because he was a leader and a good role model, while Steve Van Allen gave Callison kudos because he was well-loved by Phillies fans.

Year	Team	Lg	G	AB	R	H	HR	RBI	SB	Avg	SLG
1958	Chisox	A.L.	18	64	10	19	1	12	1	.297	.469
1959	Chisox	A.L.	49	104	12	18	3	12	0	.173	.288
1960	Phillies	N.L.	99	288	36	75	9	30	0	.260	.427
1961	Phillies	N.L.	138	455	74	121	9	47	10	.266	.418
1962	Phillies	N.L.	157	603	107	181	23	83	10	.300	.491
1963	Phillies	N.L.	157	626	96	178	26	78	8	.284	.502
1964	Phillies	N.L.	162	654	101	179	31	104	6	.274	.492
1965	Phillies	N.L.	160	619	93	162	32	101	6	.262	.509
1966	Phillies	N.L.	155	612	93	169	11	55	8	.276	.418
1967	Phillies	N.L.	149	556	62	145	14	64	6	.261	.408
1968	Phillies	N.L.	121	398	46	97	14	40	4	.244	.415
1969	Phillies	N.L.	134	495	66	131	16	64	2	.265	.440
1970	Chi. Cubs	N.L.	147	477	65	126	19	68	7	.264	.440
1971	Chi. Cubs	N.L.	103	290	27	61	8	38	2	.210	.341
1972	N.Y. Yankees	A.L.	92	275	28	71	9	34	3	.258	.393
1973	N.Y. Yankees	A.L.	45	136	10	24	1	10	1	.176	.228
	Phillies Totals		1432	5306	774	1438	185	666	60	.271	.457
	Career Totals		1886	6652	926	1757	226	840	74	.264	.441

National League All-Star (1962, 1964–65)

51 Pete Retzlaff

RANK	POINTS	VOTES RECEIVED
1st	50	0
2nd	49	0
3rd	48	0
4th	47	0
5th	46	0
6th	45	0
7th	44	0
8th	43	0
9th	42	0
10th	41	0
11th	40	0
12th	39	2
13th	38	0
14th	37	0
15th	36	0
16th	35	1
17th	34	0
18th	33	0
19th	32	1
20th	31	0
21st	30	0
22nd	29	1
23rd	28	1
24th	27	0
25th	26	1
26th	25	1
27th	24	2
28th	23	1
29th	22	1
30th	21	2

RANK	POINTS	VOTES RECEIVED
31st	20	5
32nd	19	2
33rd	18	0
34th	17	1
35th	16	0
36th	15	2
37th	14	2
38th	13	1
39th	12	1
40th	11	0
41st	10	2
42nd	9	2
43rd	8	0
44th	7	0
45th	6	3
46th	5	0
47th	4	0
48th	3	0
49th	2	0
50th	1	0
Not on List	0	65

TOP 10 VOTES	0
2ND 10 VOTES	4
3RD 10 VOTES	10
4TH 10 VOTES	14
5TH 10 VOTES	7
TOTAL VOTES	35
TOTAL POINTS	682

▼ **TEAM**
Eagles

▼ **YEARS PLAYED**
1956–1966

▼ **POSITION**
Tight End

The Eagles are not in the habit of retiring players' numbers. When they honored Reggie White by retiring his number 92 in 2005, it was only the seventh time the team bestowed that honor on a player. Pete Retzlaff, described by John Senkow as one of the best all-time Eagles, was one of those players. What did Retzlaff accomplish for the Eagles organization to retire his number 44?

In his 11 years in town, he led the Eagles in receptions and receiving yards six times, including the 1960 championship year. Merrill Reese and Terry Bickhart had nice things to say about Retzlaff. Merrill: "He ran like a gazelle; he was graceful; he looked effortless. He glided under the ball. He ran beautiful patterns." Terry: "He was classy and dependable. Tommy McDonald made the spectacular plays, but Retzlaff was dependable. He was the guy the Eagles went to on third and six. He was sure-handed." Bob Anderson also mentioned Retzlaff's sure-handedness. "He didn't fumble or drop passes." Bob also said that Retzlaff "invented the 'receiving tight end'"; previously, tight ends usually were utilized more for their blocking than receiving. That is not to say that Retzlaff couldn't block. Bob, as well as Jerry McDonough, commended Retzlaff on his blocking ability.

Fred Warren and Bill McElroy pointed to Retzlaff's 11-year tenure. Not many Eagles have played for the team longer. Neil Goldstein and Paul Lightkep voted for Retzlaff because they thought he was one of the top Eagles of the 1960s, and one of the stars on some bad Eagles teams. Retzlaff was at his peak from 1963 to 1965, toward the end of his career, when he averaged 58 catches, 980 yards and eight touchdowns per season on Eagles teams that did not post a winning record.

The problem with Retzlaff, according to some voters, notably Michael Beirne and John Mitchell, was that notwithstanding his retired number status, he wasn't one of the top receivers of his time, nor was he one of the best Eagles receivers of all time. Michael pointed out that Retzlaff rarely finished in the top five of the NFL in a category: in 1960, he finished fifth in the league in receptions, and in 1965, he finished second in yards, third in receptions and tied for third in touchdowns. Those were his only top-five finishes. John compared Retzlaff to other Eagles wide receivers and tight ends over the years. "He is not comparable to Carmichael or Quick. A better comparison would be Charles Young [he was a Pro Bowl tight end from 1973 to 1975] or John Spagnola [he had consecutive 60-reception seasons in 1984-85]. Retzlaff played with Ben Hawkins [in 1967, the year after Retzlaff retired, he led the NFL with 1265 receiving yards], who was comparable to Carmichael and Quick."

Year	Team	Lg	G	Rec	Yds	Avg	TD
1956	Eagles	NFL	10	12	159	13.2	0
1957	Eagles	NFL	12	10	120	12.0	0
1958	Eagles	NFL	12	56	766	13.7	2
1959	Eagles	NFL	10	34	595	17.5	1
1960	Eagles	NFL	12	46	826	18.0	5
1961	Eagles	NFL	14	50	769	15.4	8
1962	Eagles	NFL	8	30	584	19.5	3
1963	Eagles	NFL	14	57	895	15.7	4
1964	Eagles	NFL	12	51	855	16.8	8
1965	Eagles	NFL	14	66	1190	18.0	10
1966	Eagles	NFL	14	40	653	16.3	6
	Eagles Totals		132	452	7412	16.4	47
	Career Totals		132	452	7412	16.4	47

NFL Pro Bowl (1958, 1960, 1963–65)
Member of World Champions (1960)
NFL co-MVP (1965)
Number 44 retired by Eagles

52 Tom Brookshier

RANK	POINTS	VOTES RECEIVED
1st	50	0
2nd	49	0
3rd	48	0
4th	47	0
5th	46	0
6th	45	1
7th	44	1
8th	43	0
9th	42	0
10th	41	0
11th	40	0
12th	39	0
13th	38	0
14th	37	0
15th	36	0
16th	35	0
17th	34	2
18th	33	0
19th	32	1
20th	31	1
21st	30	1
22nd	29	0
23rd	28	0
24th	27	1
25th	26	1
26th	25	3
27th	24	0
28th	23	0
29th	22	2
30th	21	1
31st	20	0
32nd	19	0
33rd	18	3
34th	17	0
35th	16	0
36th	15	2
37th	14	0
38th	13	1
39th	12	1
40th	11	4
41st	10	1
42nd	9	2
43rd	8	3
44th	7	1
45th	6	0
46th	5	1
47th	4	2
48th	3	1
49th	2	0
50th	1	0
Not on List	0	63

TOP 10 VOTES	2
2ND 10 VOTES	4
3RD 10 VOTES	9
4TH 10 VOTES	11
5TH 10 VOTES	11
TOTAL VOTES	37
TOTAL POINTS	671

▼ TEAM
Eagles

▼ YEARS PLAYED
1953, 1956–1961

▼ POSITION
Safety

The Eagles' knack for producing punishing, hard-hitting defensive backs didn't start with Andre Waters and Wes Hopkins in the 1980s. Back in 1953, Tom Brookshier cracked the Birds' starting lineup, and in addition to grabbing eight interceptions, he quickly established his reputation as a player who could lay a hit on a running back or receiver. "He was a good guts player who could change the momentum of a game with his vicious hits," said Neil Goldstein. "He had more guts than current players. He wasn't as quick, but he could tackle as hard." Bob Cinalli extolled Brookshier not only for his ability to hit, but his overall skills: "He could cover anybody. He could defend the run and the pass. He knew how to play the receiver. Receivers avoided being in his area." Jon Grisdale: "He was nasty and tough, one of the keys to the Eagles winning the 1960 championship. He was a good tackler; other teams didn't go across the middle. He was better than Hopkins or Dawkins." Brookshier's fan appeal and likability earned him the votes of Patrick Dooley, Bob Chazin and Dave Myers.

Brookshier had a reputation for playing dirty, and it cost him a spot on Jerry McDonough's list. Jerry pointed out that when Brookshier suffered his career-ending leg injury in 1961, he was roughing up an opposing running back. Terry Bickhart thought that Brookshier was overshadowed by the future Hall of Famers on the 1960 championship team: Chuck Bednarik, Norm Van Brocklin and Tommy McDonald. Harvey Feldman watched Brookshier during his childhood and was decidedly unimpressed: "I do not think he was terribly talented. Certainly he was better than Bobby Taylor—but so am I." Taylor was a starting cornerback for the Eagles for the better part of his nine years in town (1995–2003). He made the Pro Bowl once, but he incurred the wrath of some Eagles fans—including Harvey, obviously—for his shoddy tackling.

Year	Team	Lg	G	Int	Yds	TD
1953	Eagles	NFL	11	8	41	0
1954		Military service				
1955		Military service				
1956	Eagles	NFL	11	1	31	0
1957	Eagles	NFL	12	4	74	0
1958	Eagles	NFL	11	1	0	0
1959	Eagles	NFL	12	3	13	0
1960	Eagles	NFL	12	1	14	0
1961	Eagles	NFL	7	2	20	0
		Eagles Totals	76	20	193	0
		Career Totals	76	20	193	0

NFL Pro Bowl (1959–60)
Member of NFL Champions (1960)
Number 40 retired by Eagles

53 Doug Collins

RANK	POINTS	VOTES RECEIVED
1st	50	0
2nd	49	0
3rd	48	0
4th	47	0
5th	46	0
6th	45	0
7th	44	0
8th	43	0
9th	42	0
10th	41	0
11th	40	0
12th	39	0
13th	38	0
14th	37	0
15th	36	1
16th	35	1
17th	34	0
18th	33	0
19th	32	0
20th	31	0
21st	30	2
22nd	29	0
23rd	28	1
24th	27	0
25th	26	1
26th	25	1
27th	24	4
28th	23	3
29th	22	1
30th	21	1
31st	20	0
32nd	19	0
33rd	18	2
34th	17	1
35th	16	2
36th	15	1
37th	14	2
38th	13	1
39th	12	1
40th	11	0
41st	10	3
42nd	9	2
43rd	8	2
44th	7	1
45th	6	1
46th	5	0
47th	4	3
48th	3	0
49th	2	1
50th	1	1
Not on List	0	60

TOP 10 VOTES	0
2ND 10 VOTES	2
3RD 10 VOTES	14
4TH 10 VOTES	10
5TH 10 VOTES	14
TOTAL VOTES	40
TOTAL POINTS	663

▼ TEAM
Sixers

▼ YEARS PLAYED
1974–1981

▼ POSITION
Guard

When the Sixers selected Allen Iverson as the first overall pick in the 1997 draft, it was the first time they had the top choice in the draft since 1973 when they practically clinched the number one pick by the All-Star break by starting the season 4-58 under immortal coaches Roy Rubin and Kevin Loughery. The Sixers chose Doug Collins. Did they make a good choice?

Lee Fiederer didn't think so. He said that Collins, while good, didn't quite live up to expectations. Neil Goldstein thought that Collins was a fundamentally good player, but not good enough to make his list. Neil added that Collins didn't have as much of an impact on the Sixers as Hal Greer, who retired the season before the team snagged Collins. Doug Brown said that the Sixers were not that good in the 1970s (although they turned the corner in 1976), and he considered Julius Erving and George McGinnis the stars of that decade, not Collins. John Bergmann added, "He was a better coach and commentator than player."

Although injuries forced Collins to retire at the age of 30 after just eight seasons, many voters believed that Collins' play with the Sixers during those years was stellar enough that he deserved a top 50 spot. Andy Musser liked Doug's play-making and energy, while Ralph Antonelli remembered Collins as a team player and a good ball-handler and shooter who was always hustling. Ralph as well as Dan McCarthy liked Collins' game so much that they put him in their top 20. Dan: "He was a great shooter...fast...better offensively than Mo Cheeks." Glenn Young admired Collins' relentless efforts on the court to get open. "Collins never, ever stopped unselfishly moving without the ball." Jim Robinson raved about Collins' leadership and attitude—Doug didn't think that he was "bigger than the game," according to Jim.

Dan Brown rated Collins high for the same reason that he did Larry Bowa. "He was a spark plug; when he was down, the team went down."

Year	Team	Lg	G	Min	FGM	FGA	FGP	FTM	FTA	FTP	AST	REB	Pts	PPG
1973–74	Sixers	NBA	25	436	72	194	.371	55	72	.764	40	46	199	8.0
1974–75	Sixers	NBA	81	2820	561	1150	.488	331	392	.844	213	315	1453	17.9
1975–76	Sixers	NBA	77	2995	614	1196	.513	372	445	.836	191	307	1600	2.8
1976–77	Sixers	NBA	58	2037	426	823	.518	210	250	.840	271	195	1062	18.3
1977–78	Sixers	NBA	79	2770	643	1223	.526	267	329	.812	320	230	1553	19.7
1978–79	Sixers	NBA	47	1595	358	717	.499	201	247	.814	191	123	917	19.5
1979–80	Sixers	NBA	36	963	191	410	.466	113	124	.911	100	94	495	13.8
1980–81	Sixers	NBA	12	329	62	126	.492	24	29	.828	42	29	148	12.3
Sixers Totals			415	13945	2927	5839	.501	1573	1888	.833	1368	1339	7427	17.9
Career Totals			415	13945	2927	5839	.501	1573	1888	.833	1368	1339	7427	17.9

NBA All-Star (1976–79)

Brian Propp

RANK	POINTS	VOTES RECEIVED
1st	50	0
2nd	49	0
3rd	48	0
4th	47	0
5th	46	0
6th	45	0
7th	44	0
8th	43	0
9th	42	0
10th	41	0
11th	40	0
12th	39	0
13th	38	0
14th	37	0
15th	36	0
16th	35	0
17th	34	0
18th	33	0
19th	32	0
20th	31	1
21st	30	1
22nd	29	0
23rd	28	1
24th	27	3
25th	26	0
26th	25	1
27th	24	1
28th	23	1
29th	22	1
30th	21	2
31st	20	0
32nd	19	0
33rd	18	3
34th	17	3
35th	16	3
36th	15	0
37th	14	2
38th	13	1
39th	12	2
40th	11	3
41st	10	2
42nd	9	1
43rd	8	2
44th	7	0
45th	6	1
46th	5	2
47th	4	1
48th	3	2
49th	2	3
50th	1	2
Not on List	0	55

TOP 10 VOTES	0
2ND 10 VOTES	1
3RD 10 VOTES	11
4TH 10 VOTES	17
5TH 10 VOTES	16
TOTAL VOTES	45
TOTAL POINTS	636

▼ **TEAM**
Flyers

▼ **YEARS PLAYED**
1980–1990

▼ **POSITION**
Left Wing

In the 1980s, the Flyers were one of the best teams in the NHL. They made the playoffs every year, posted a winning record every season except one (and played .500 hockey that year), and advanced to the Stanley Cup Finals in 1980, 1985 and 1987. Only one player wore the orange and black for the entire decade: Brian Propp. "He was the Flyers' next big scorer after Clarke and Barber," said Joe Fee. "He was an awesome player that produced great numbers," said Andy Salayda, who ranked Propp 21st. The record book supports Andy's argument. Propp ranks second on the Flyers' career assists list, and third in goals and points. Steve Kennedy was impressed enough with Propp's numbers to rank him 35th. Jeff Skow: "He had consistency and longevity. He was a guy you could count on. He, Howe and Kerr made up the superstar nucleus of the Flyers of the '80s." Bob Anderson also liked Propp. "He was workmanlike. He did his job, night after night."

If the Flyers had beaten the Islanders in the '80 Finals or the Oilers in the '85 or '87 Finals, John Surbeck may have found a spot for Propp on his list. But because Propp didn't play on any Cup-winners and he was a one-dimensional player (he generated offense, but didn't play much defense), John passed on Propp. "He was good, he got his goals, but didn't make that much of an impression on me," said Mike Koob. David Berky thought Propp was a relentless player but not colorful. Jon Grisdale acknowledged Propp's consistency, but didn't think that Propp was outstanding. If you take a close look at Propp's numbers, it appears that Jon hit the nail on the head. Propp had eight 30-goal and nine 40-assist seasons for the Flyers, and between '82 and '86, when he was at his peak, he averaged 41 goals and 51 assists per season. Propp, though, never cracked the 50-goal, 60-assist or 100-point mark, although several Flyers have achieved each of those milestones. Propp was traded to the Bruins in the middle of the 1989-90 season and the Flyers, without him, then went into a tailspin, failing to make the playoffs in each of the next five seasons.

Year	Team	Lg	Gm	G	A	Pts	PM
1979–80	Flyers	NHL	80	34	41	75	54
1980–81	Flyers	NHL	79	26	40	66	110
1981–82	Flyers	NHL	80	44	47	91	117
1982–83	Flyers	NHL	80	40	42	82	72
1983–84	Flyers	NHL	79	39	53	92	37
1984–85	Flyers	NHL	76	43	54	97	43
1985–86	Flyers	NHL	72	40	57	97	47
1986–87	Flyers	NHL	53	31	36	67	45
1987–88	Flyers	NHL	74	27	49	76	76
1988–89	Flyers	NHL	77	32	46	78	37
1989–90	Flyers	NHL	40	13	15	28	31
1989–90	Boston	NHL	14	3	9	12	10
1990–91	Minnesota	NHL	79	26	47	73	58
1991–92	Minnesota	NHL	51	12	23	35	49
1992–93	Minnesota	NHL	17	3	3	6	0
1993–94	Hartford	NHL	65	12	17	29	44
	Flyers Totals		790	369	480	849	669
	Career Totals		1016	425	579	1004	830

NHL All-Star (1980, 1982, 1984, 1986, 1990)

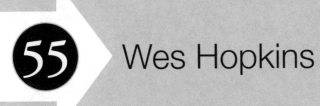

55 Wes Hopkins

RANK	POINTS	VOTES RECEIVED
1st	50	0
2nd	49	0
3rd	48	0
4th	47	0
5th	46	0
6th	45	0
7th	44	0
8th	43	0
9th	42	0
10th	41	0
11th	40	0
12th	39	0
13th	38	0
14th	37	0
15th	36	0
16th	35	1
17th	34	0
18th	33	0
19th	32	1
20th	31	1
21st	30	0
22nd	29	0
23rd	28	0
24th	27	1
25th	26	2
26th	25	3
27th	24	1
28th	23	1
29th	22	1
30th	21	2
31st	20	0
32nd	19	0
33rd	18	0
34th	17	1
35th	16	1
36th	15	0
37th	14	2
38th	13	6
39th	12	0
40th	11	1
41st	10	3
42nd	9	2
43rd	8	1
44th	7	1
45th	6	1
46th	5	0
47th	4	2
48th	3	1
49th	2	1
50th	1	0
Not on List	0	63

TOP 10 VOTES	0
2ND 10 VOTES	3
3RD 10 VOTES	11
4TH 10 VOTES	11
5TH 10 VOTES	12
TOTAL VOTES	37
TOTAL POINTS	595

▼ TEAM
Eagles

▼ YEARS PLAYED
1983–1993

▼ POSITION
Safety

Ed Brittingham stated it quite well: "Philly fans hold a special place in their hearts for tough defensive football players. They just identify with 'Smash-mouth' football like nothing else. Guys like Wes Hopkins will always have a connection with Philly fans that other athletes can't have regardless of what stats they put up." Like Ed, many voters rated Hopkins high because he was tough and tackled hard. "He was a tremendous, hard-hitting safety," said Merrill Reese. "Receivers didn't want to meet him in the open field." Cliff Patterson described why Hopkins made his top 20. "He was a good leader and a hard hitter; he gave the Eagles respectability when they were coming around. He was one of Buddy Ryan's first All-Star-caliber players." In 1985, when the Eagles were still in the "coming around" stage, Hopkins led the Birds in tackles and interceptions and earned a plane ticket to Honolulu after the season. Mike Koob put Hopkins high on his list not only because he was a heavy hitter, but because he could cover and was a fan favorite. Greg Geier gave Hopkins a lot of credit for bouncing back from a serious injury (Hopkins sustained a knee injury in 1986, which forced him to miss the rest of the season and the entire 1987 season) to play at a high level. Greg also cited Hopkins' longevity; he was a standout on the Eagles' defense for 10 seasons, as long as any Birds defensive player in the Ryan/Kotite era.

Mark Eckel passed on Hopkins because his Pro Bowl selection appearance after the 1985 season was the lone selection in his career. "Hopkins was never the best safety in the league," said Mike Sielski, "unlike Brian Dawkins." Jody McDonald said that the Eagles' defense, largely because of Reggie White, was great as a unit, which reduced the individual value of Wes and some of the other players like Clyde Simmons and Andre Waters. Jeff Skow felt that Wes got lost when compared to players from other teams in the city who played on championship teams and runners-up.

Year	Team	Lg	G	Int	Yds	TD	Sacks
1983	Eagles	NFL	14	0	0	0	1
1984	Eagles	NFL	16	5	107	0	1.5
1985	Eagles	NFL	15	6	36	1	2
1986	Eagles	NFL	4	0	0	0	0
1988	Eagles	NFL	16	5	21	0	0
1989	Eagles	NFL	16	0	0	0	3.5
1990	Eagles	NFL	15	5	45	0	2
1991	Eagles	NFL	16	5	26	0	2
1992	Eagles	NFL	10	3	6	0	0
1993	Eagles	NFL	15	1	0	0	0
	Eagles Totals		137	30	241	1	12
	Career Totals		137	30	241	1	12

NFL Pro Bowl (1985)

TERRY BICKHART'S TOP 10

1. Wilt Chamberlain
2. Bobby Clarke
3. Julius Erving
4. Reggie White
5. Richie Ashburn
6. Bernie Parent
7. Charles Barkley
8. Steve Carlton
9. Chuck Bednarik
10. Mike Schmidt

Bob Boone

RANK	POINTS	VOTES RECEIVED
1st	50	0
2nd	49	0
3rd	48	0
4th	47	0
5th	46	0
6th	45	0
7th	44	0
8th	43	0
9th	42	0
10th	41	0
11th	40	0
12th	39	0
13th	38	0
14th	37	0
15th	36	0
16th	35	0
17th	34	0
18th	33	0
19th	32	1
20th	31	0
21st	30	0
22nd	29	0
23rd	28	1
24th	27	1
25th	26	2
26th	25	3
27th	24	1
28th	23	1
29th	22	1
30th	21	2
31st	20	0
32nd	19	0
33rd	18	2
34th	17	2
35th	16	1
36th	15	3
37th	14	0
38th	13	1
39th	12	0
40th	11	0
41st	10	2
42nd	9	3
43rd	8	0
44th	7	1
45th	6	2
46th	5	1
47th	4	4
48th	3	2
49th	2	2
50th	1	1
Not on List	0	60

TOP 10 VOTES	0
2ND 10 VOTES	1
3RD 10 VOTES	12
4TH 10 VOTES	9
5TH 10 VOTES	18
TOTAL VOTES	40
TOTAL POINTS	567

▼ **TEAM**
Phillies

▼ **YEARS PLAYED**
1972–1981

▼ **POSITION**
Catcher

He didn't have Schmidt's numbers, McGraw's personality or Bowa's fire, but Bob Boone, who held down the Phillies' starting job as catcher for nearly a decade, including the 1980 season, was praised by many voters, including Bob Chazin, Dennis Brady and Joe Brown, for his steadiness, consistency and longevity.

Boone received the nicest compliments, though, from Adam Kimelman, Gordie Jones and Bob Anderson. Adam described him as a well-rounded player who played a tough position and helped the Phillies with his glove and bat. Gordie Jones pointed to Boone's defensive presence, his skill at handling pitchers, and his knack for delivering clutch hits. Bob felt that while Boone was not in the class of Johnny Bench, Carlton Fisk or Thurman Munson, he was still fairly good. "He made pitchers better—Steve Carlton, Ron Reed, Larry Christenson and Dick Ruthven. He was great at blocking the plate. Nobody bunted on him. He had longevity, leadership and a tremendous World Series against Kansas City." Boone hit .412 with four RBIs in the '80 series against the Royals, and won a pair of Gold Gloves for the Phillies. He won five more Gold Gloves for the Angels and Royals after he left Philadelphia.

The consensus among the voters who passed on Boone was that he was not a star. "He was good, but not an offensive force or a clubhouse leader" (John Clark). "He was steady for a number of years but not spectacular" (John Mitchell). "He was good, but not great. [If he earned] another ring, he may have made my list" (Greg Veith). "He was a good catcher, but a career .260 hitter at best" (Rod Smith). To be exact, his lifetime batting average was .254, and he hit .259 during his 10 years with the Phillies. His single-season highs in home runs and RBIs were 12 and 66. Johnny Bench had those numbers by the All-Star break in some years.

Year	Team	Lg	G	AB	R	H	HR	RBI	SB	Avg	SLG
1972	Phillies	N.L.	16	51	4	14	1	4	1	.275	.353
1973	Phillies	N.L.	145	521	42	136	10	61	3	.261	.365
1974	Phillies	N.L.	146	488	41	118	3	52	3	.242	.322
1975	Phillies	N.L.	97	289	28	71	2	20	1	.246	.329
1976	Phillies	N.L.	121	361	40	98	4	54	2	.271	.366
1977	Phillies	N.L.	132	440	55	125	11	66	5	.284	.436
1978	Phillies	N.L.	132	435	48	123	12	62	2	.283	.425
1979	Phillies	N.L.	119	398	38	114	9	58	1	.286	.422
1980	Phillies	N.L.	141	480	34	110	9	55	3	.229	.338
1981	Phillies	N.L.	76	227	19	48	4	24	2	.211	.295
1982	California	A.L.	143	472	42	121	7	58	0	.256	.337
1983	California	A.L.	142	468	46	120	9	52	4	.256	.353
1984	California	A.L.	139	450	33	91	3	32	3	.202	.262
1985	California	A.L.	150	460	37	114	5	55	1	.248	.317
1986	California	A.L.	144	442	48	98	7	49	1	.222	.305
1987	California	A.L.	128	389	42	94	3	33	0	.242	.311
1988	California	A.L.	122	352	38	104	5	39	2	.295	.386
1989	Kansas City	A.L.	131	405	33	111	1	43	3	.274	.323
1990	Kansas City	A.L.	40	117	11	28	0	9	1	.239	.265
Phillies Totals			1125	3690	349	957	65	456	23	.259	.370
Career Totals			2264	7245	679	1838	105	826	38	.254	.346

National League All-Star (1976, 1978–79)
American League All-Star (1983)
National League Gold Glove (1978–79)
American League Gold Glove (1982, 1986–89)
Member of World Champions (1980)

57 Chris Short

RANK	POINTS	VOTES RECEIVED
1st	50	0
2nd	49	0
3rd	48	0
4th	47	0
5th	46	0
6th	45	0
7th	44	0
8th	43	0
9th	42	0
10th	41	0
11th	40	1
12th	39	1
13th	38	0
14th	37	0
15th	36	0
16th	35	0
17th	34	0
18th	33	0
19th	32	0
20th	31	0
21st	30	1
22nd	29	0
23rd	28	1
24th	27	3
25th	26	1
26th	25	0
27th	24	0
28th	23	1
29th	22	0
30th	21	0
31st	20	0
32nd	19	0
33rd	18	1
34th	17	0
35th	16	1
36th	15	0
37th	14	2
38th	13	2
39th	12	1
40th	11	1
41st	10	1
42nd	9	0
43rd	8	0
44th	7	1
45th	6	2
46th	5	0
47th	4	3
48th	3	0
49th	2	1
50th	1	3
Not on List	0	72

TOP 10 VOTES	0
2ND 10 VOTES	2
3RD 10 VOTES	7
4TH 10 VOTES	8
5TH 10 VOTES	11
TOTAL VOTES	28
TOTAL POINTS	424

▼ TEAM
Phillies

▼ YEARS PLAYED
1959–1972

▼ POSITION
Pitcher

Only one man played for the Phillies in the 1950s, 1960s and 1970s: left-handed pitcher Chris Short. When he broke in with the Phils in 1959, Robin Roberts was one of his teammates; in Short's last year in Philadelphia, 1972, he was on the same staff as first-year Phillie Steve Carlton. He wasn't in the class of those two icons, but Short strung together a few strong seasons in the 1960s. Jon Grisdale considered Short the second-best left-handed National League starting pitcher in the '60s, behind Hall of Famer Sandy Koufax. (Hall of Famer Warren Spahn was outstanding in the early '60s, but retired in 1965.) Between 1964 and 1968, Short was 83-54 (a .606 winning percentage); Shorty's 83 wins ranked third among National League pitchers behind Juan Marichal and Bob Gibson during that period. Andy Musser credited Short's success to his hook. "He had one of the greatest curve balls of all time." Jerry McDonough was impressed with Short's longevity and performance ("a good, solid pitcher for a few years"). "He was not as good as Jim Bunning," said Jerry, "but he was better than Rick Wise." (Wise, who was traded by the Phillies to acquire Steve Carlton, led the staff in wins from 1969 to 1971 and threw a no-hitter in 1971.)

Short's character and work ethic also helped him in the voting. "He was a good citizen who represented the city of Philadelphia" (Dave Beck). "He was a good guy who never complained. He was always ready to go, [even] on two days' rest" (Bob Chazin). In fact, manager Gene Mauch was criticized for his overuse of Short and Bunning during the 1964 collapse. Mauch started Short and Bunning three different times each on two days' rest over the final 12 games that season.

No doubt, Short would have finished higher in the voting if he were able to maintain his top-notch form after 1968. But, as Ned Hark said, Short had a tendency to get injured. In 1969, a back injury sidelined him for almost the entire season, and he was never effective after that. Ned also felt, as did Bill McElroy, that even at Short's best, he was not a dominating pitcher like Bunning. John Mitchell compared Short to Curt Simmons—a good, solid number two pitcher— but not good enough to make his list. Mike Rad recalled that Short's pitching ran the gamut from outstanding to awful. "He could be very good or get hammered."

Year	Team	Lg	G	W	L	CG	SH	IP	H	BB	SO	ER	ERA
1959	Phillies	N.L.	3	0	0	0	0	14.1	19	10	8	13	8.16
1960	Phillies	N.L.	42	6	9	2	0	107.1	101	52	54	47	3.94
1961	Phillies	N.L.	39	6	12	1	0	127.1	157	71	80	84	5.94
1962	Phillies	N.L.	47	11	9	4	0	142	149	56	91	54	3.42
1963	Phillies	N.L.	38	9	12	6	3	198	185	69	160	65	2.95
1964	Phillies	N.L.	42	17	9	12	4	220.2	174	51	181	54	2.20
1965	Phillies	N.L.	47	18	11	15	5	297.1	260	89	237	93	2.82
1966	Phillies	N.L.	42	20	10	19	4	272	257	68	177	107	3.54
1967	Phillies	N.L.	29	9	11	8	2	199.1	163	74	142	53	2.39
1968	Phillies	N.L.	42	19	13	9	2	269.2	236	81	202	88	2.94
1969	Phillies	N.L.	2	0	0	0	0	10	11	4	5	8	7.20
1970	Phillies	N.L.	36	9	16	7	2	199	211	66	133	95	4.30
1971	Phillies	N.L.	31	7	14	5	2	173	182	63	95	74	3.85
1972	Phillies	N.L.	19	1	1	0	0	23	24	8	20	10	3.91
1973	Milwaukee	A.L.	42	3	5	0	0	72	86	44	44	41	5.13
Phillies Totals			459	132	127	88	24	2253	2129	762	1585	845	3.38
Career Totals			501	135	132	88	24	2325.00	2215	806	1629	886	3.43

National League All-Star (1964, 1967)

58 Pelle Lindbergh

RANK	POINTS	VOTES RECEIVED
1st	50	0
2nd	49	0
3rd	48	0
4th	47	0
5th	46	0
6th	45	0
7th	44	0
8th	43	0
9th	42	0
10th	41	1
11th	40	0
12th	39	0
13th	38	0
14th	37	0
15th	36	0
16th	35	0
17th	34	1
18th	33	1
19th	32	0
20th	31	1
21st	30	0
22nd	29	0
23rd	28	0
24th	27	1
25th	26	1
26th	25	0
27th	24	0
28th	23	1
29th	22	0
30th	21	0
31st	20	0
32nd	19	3
33rd	18	0
34th	17	0
35th	16	0
36th	15	1
37th	14	1
38th	13	1
39th	12	0
40th	11	1
41st	10	2
42nd	9	3
43rd	8	0
44th	7	0
45th	6	3
46th	5	1
47th	4	1
48th	3	3
49th	2	1
50th	1	0
Not on List	0	72

TOP 10 VOTES	1
2ND 10 VOTES	3
3RD 10 VOTES	3
4TH 10 VOTES	7
5TH 10 VOTES	14
TOTAL VOTES	28
TOTAL POINTS	410

▼ **TEAM**
Flyers

▼ **YEARS PLAYED**
1982–1986

▼ **POSITION**
Goalie

It's hard to deny that two of the best NHL goalies of this generation are Dominik Hasek and Martin Brodeur. Hasek won two MVPs and six Vezina Trophies for the Sabres, while Brodeur helped the New Jersey Devils win three Stanley Cups and captured two Vezina Trophies. Michael Barkann paid Pelle Lindbergh quite a compliment when he compared the Swedish-born goaltender to Hasek and Brodeur. "He was so dominating; he was a 'shutdown' goalie. When Pelle was in goal, you knew the other team wasn't going to score much." Like Jerome Brown, Pelle died in a car accident in his 20s at a time when his career was on the upside. Jerome's best season was in '91, and he died the following June. Pelle had his best year in '85 when he won 40 games during the regular season and added 12 in the postseason in which the Flyers lost to the Oilers in the finals. Pelle had his tragic accident early the following season.

While Lindbergh only held the Flyers' starting goalie job for three years, he made a notable impression on many voters besides Michael. "He was a phenomenal goalie with great reflexes," said Paul Troy. "Had he not died, the Flyers could have won another Cup." Bryan Davis also thought that but for Pelle's death, Flyers fans would have enjoyed another parade. "He was outstanding—one of the best in the league." Many people talked about what Pelle could have been. Dave Sautter: "He had the potential to be a Hall of Famer." Paul Lightkep: "He was on the edge of greatness. He could have been one of the greatest goalies ever." Rob Betts: "He had the potential to be better than Bernie."

Lindbergh's small body of work stood in the way of his picking up more votes. "He was on his way to becoming a Hall of Famer," said Ray Didinger, "but he was hard to judge because of the brevity of his career." Dave Myers and Greg Veith had similar comments. Dave: "He was very talented, but didn't play long enough to be included on my list." Greg: "He was the second best Flyers goalie behind Bernie, but his career was too short."

What if . . .? Had it not been for his untimely death, Pelle may have finished in the top 10; perhaps the Flyers would have retired his jersey, and his plaque just might be displayed in the Hockey Hall of Fame in Toronto.

Year	Team	Lg	Gm	W	L	T	Sh	Avg
1981–82	Flyers	NHL	8	2	4	2	0	4.38
1982–83	Flyers	NHL	40	23	13	3	3	2.98
1983–84	Flyers	NHL	36	16	13	3	1	4.05
1984–85	Flyers	NHL	65	40	17	7	2	3.02
1985–86	Flyers	NHL	8	6	2	0	1	2.88
		Flyers Totals	157	87	49	15	7	3.30
		Career Totals	157	87	49	15	7	3.30

NHL All-Star (1983, 1985)
Vezina Trophy (1985)

STEVE KENNEDY'S TOP 10

1. Wilt Chamberlain
2. Mike Schmidt
3. Bobby Clarke
4. Allen Iverson
5. Steve Carlton
6. Reggie White
7. Charles Barkley
8. Julius Erving
9. Donovan McNabb
10. Chuck Bednarik

59 Eric Allen

RANK	POINTS	VOTES RECEIVED
1st	50	0
2nd	49	0
3rd	48	0
4th	47	0
5th	46	0
6th	45	0
7th	44	0
8th	43	0
9th	42	0
10th	41	0
11th	40	0
12th	39	0
13th	38	0
14th	37	0
15th	36	0
16th	35	0
17th	34	0
18th	33	0
19th	32	0
20th	31	0
21st	30	1
22nd	29	0
23rd	28	2
24th	27	0
25th	26	0
26th	25	1
27th	24	0
28th	23	2
29th	22	0
30th	21	0
31st	20	0
32nd	19	2
33rd	18	0
34th	17	2
35th	16	4
36th	15	0
37th	14	1
38th	13	0
39th	12	0
40th	11	0
41st	10	1
42nd	9	2
43rd	8	1
44th	7	1
45th	6	2
46th	5	2
47th	4	0
48th	3	1
49th	2	1
50th	1	3
Not on List	0	71

TOP 10 VOTES	0
2ND 10 VOTES	0
3RD 10 VOTES	6
4TH 10 VOTES	9
5TH 10 VOTES	14
TOTAL VOTES	29
TOTAL POINTS	380

▼ **TEAM**
Eagles

▼ **YEARS PLAYED**
1988–1994

▼ **POSITION**
Cornerback

Merrill Reese's description of the play on radio earned him ESPN's "Call of the Year." It was October 1993, and the Eagles were playing the Jets at the Meadowlands. Eric Allen picked off a Boomer Esiason pass at the Eagles' six-yard line, wove in and out of traffic, and ran 94 yards for a touchdown in the Birds' 35-30 win. That was one of four interceptions which Allen returned for touchdowns in '93. He was one of the best cornerbacks that Merrill has ever seen. "He had the most remarkable sense of anticipation; he could sense and diagnose a play instantly. He had outstanding athletic ability. He could run the open field as well as any running back or return man."

Eric's ability to cover and intercept earned him raves from other voters. "He was not the biggest [5'10", 180 lbs.] or strongest," said Bob Bookbinder, "but opponents made a point of not throwing in his direction. He was capable of the big interception and with his speed made some big plays. He made other teams change their offensive approach to the game. He was a quiet leader." Jason Garber: "He was one of the top five cornerbacks in his time. He allowed the Eagles to blitz more due to his man-to-man coverage. He always covered the other team's best receiver." Michael Barkann described him as a "lock-down" cornerback. Brent Saunders called him "the best Eagles' corner ever." Dave Sautter put Allen in the category of "borderline Hall of Famer." His numbers support Dave's point. In his 14-year NFL career (half of which was spent with the Eagles), he intercepted 54 passes (which puts him in the top 20 on the all-time list), 34 of which were with the Eagles, and made six Pro Bowl appearances, five with the Eagles.

But did Allen cover so well and rack up all those interceptions because he was so good or because the Eagles' defense, notably the defensive line, was so superb? According to Ned Hark, it was the latter. "A good cornerback is only as good as his front four. The Eagles' defensive line wreaked havoc on quarterbacks. Allen was a product of a lot of guys around him." Sean Bergin felt the same way, noting that two of the stars of the defensive line, Reggie White and Jerome Brown, overshadowed him. John Mitchell acknowledged that Allen was a solid cover man and a quiet, unassuming leader, but did not have quite enough to make John's top 50. Philly fans often are not forgiving when a player leaves the city to sign as a free-agent with another team. Allen did that when he signed with the Saints in 1995, and Randy Axelrod held it against him. "He bailed out on the Eagles."

Year	Team	Lg	G	Int	Yds	Td	Sacks
1988	Eagles	NFL	16	5	76	0	0
1989	Eagles	NFL	15	8	38	0	0
1990	Eagles	NFL	16	3	37	1	0
1991	Eagles	NFL	16	5	20	0	0
1992	Eagles	NFL	16	4	49	0	0
1993	Eagles	NFL	16	6	201	4	2
1994	Eagles	NFL	16	3	61	0	0
1995	New Orleans	NFL	16	2	28	0	0
1996	New Orleans	NFL	16	1	33	0	0
1997	New Orleans	NFL	16	2	27	0	0
1998	Oakland	NFL	10	5	59	0	0
1999	Oakland	NFL	16	3	33	0	0
2000	Oakland	NFL	16	6	145	3	1
2001	Oakland	NFL	16	1	19	1	0
	Eagles Totals		111	34	482	5	2
	Career Totals		217	54	826	9	3

NFL Pro Bowl (1989, 1991–95)

Bobby Abreu

RANK	POINTS	VOTES RECEIVED
1st	50	0
2nd	49	0
3rd	48	0
4th	47	0
5th	46	0
6th	45	0
7th	44	0
8th	43	0
9th	42	0
10th	41	0
11th	40	0
12th	39	0
13th	38	1
14th	37	0
15th	36	0
16th	35	1
17th	34	0
18th	33	0
19th	32	0
20th	31	0
21st	30	0
22nd	29	0
23rd	28	0
24th	27	1
25th	26	1
26th	25	1
27th	24	1
28th	23	0
29th	22	3
30th	21	0

RANK	POINTS	VOTES RECEIVED
31st	20	0
32nd	19	0
33rd	18	1
34th	17	0
35th	16	1
36th	15	1
37th	14	2
38th	13	0
39th	12	0
40th	11	1
41st	10	1
42nd	9	1
43rd	8	0
44th	7	2
45th	6	0
46th	5	0
47th	4	0
48th	3	0
49th	2	1
50th	1	3
Not on List	0	77

TOP 10 VOTES	0
2ND 10 VOTES	2
3RD 10 VOTES	7
4TH 10 VOTES	6
5TH 10 VOTES	8
TOTAL VOTES	23
TOTAL POINTS	367

▼ TEAM
Phillies

▼ YEARS PLAYED
1998–2006

▼ POSITION
Outfielder

Bobby Abreu just might be the most underrated Philadelphia athlete in history. Despite a string of outstanding seasons statistically, more than half of the voters did not include Bobby in their top 50. Bill McElroy pulled no punches in expressing his dislike for Abreu: "He defined what was wrong with the Phillies [from the mid-1990s to the mid-2000s], a self-centered player who worried about statistics instead of wins. If he played for any other team, his selfishness would make them losers also." (Would Joe Torre agree?) Mike Mastalski covered all the bases when taking shots at Abreu—his attitude, glove and ability to hit in the clutch. "He is a slacker. His Gold Glove [in 2005] was a disgrace. His stats [for the Phillies] were inflated by non-clutch home runs. If the Phillies were down 7-2 in the ninth inning, he'd hit a two-run homer."

Other voters, although not as critical as Bill or Mike, didn't think that Abreu deserved a spot on their lists. "He's a nice ballplayer, but what [did] he [do] to lead the team?" (Greg Geier). "He has great skills, but something about his demeanor bothers me. He's too nonchalant" (Ned Hark). "He's a lifetime .300 hitter, which is extremely hard to do…[but] to make my list, you have to play hard on both sides of the ball" (Ryan Kent). "He's not a clutch hitter. And he's no Roberto Clemente in right field" [Clemente won 12 Gold Gloves for the Pirates] (Ken Berky).

But Bobby has his staunch defenders; Steve Kennedy was among his biggest. "He's the best five-tool [hit for average, hit for power, run, field and throw] right fielder in all of baseball. Abreu gets a bad rap because he's not emotional, and is misunderstood because he's not from the U.S.A. But talk to baseball people, and he's the best all-around offensive right fielder in the game." Mike DiColla and Harvey Feldman were also huge Abreu fans, ranking the Venezuelan in their top 20. Mike: "He's 'Mr. Consistency'—a good all-around player every year. He's the kind of player Phillies fans won't appreciate until he's gone." Mike also disagreed with the notion that Abreu doesn't hustle. "He's laid-back, but he hustles." Harvey admitted that he was not thrilled about Abreu's attitude (with the Phillies), but said that his statistics speak for themselves. He also was impressed with Bobby's membership in the 30 home run/30 stolen base club. No doubt, Abreu's stats with the Phillies were terrific, including several seasons in which he hit .300, scored 100 runs, and drove in 100 runs. He had two seasons in which he both hit 30 home runs and stole 30 bases, which puts him in the same company as Willie Mays, Bobby Bonds and Barry Bonds. Not bad company.

JOHN CLARK'S TOP 10

1. Wilt Chamberlain
2. Mike Schmidt
3. Bobby Clarke
4. Reggie White
5. Allen Iverson
6. Donovan McNabb
7. Charles Barkley
8. Steve Carlton
9. Julius Erving
10. Mo Cheeks

Year	Team	Lg	G	AB	R	H	HR	RBI	SB	Avg	SLG
1996	Houston	N.L.	15	22	1	5	0	1	0	.227	.273
1997	Houston	N.L.	59	188	22	47	3	26	7	.250	.372
1998	Phillies	N.L.	151	497	68	155	17	74	19	.312	.497
1999	Phillies	N.L.	152	546	118	183	20	93	27	.335	.549
2000	Phillies	N.L.	154	576	103	182	25	79	28	.316	.554
2001	Phillies	N.L.	162	588	118	170	31	110	36	.289	.543
2002	Phillies	N.L.	157	572	102	176	20	85	31	.308	.521
2003	Phillies	N.L.	158	577	99	173	20	101	22	.300	.468
2004	Phillies	N.L.	159	574	118	173	30	105	40	.301	.544
2005	Phillies	N.L.	162	588	104	168	24	102	31	.286	.474
2006	Phillies	N.L.	98	339	61	94	8	65	20	.277	.434
2006	N.Y. Yankees	A.L.	58	209	37	69	7	42	10	.330	.507
	Phillies Totals		1353	4857	891	1474	195	814	254	.303	.513
	Career Totals		1485	5276	951	1595	205	883	271	.302	.507

National League All-Star (2004–05)
National League Gold Glove (2005)

Seth Joyner

RANK	POINTS	VOTES RECEIVED
1st	50	0
2nd	49	0
3rd	48	0
4th	47	0
5th	46	0
6th	45	0
7th	44	0
8th	43	0
9th	42	0
10th	41	0
11th	40	0
12th	39	0
13th	38	0
14th	37	0
15th	36	0
16th	35	0
17th	34	0
18th	33	0
19th	32	0
20th	31	0
21st	30	0
22nd	29	1
23rd	28	3
24th	27	0
25th	26	0
26th	25	0
27th	24	2
28th	23	1
29th	22	1
30th	21	0

RANK	POINTS	VOTES RECEIVED
31st	20	0
32nd	19	0
33rd	18	1
34th	17	1
35th	16	1
36th	15	1
37th	14	1
38th	13	1
39th	12	1
40th	11	1
41st	10	0
42nd	9	0
43rd	8	0
44th	7	0
45th	6	0
46th	5	3
47th	4	2
48th	3	2
49th	2	2
50th	1	2
Not on List	0	73

TOP 10 VOTES	0
2ND 10 VOTES	0
3RD 10 VOTES	8
4TH 10 VOTES	8
5TH 10 VOTES	11
TOTAL VOTES	27
TOTAL POINTS	357

▼ TEAM
Eagles

▼ YEARS PLAYED
1986–1993

▼ POSITION
Linebacker

From 1988 to 1992, the Eagles made the playoffs four out of five years, due in large part to their tenacious and dominating defense. It's indisputable that Reggie White was the Eagles' best defensive player during that run. But who was second best? Seth Joyner, according to some. "Other than Reggie, Seth was the best player on the defense," declared Tom Walter. "He made big plays. He was always around the ball. He was all over the field. He made timely interceptions." "Reggie got a lot of the ink," said John Mitchell, "but Seth was the glue at linebacker. He was the heart of the Eagles' defense—he played with emotion." Bob Bookbinder, another big Joyner supporter, said, "He could make the big play, whether it be a stop or turnover for a touchdown. I remember his determination in breaking down the offensive momentum of the other team."

"No Eagles linebacker has been as good since Joyner," said Greg Geier. "He took over games by himself," added Randy Axelrod. Joyner was also praised for his aggressiveness (Andy Dziedzic), dominance (John Bergmann) and leadership (Andy Paul).

Michael Barkann and Jeff Skow didn't think that Joyner was the second-best Eagles defensive player of the Ryan-Kotite era and, in fact, didn't think he was worthy of a top 50 spot. Michael thought that Eric Allen, among others, was a better defensive player; Jeff felt that Seth wasn't as good at his position as Jerome Brown. Bill McElroy and Brent Saunders didn't believe that Joyner deserved much credit because the defensive line, which Reggie anchored, was the key to the D. Bill was blunt in his dismissal of Joyner. "He played behind a great line. Big deal." Brent pointed out that when Joyner went to other teams (Arizona, Green Bay) where the line wasn't as strong, "he wasn't as good, and was exposed against the run."

Year	Team	Lg	G	Int	Yds	TD	Sacks
1986	Eagles	NFL	14	1	4	0	2
1987	Eagles	NFL	12	2	42	0	4
1988	Eagles	NFL	16	4	96	0	3.5
1989	Eagles	NFL	14	1	0	0	4.5
1990	Eagles	NFL	16	1	9	0	7.5
1991	Eagles	NFL	16	3	41	0	6.5
1992	Eagles	NFL	16	4	88	2	6.5
1993	Eagles	NFL	16	1	6	0	2
1994	Arizona	NFL	16	3	2	0	6
1995	Arizona	NFL	16	3	9	0	1
1996	Arizona	NFL	16	1	10	0	5
1997	Green Bay	NFL	11	0	0	0	3
1998	Denver	NFL	16	0	0	0	0
	Eagles Totals		120	17	286	2	36.5
	Career Totals		195	24	307	2	51.5

NFL Pro Bowl (1991, 1993–94)
Member of Super Bowl Champions (1998)

62 Darren Daulton

RANK	POINTS	VOTES RECEIVED
1st	50	0
2nd	49	0
3rd	48	0
4th	47	0
5th	46	0
6th	45	0
7th	44	0
8th	43	0
9th	42	0
10th	41	0
11th	40	0
12th	39	0
13th	38	0
14th	37	0
15th	36	0
16th	35	0
17th	34	0
18th	33	0
19th	32	0
20th	31	1
21st	30	0
22nd	29	0
23rd	28	0
24th	27	0
25th	26	1
26th	25	0
27th	24	2
28th	23	0
29th	22	0
30th	21	0

RANK	POINTS	VOTES RECEIVED
31st	20	0
32nd	19	0
33rd	18	2
34th	17	2
35th	16	0
36th	15	0
37th	14	0
38th	13	1
39th	12	1
40th	11	4
41st	10	1
42nd	9	3
43rd	8	3
44th	7	2
45th	6	2
46th	5	0
47th	4	1
48th	3	3
49th	2	4
50th	1	1
Not on List	0	66

TOP 10 VOTES	0
2ND 10 VOTES	1
3RD 10 VOTES	3
4TH 10 VOTES	10
5TH 10 VOTES	20
TOTAL VOTES	34
TOTAL POINTS	353

▼ **TEAM**
Phillies

▼ **YEARS PLAYED**
1983, 1985–1997

▼ **POSITION**
Catcher

If you asked five Phillies fans to name the most important member of the 1993 team, you might get five different answers. Lenny Dykstra, John Kruk, Tommy Greene, Curt Schilling and Mitch "The Wild Thing" Williams are all reasonable responses. Steve Bucci didn't have to think long when posed the question: Darren Daulton. "He was the heart and soul and backbone of the '93 Phillies. He was loved by the fans." Chris Wheeler also saluted Dutch for his clubhouse leadership. "[Manager Jim] Fregosi asked him to take charge. He was a physical presence." Daulton also scored high on Wheels' likability scale. "He doesn't have a mean bone in his body." Steve and Chris ranked Daulton 33rd and 34th, respectively. John Clark thought Daulton was a more important piece to the '93 Phillies than catcher Bob Boone was to the '80 Phillies. "Daulton was an offensive force, clubhouse leader, he handled the pitching staff, and was popular with his 'Macho Row' teammates." Cliff Patterson and Dick Streeter also cited Dutch's leadership, while Bob Chazin picked Daulton for his ability to produce home runs and RBIs, notably in 1992 and 1993 when he posted back-to-back 20-home run, 100-RBI seasons, making him one of a few catchers in history with consecutive 100-RBI seasons.

The main reason that Michael Beirne and Lee Fiederer didn't include Daulton on their lists is that aside from 1992 and 1993, he wasn't very productive. "He had a bad streak of years before '92 and '93," said Lee. Entering the 1992 season, Daulton had been, for the most part, a part-time player for the Phillies for eight years; his career batting average was only .222 and his season highs in home runs and RBIs were just 12 and 57. After '93, knee injuries significantly hampered Dutch, and he did not play in 100 games in a season again. Other voters looked at all the mediocre seasons and declined to include him. Jody McDonald: "He was the leader of the '93 Phillies, but not quite good enough for the list." Greg Geier: "He was not a great player, although he was colorful and a fan favorite."

Daulton was almost a career Phillie, playing all but a half-season for the team. Ironically, he earned a world championship ring for the Marlins in that half-season.

Year	Team	Lg	G	AB	R	H	HR	RBI	SB	Avg	SLG
1983	Phillies	N.L.	2	3	1	1	0	0	0	.333	.333
1985	Phillies	N.L.	36	103	14	21	4	11	3	.204	.369
1986	Phillies	N.L.	49	138	18	31	8	21	2	.225	.428
1987	Phillies	N.L.	53	129	10	25	3	13	0	.194	.310
1988	Phillies	N.L.	58	144	13	30	1	12	2	.208	.271
1989	Phillies	N.L.	131	368	29	74	8	44	2	.201	.310
1990	Phillies	N.L.	143	459	62	123	12	57	7	.268	.416
1991	Phillies	N.L.	89	285	36	56	12	42	5	.196	.365
1992	Phillies	N.L.	145	485	80	131	27	109	11	.270	.524
1993	Phillies	N.L.	147	510	90	131	24	105	5	.257	.482
1994	Phillies	N.L.	69	257	43	77	15	56	4	.300	.549
1995	Phillies	N.L.	98	342	44	85	9	55	3	.249	.401
1996	Phillies	N.L.	5	12	3	2	0	0	0	.167	.167
1997	Phillies	N.L.	84	269	46	71	11	42	6	.264	.480
1997	Florida	N.L.	52	126	22	33	3	21	2	.262	.429
Phillies Totals			1109	3504	489	858	134	567	48	.245	.427
Career Totals			1161	3630	511	891	137	588	50	.245	.427

National League All-Star (1992–93, 1995)
Member of World Champions (1997)

Scott Rolen

RANK	POINTS	VOTES RECEIVED
1st	50	0
2nd	49	0
3rd	48	0
4th	47	0
5th	46	0
6th	45	0
7th	44	0
8th	43	0
9th	42	0
10th	41	0
11th	40	0
12th	39	0
13th	38	0
14th	37	0
15th	36	0
16th	35	0
17th	34	0
18th	33	1
19th	32	0
20th	31	0
21st	30	0
22nd	29	0
23rd	28	2
24th	27	1
25th	26	0
26th	25	1
27th	24	1
28th	23	1
29th	22	0
30th	21	0
31st	20	0
32nd	19	2
33rd	18	1
34th	17	0
35th	16	3
36th	15	1
37th	14	0
38th	13	0
39th	12	0
40th	11	0
41st	10	0
42nd	9	1
43rd	8	0
44th	7	2
45th	6	1
46th	5	2
47th	4	1
48th	3	0
49th	2	0
50th	1	1
Not on List	0	78

TOP 10 VOTES	0
2ND 10 VOTES	1
3RD 10 VOTES	6
4TH 10 VOTES	7
5TH 10 VOTES	8
TOTAL VOTES	22
TOTAL POINTS	351

▼ **TEAM**
Phillies

▼ **YEARS PLAYED**
1996–2002

▼ **POSITION**
Third Baseman

After five and a half productive seasons with the Phillies, Scott Rolen parted acrimoniously in July 2002 when he was traded to the Cardinals, along with Doug Nickle, for Placido Polanco, Mike Timlin and Bud Smith. Mike Mastalski thought it was the fault of both Rolen and the Phillies brass that things couldn't be worked out, but Scott's whining didn't help matters. Randy Axelrod added some caustic comments about Rolen's departure and his performance while he was here: "He screwed the Phillies, wasn't a clutch hitter, and sometimes didn't play when he had minor injuries." Jeff Skow believed that Rolen had a tendency to sit out when other players would have stayed in the lineup.

Jeff also felt that Rolen didn't play to his potential with the Phillies which leads to one of the main reasons that neither John Clark nor Andy Dziedzic included Rolen on their lists: he was better as a Cardinal than as a Phillie. Indeed, in 2004, Rolen hit .314 with 34 home runs and 124 RBIs (he never reached any of those figures as a Phillie) and finished fourth in the National League MVP vote. In 2006, Rolen helped the Redbirds win the World Series. Steve Kennedy predicted that if Rolen stays healthy, he will be a Hall of Famer—as a Cardinal, not as a Phillie—although Steve thought Rolen got a raw deal in 2002.

Rolen also lost points in the popularity category. Dick Streeter was critical of Rolen because he didn't reach out to the fans, while Bob Bookbinder was more harsh. Bob works at a store in the King of Prussia area which Rolen, who lived nearby when he played for the Phillies, frequented. Bob lamented that Rolen's demeanor was the same on every visit to the store: unfriendly and aloof.

Chris Wheeler didn't include Rolen on his list, but paid Scott quite a compliment. Wheels said Rolen was a better defensive third baseman than 10-time Gold Glove winner Mike Schmidt, citing Scott's quickness and strong arm. (Rolen won three Gold Gloves for the Phillies.) Wheels, however, thought that Rolen's tenure in Philadelphia was too short to warrant inclusion on his top 50 list.

Rolen had his share of supporters, most notably Greg Veith and Bill McClain. Greg was in Rolen's corner in the management dispute and raved about him as a hitter: "Generally, I side with management, but in the Rolen affair, it's impossible to side with management. In my mind, the Rolen affair boiled down mostly to Rolen vs. [general manager Ed] Wade; I was always on Scotty's side and I think if people stop and think about what he was up against with that clown Wade, most would agree. I never want to hear another jackass in or out of the media say, 'All Philadelphia asks is that you play hard.' Rolen played hard night in and night out and look how he was rewarded. Most impressive [about Scott] was his glove, second most impressive was his genuine hustle and all-out style (the same thing people love Utley for now), and third, Rolen is a very good, very smart hitter with power."

Bill called Rolen the most identifiable player with the Phillies franchise after 1993. "He was the best player on a lot of the Phillies teams." In the forgettable four years that Terry Francona managed the Phillies (1997-2000), Rolen led the team in home runs and RBIs three times. "He's one of the best third basemen of this generation," added Bill.

Dave Sautter used historical perspective to explain ranking Rolen in his top 25. "He's the Phillies' second-best third baseman ever behind Schmidt." What about David Bell?

Year	Team	Lg	G	AB	R	H	HR	RBI	SB	Avg	SLG
1996	Phillies	N.L.	37	130	10	33	4	18	0	.254	.400
1997	Phillies	N.L.	156	561	93	159	21	92	16	.283	.469
1998	Phillies	N.L.	160	601	120	174	31	110	14	.290	.532
1999	Phillies	N.L.	112	421	74	113	26	77	12	.268	.525
2000	Phillies	N.L.	128	483	88	144	26	89	8	.298	.551
2001	Phillies	N.L.	151	554	96	160	25	107	16	.289	.498
2002	Phillies	N.L.	100	375	52	97	17	66	5	.259	.472
2002	St. Louis	N.L.	55	205	37	57	14	44	3	.278	.561
2003	St. Louis	N.L.	154	559	98	160	28	104	13	.286	.528
2004	St. Louis	N.L.	142	500	109	157	34	124	4	.314	.598
2005	St. Louis	N.L.	56	196	28	46	5	28	1	.235	.383
2006	St. Louis	N.L.	142	521	94	154	22	95	7	.296	.518
	Phillies Totals		844	3125	533	880	150	559	71	.282	.504
	Career Totals		1393	5106	899	1454	253	954	99	.285	.515

National League Rookie of the Year (1997)
National League Gold Glove (1998, 2000–04, 2006)
National League All-Star (2002–06)
Member of World Champions (2006)

64 David Akers

RANK	POINTS	VOTES RECEIVED
1st	50	0
2nd	49	0
3rd	48	0
4th	47	0
5th	46	0
6th	45	0
7th	44	0
8th	43	0
9th	42	0
10th	41	0
11th	40	0
12th	39	0
13th	38	0
14th	37	0
15th	36	1
16th	35	1
17th	34	1
18th	33	0
19th	32	0
20th	31	0
21st	30	0
22nd	29	1
23rd	28	1
24th	27	0
25th	26	0
26th	25	0
27th	24	0
28th	23	1
29th	22	0
30th	21	1
31st	20	1
32nd	19	0
33rd	18	0
34th	17	0
35th	16	0
36th	15	1
37th	14	0
38th	13	2
39th	12	1
40th	11	0
41st	10	0
42nd	9	0
43rd	8	4
44th	7	0
45th	6	1
46th	5	3
47th	4	2
48th	3	2
49th	2	1
50th	1	0
Not on List	0	75

TOP 10 VOTES	0
2ND 10 VOTES	3
3RD 10 VOTES	4
4TH 10 VOTES	5
5TH 10 VOTES	13
TOTAL VOTES	25
TOTAL POINTS	348

▼ TEAM
Eagles

▼ YEARS PLAYED
1999–Present

▼ POSITION
Kicker

The name of David Akers sparked a heated debate on this question: Is a field goal kicker worthy of inclusion on a list of best athletes? Some voters emphatically believed that no matter how good Akers has been with the Eagles, because he is a kicker, he doesn't belong. "He is one of the best in the business," conceded Mike Mastalski, "but still he is only a kicker. A team can sign a kicker off his day job." Funny you say that, Mike. Akers was a waiter at a steak house when the Eagles signed him in 1999. Joe Fee also used sarcasm to make his point. "No kicker will ever make any list [of top athletes] that I author—unless it's as a soccer player." Fran Garvin passed on Akers for similar reasons. "Kickers are not great athletes. They don't compare to the other great athletes on the list."

A few voters strongly disagreed. Ralph Antonelli and Bob Bookbinder were two of Akers' biggest supporters. Ralph: "A field goal kicker is important because three points can make or break a game. Akers is the Eagles' best field goal kicker ever. He is consistent; he has a strong leg. He has a good attitude." Bob: "He has been the difference in a lot of Eagles wins. He is a great leader. I also like the pride he has taken in making runback-saving tackles. There have been a number of Eagles teams that looked like they had no clue about how to score in the red zone. Regardless of the performance of some of those Eagles offenses, Akers has continued to get the job done." Sean Bergin and Bill McElroy considered Akers one of the best kickers in the league and included him for that reason. "A kicker is like a closer in baseball," said Sean. "Akers is 'lights out' when you need him. Automatic." Akers is the Eagles' all-time leader in field goals and points. He has nailed many a clutch field goal—among the most memorable came against Green Bay in the NFC divisional playoff game in January 2004. Soon after Freddy Mitchell's dramatic fourth and 26 catch, which prolonged the Eagles' fourth-quarter drive, Akers tied the game with a field goal with five seconds left in regulation, and then nailed a three-pointer in overtime for the win.

Mike Koob did not include Akers because he has had some key misses. Mike recalled the 35-yarder that Akers missed at the Meadowlands in the last week of the 2002 season, which would have won the game and clinched the division; the Birds lost the game in overtime. "He always seems to miss a lot of field goals against the Giants." Akers only connected on eight of his first 16 field goal attempts against the Giants.

STEVE BUCCI'S TOP 10

1. Wilt Chamberlain
2. Mike Schmidt
3. Steve Carlton
4. Chuck Bednarik
5. Julius Erving
6. Bobby Clarke
7. Bernie Parent
8. Reggie White
9. Allen Iverson
10. Charles Barkley

Year	Team	Lg	G	XP	XPA	XP Pct	FG	FGA	FG Pct	Long	Pts
1998	Eagles	NFL	1	2	2	100.0	0	2	0	—	2
1999	Eagles	NFL	16	2	2	100.0	3	6	50.0	53	11
2000	Eagles	NFL	16	34	36	94.4	29	33	87.9	51	121
2001	Eagles	NFL	16	37	38	94.4	26	31	83.9	50	115
2002	Eagles	NFL	16	43	43	100.0	30	34	88.2	51	133
2003	Eagles	NFL	16	42	42	100.0	24	29	82.8	57	114
2004	Eagles	NFL	16	41	42	100.0	27	32	84.4	51	122
2005	Eagles	NFL	12	23	23	100.0	16	22	72.7	50	71
2006	Eagles	NFL	16	48	48	100.0	18	23	78.3	47	102
	Eagles Totals		125	272	276	98.6	173	212	81.6	57	791
	Career Totals		125	272	276	98.6	173	212	81.6	57	791

NFL Pro Bowl (2001–02, 2004)

John Kruk

RANK	POINTS	VOTES RECEIVED
1st	50	0
2nd	49	0
3rd	48	0
4th	47	0
5th	46	0
6th	45	0
7th	44	0
8th	43	0
9th	42	0
10th	41	0
11th	40	0
12th	39	0
13th	38	0
14th	37	0
15th	36	0
16th	35	0
17th	34	0
18th	33	0
19th	32	0
20th	31	2
21st	30	0
22nd	29	0
23rd	28	0
24th	27	0
25th	26	0
26th	25	0
27th	24	0
28th	23	0
29th	22	3
30th	21	1

RANK	POINTS	VOTES RECEIVED
31st	20	0
32nd	19	1
33rd	18	1
34th	17	1
35th	16	0
36th	15	2
37th	14	1
38th	13	1
39th	12	0
40th	11	1
41st	10	2
42nd	9	1
43rd	8	1
44th	7	0
45th	6	1
46th	5	3
47th	4	2
48th	3	0
49th	2	2
50th	1	2
Not on List	0	72

TOP 10 VOTES	0
2ND 10 VOTES	2
3RD 10 VOTES	4
4TH 10 VOTES	8
5TH 10 VOTES	14
TOTAL VOTES	28
TOTAL POINTS	343

▼ TEAM
Phillies

▼ YEARS PLAYED
1989–1994

▼ POSITION
First Baseman

On the Phillies' all-time team of colorful players, John Kruk undoubtedly is the starting first baseman. "He was such a personality, a character, he was enjoyable to watch," said Andy Paul. "He was lovable, a fan favorite," said Bob Chazin. Who else but the Krukker, when told by a woman at a restaurant that his eating and drinking habits were not becoming for a professional athlete, would respond, "I ain't no athlete, lady. I'm a baseball player." Patrick Dooley recalled that classic Krukism, noting that the roly-poly first baseman connected with the average fan. Michael Barkann thought that Kruk connected, not only with the fans, but with his teammates. "He helped police the locker room. He had the intangibles. He made the team better."

Kruk didn't earn the votes of these and other survey participants just because he was colorful. He could, as Patrick Dooley put it, "hit a ton." During his five and a half years in Philadelphia, he hit .309 and never hit less than .291 in a season. Jeff Skow: "He was very consistent [during his years with the Phillies], especially the magical '93 season."

A few people, including Greg Geier, Paul Troy, Mike Koob and Mike Mastalski, felt that Kruk, while a fan favorite, didn't have enough productive years with the Phillies. While Kruk's average was consistently high, his season highs for the Phillies in home runs and RBIs were 21 and 92 in 1991; he didn't hit as many as 15 long balls in any other season for the Phillies and only drove in more than 70 runs in one other season.

Joe Brown put a different spin on Kruk's likability. "He was such a personality and because of that, he got more notoriety than he would have otherwise. If he had played on a bad team, we probably wouldn't be talking about him. He would have had a longer, better career if he took care of himself better."

Year	Team	Lg	G	AB	R	H	HR	RBI	SB	Avg	SLG
1986	San Diego	N.L.	122	278	33	86	4	38	2	.309	.424
1987	San Diego	N.L.	138	447	72	140	20	91	18	.313	.488
1988	San Diego	N.L.	120	378	54	91	9	44	5	.241	.362
1989	San Diego	N.L.	31	76	7	14	3	6	0	.184	.303
1989	Phillies	N.L.	81	281	46	93	5	38	3	.331	.473
1990	Phillies	N.L.	142	443	52	129	7	67	10	.291	.431
1991	Phillies	N.L.	152	538	84	158	21	92	7	.294	.483
1992	Phillies	N.L.	144	507	86	164	10	70	3	.323	.458
1993	Phillies	N.L.	150	535	100	169	14	85	6	.316	.475
1994	Phillies	N.L.	75	255	35	77	5	38	4	.302	.427
1995	Chisox	A.L.	45	159	13	49	2	23	0	.308	.390
	Phillies Totals		744	2559	403	790	62	390	33	.309	.461
	Career Totals		1200	3897	582	1170	100	592	58	.300	.446

National League All-Star (1991–93)

Guy Rodgers

RANK	POINTS	VOTES RECEIVED
1st	50	0
2nd	49	0
3rd	48	0
4th	47	0
5th	46	0
6th	45	0
7th	44	0
8th	43	0
9th	42	1
10th	41	0
11th	40	0
12th	39	0
13th	38	0
14th	37	1
15th	36	0
16th	35	0
17th	34	0
18th	33	0
19th	32	1
20th	31	0
21st	30	0
22nd	29	0
23rd	28	0
24th	27	1
25th	26	1
26th	25	0
27th	24	0
28th	23	0
29th	22	0
30th	21	1
31st	20	0
32nd	19	0
33rd	18	3
34th	17	2
35th	16	0
36th	15	1
37th	14	0
38th	13	0
39th	12	1
40th	11	1
41st	10	2
42nd	9	1
43rd	8	0
44th	7	0
45th	6	0
46th	5	0
47th	4	0
48th	3	0
49th	2	1
50th	1	0
Not on List	0	82

TOP 10 VOTES	1
2ND 10 VOTES	2
3RD 10 VOTES	3
4TH 10 VOTES	8
5TH 10 VOTES	4
TOTAL VOTES	18
TOTAL POINTS	342

▼ **TEAM**
Warriors

▼ **YEARS PLAYED**
1959–1962

▼ **POSITION**
Guard

Jim Rosen waxed sentimental when he was asked about one of his childhood heroes, Guy Rodgers. "He was the first to be called a great 'Philly guard' and we should all be very proud of that as Philadelphians. He became a symbol of something about us." Rodgers, a native of Philadelphia, played college ball at Temple and was drafted by the Warriors in 1958. In his second NBA season, he finished second in the league in assists per game; he finished second in that category again in 1961 and 1962. Wilt Chamberlain was the beneficiary of many of those assists.

The Warriors headed west after the 1962 season, so Guy's time in Philadelphia as a pro player was limited to four years. However, he left such an indelible impression during that short time that many voters rated him high on their lists. Like Jim Rosen, Ray Didinger is well aware of Philadelphia's reputation for producing first-rate basketball players, especially guards. "Some people think he was the greatest guard that the city of Philadelphia ever produced," said Ray, who ranked Rodgers 15th. "He was a classic point guard—ahead of his time. He was revolutionary, tremendously influential. He had great ability to handle the ball and pass."

Others, notably Bob Cinalli, Neil Goldstein, Jon Grisdale and Steve Danawitz, marveled at Guy's speed, passing and ball-handling. Bob: "He and [Celtics star] Bob Cousy were the two best guards in the league, head and shoulders above anybody else in the league. Guy played a pure game of basketball; he was a magician with the ball." Jon: "He was very fast. He could score eight points in a game and he would be the star of the game because of the other things he did." Neil and Steve remember Guy's passing, dribbling behind his back, and feeding the ball to Wilt.

After Rodgers left Philadelphia, he played eight more NBA seasons, and his numbers improved over the years. He led the NBA in assists for the San Francisco Warriors in 1963 and the Chicago Bulls in 1967. While he averaged only 10.8 points per game in Philadelphia, he had 18-point-per-game seasons in San Francisco and Chicago.

Some of the voters who passed on Guy compared him to two other star players for the Warriors, Paul Arizin and Tom Gola. While Rodgers' NBA career was good, he wasn't elected to the Hall of Fame, while Arizin and Gola made the Hall. "I realize that is hair-splitting, but that is sort of the differentiation you have to make when considering so many great players," said Gordie Jones. Jack Guziewicz mimicked Gordie by stating that Arizin and Gola were more prominent than Rodgers. Jack made another interesting point when comparing Rodgers to Allen Iverson. Rodgers, like Iverson, stood about six feet, but the average height of NBA players has increased dramatically since Guy's day and, therefore, Guy played against shorter players. "Iverson has been able to dominate despite playing against players much taller," said Jack. "Rodgers didn't have nearly the height disadvantage that Iverson did."

If a player's college career could be considered, Terry Bickhart may have included Rodgers. He was an outstanding player at Temple—he was their all-time leading scorer until the 1980s. Arizin was a better pro player," said Terry; "Rodgers was a better college player."

Year	Team	Lg	G	Min	FGM	FGA	FGP	FTM	FTA	FTP	AST	REB	Pts	PPG
1958–59	Warriors	NBA	45	1565	211	535	.394	61	112	.545	261	281	483	1.7
1959–60	Warriors	NBA	68	2483	338	870	.389	111	181	.613	482	391	787	11.6
1960–61	Warriors	NBA	78	2905	397	1029	.386	206	300	.687	677	509	1000	12.8
1961–62	Warriors	NBA	80	2650	267	749	.356	121	182	.665	643	348	655	8.2
1962–63	San Francisco	NBA	79	3249	445	1150	.387	208	286	.727	825	394	1098	13.9
1963–64	San Francisco	NBA	79	2695	337	923	.365	198	280	.707	556	328	872	11.0
1964–65	San Francisco	NBA	79	2699	465	1225	.380	223	325	.686	565	323	1153	14.6
1965–66	San Francisco	NBA	79	2902	586	1571	.373	296	407	.727	846	421	1468	18.6
1966–67	Chicago	NBA	81	3063	538	1377	.391	383	475	.806	908	346	1459	18.0
1967–68	Chic.-Cinn.	NBA	4	129	16	54	.296	9	11	.818	28	150	41	1.3
1968–69	Milwaukee	NBA	81	2157	325	862	.377	184	232	.793	561	226	834	1.3
1969–70	Milwaukee	NBA	64	749	68	191	.356	67	90	.744	213	74	203	3.2
Warriors Totals			271	9603	1213	3183	.381	499	775	.644	2063	1529	2925	1.8
Career Totals			892	28663	4125	10908	.378	2165	3003	.721	6917	3791	10415	11.7

NBA All-Star (1963–64, 1966–67)

Timmy Brown

RANK	POINTS	VOTES RECEIVED
1st	50	0
2nd	49	0
3rd	48	0
4th	47	0
5th	46	0
6th	45	0
7th	44	0
8th	43	0
9th	42	0
10th	41	0
11th	40	0
12th	39	0
13th	38	1
14th	37	1
15th	36	0
16th	35	0
17th	34	0
18th	33	0
19th	32	0
20th	31	0
21st	30	0
22nd	29	0
23rd	28	2
24th	27	0
25th	26	0
26th	25	0
27th	24	0
28th	23	0
29th	22	1
30th	21	1

RANK	POINTS	VOTES RECEIVED
31st	20	0
32nd	19	0
33rd	18	2
34th	17	0
35th	16	0
36th	15	0
37th	14	0
38th	13	2
39th	12	1
40th	11	3
41st	10	0
42nd	9	0
43rd	8	1
44th	7	4
45th	6	1
46th	5	1
47th	4	0
48th	3	2
49th	2	1
50th	1	1
Not on List	0	75

TOP 10 VOTES	0
2ND 10 VOTES	2
3RD 10 VOTES	4
4TH 10 VOTES	8
5TH 10 VOTES	11
TOTAL VOTES	25
TOTAL POINTS	337

▼ TEAM
Eagles

▼ YEARS PLAYED
1960–1967

▼ POSITION
Running Back

For more than a half-century, Bob Cinalli has spent his Sundays in the fall cheering for the Eagles. The best three Birds running backs he has ever seen are: (1) 1940s star Steve Van Buren, (2) Wilbert Montgomery and (3) Timmy Brown. "Brown was just a little below the caliber of [Hall of Famer] Tony Dorsett," said Bob. Cliff Patterson didn't see Van Buren play but saw Timmy and thought he may have been more talented than Wilbert. Merrill Reese rattled off Brown's attributes: "Dazzling runner, tremendous moves and explosive speed." Mike Rad and Bill McClain described Brown as one of the best players on some bad Eagles teams of the 1960s. From 1962 to 1964, the Eagles won a total of 11 games, but Brown led them in touchdowns in all three seasons, scoring 10 or more each year. In 1965 and 1966, he continued to rack up six-pointers, ranking second on the Birds in touchdowns both years. Jon Grisdale said that Brown was a great all-purpose player, likening him to Brian Westbrook. Timmy was a threat to score on the ground, in the air and, as Neil Goldstein and Mike Rad pointed out, as a return man. "He could take a ball coast-to-coast on a kickoff," said Neil. He certainly could. Timmy returned five kickoffs for touchdowns for the Eagles in his career, including two in 1966; he also took a punt all the way and went the distance after a missed field goal.

Brown's stardom was relatively short-lived, though, and by 1968, after a year with the Colts, his NFL career was over. Many voters thought that Timmy's star did not shine long enough to make their lists. "He was spectacular in his heyday," said Terry Bickhart, "but it was too short a period to be included." Harvey Feldman acknowledged that Brown had some good seasons, but then, Harvey said, tongue-in-cheek, so did Clarence Peaks. Peaks ranked first or second in rushing for the Birds from 1957 to 1961, although he topped out at 495 yards. While Dennis Brady picked Brown over Westbrook because Timmy played every down on offense, Jack Guziewicz thought

Westbrook was a more versatile player, and picked him over Brown. Jerry McDonough also couldn't find room for Timmy in his top 50 because of Brown's relatively short stretch of stardom in Philly.

Year	Team	Lg	G	Att	Rushing Yds	Avg	TD	Rec	Receiving Yds	Avg	TD
1959	Green Bay	NFL	1	0	0	0	0	0	0	0	0
1960	Eagles	NFL	12	9	35	3.9	2	9	247	27.4	2
1961	Eagles	NFL	14	50	338	6.8	1	14	264	18.9	2
1962	Eagles	NFL	14	137	545	4.0	5	52	849	16.3	6
1963	Eagles	NFL	14	192	841	4.4	6	36	487	13.5	4
1964	Eagles	NFL	10	90	356	4.0	5	15	244	16.3	5
1965	Eagles	NFL	13	158	861	5.4	6	50	682	13.6	3
1966	Eagles	NFL	13	161	548	3.4	3	33	371	11.2	3
1967	Eagles	NFL	7	53	179	3.4	1	22	202	9.2	1
1968	Baltimore	NFL	11	39	159	4.1	2	4	53	13.3	0
Eagles Totals			97	850	3703	4.3	29	231	3346	14.5	26
Career Totals			109	889	3862	4.3	31	235	3399	14.5	26

Member of NFL Champions (1960)
NFL Pro Bowl (1962–63, 1965)

68 Ed Van Impe

RANK	POINTS	VOTES RECEIVED		RANK	POINTS	VOTES RECEIVED
1st	50	0		31st	20	1
2nd	49	0		32nd	19	0
3rd	48	0		33rd	18	0
4th	47	0		34th	17	0
5th	46	0		35th	16	0
6th	45	0		36th	15	0
7th	44	0		37th	14	1
8th	43	0		38th	13	0
9th	42	0		39th	12	0
10th	41	0		40th	11	3
11th	40	0		41st	10	0
12th	39	0		42nd	9	0
13th	38	0		43rd	8	0
14th	37	0		44th	7	1
15th	36	0		45th	6	0
16th	35	0		46th	5	2
17th	34	0		47th	4	1
18th	33	2		48th	3	0
19th	32	0		49th	2	2
20th	31	2		50th	1	0
21st	30	0		Not on List	0	81
22nd	29	0				
23rd	28	0				
24th	27	0		TOP 10 VOTES		0
25th	26	1		2ND 10 VOTES		4
26th	25	1		3RD 10 VOTES		4
27th	24	0		4TH 10 VOTES		5
28th	23	0		5TH 10 VOTES		6
29th	22	0		TOTAL VOTES		19
30th	21	2		TOTAL POINTS		313

▼ **TEAM**
Flyers

▼ **YEARS PLAYED**
1968–1976

▼ **POSITION**
Defenseman

If you watched a lot of Phillies baseball and Flyers hockey in the late 1960s and 1970s, there are two events which you rarely saw: a Larry Bowa home run and an Ed Van Impe goal. Bowa poked just 13 home runs in his dozen years as a Phillie, while Van Impe registered just 19 goals during his nine seasons in Philadelphia; he netted just eight in his last seven seasons for the Flyers. The infrequency with which Van Impe scored was one of the main reasons he didn't make many voters' lists, including Dennis Brady's: "He was no offensive threat."

To a lot of voters, though, including Bill McElroy, Ned Hark and Paul Lightkep, it didn't matter that Van Impe rarely got on the scoreboard—his job was to play defense, and he did it well. Ned noted that when "Steady Eddie" Van Impe was on the ice, opposing players did not hang around the Flyers' net. Paul described Van Impe as one of the best defensemen he has ever seen. Fred Warren credited Van Impe for being an original Flyer who had longevity with the team and solidified the defense. Van Impe earned the votes of Ralph Antonelli and Harvey Feldman because he was the consummate team player. Harvey elaborated: "Van Impe [along with other Flyers defensemen, including Joe Watson, Jimmy Watson and Andre 'Moose' Dupont] epitomized the kinds of players that Philadelphians love—anything for the team. The Stanley Cup victories made Philadelphia a national sports town in the eyes of the national media in a way that it was not before."

On the other hand, Gregg Asman and Greg Veith were rather vehement that Van Impe was not deserving of a top 50 spot. "He may have been a good defenseman ('a defensive defenseman')," said Gregg, "but not a great athlete. I would have picked Behn Wilson over Van Impe." Gregg also pointed out that Mark Howe could score in addition to playing defense.

Greg Veith thought that Bernie Parent "made" Van Impe and the other Flyers defensemen. In other words, they were good because

Bernie was so good. "He was a nice defenseman, but I don't think he made more than one or two All-Star Games. [He made three.] He wasn't on the same planet as [premier defensemen of that era] Bobby Orr, Larry Robinson or Denis Potvin."

Year	Team	Lg	Gm	G	A	Pts	PM
1966–67	Chicago	NHL	61	8	11	19	111
1967–68	Flyers	NHL	67	4	13	17	141
1968–69	Flyers	NHL	68	7	12	19	112
1969–70	Flyers	NHL	65	0	10	10	117
1970–71	Flyers	NHL	77	0	11	11	80
1971–72	Flyers	NHL	73	4	9	13	78
1972–73	Flyers	NHL	72	1	11	12	76
1973–74	Flyers	NHL	77	2	16	18	119
1974–75	Flyers	NHL	78	1	17	18	109
1975–76	Flyers	NHL	40	0	8	8	60
1975–76	Pittsburgh	NHL	12	0	5	5	16
1976–77	Pittsburgh	NHL	10	0	3	3	6
	Flyers Totals		617	19	107	126	892
	Career Totals		700	27	126	153	1025

NHL All-Star (1969, 1974–75)
Member of Stanley Cup Champions (1974–75)

Bob Brown

RANK	POINTS	VOTES RECEIVED
1st	50	0
2nd	49	0
3rd	48	0
4th	47	0
5th	46	0
6th	45	0
7th	44	0
8th	43	0
9th	42	0
10th	41	0
11th	40	0
12th	39	0
13th	38	0
14th	37	0
15th	36	0
16th	35	0
17th	34	0
18th	33	1
19th	32	1
20th	31	1
21st	30	0
22nd	29	0
23rd	28	1
24th	27	2
25th	26	0
26th	25	0
27th	24	1
28th	23	0
29th	22	0
30th	21	0
31st	20	0
32nd	19	1
33rd	18	1
34th	17	1
35th	16	0
36th	15	0
37th	14	0
38th	13	0
39th	12	1
40th	11	0
41st	10	0
42nd	9	0
43rd	8	1
44th	7	2
45th	6	0
46th	5	2
47th	4	1
48th	3	2
49th	2	0
50th	1	0
Not on List	0	81

TOP 10 VOTES	0
2ND 10 VOTES	3
3RD 10 VOTES	4
4TH 10 VOTES	4
5TH 10 VOTES	8
TOTAL VOTES	19
TOTAL POINTS	310

▼ TEAM
Eagles

▼ YEARS PLAYED
1964–1968

▼ POSITION
Offensive Tackle

He was a "Hall of Famer" (Jody McDonald), "a perennial Pro Bowler" (Bob Anderson), "one of the best in the league at his position throughout his career" (Harvey Feldman) and "a pioneer at his position—at least 10 years ahead of his time" (John Mitchell), but on the whole Bob Brown did not receive his due in the voting. Doug Brown explained why he didn't include "Boomer" on his list; undoubtedly, many voters excluded Brown for similar reasons. "He only played here a few years [five] and probably suffered from the lack of respect afforded offensive linemen. Also, the Eagles [stunk] in those years." (They only had one winning season during Bob's five years in town.) In a nutshell, Brown had short tenure in Philadelphia, was on a lousy team, and played an unglamorous position. Bill Jakavick watched Brown's Eagles as a kid and although he didn't dispute Brown's dominance, declined to include him in his top 50. "In my younger years, I was more interested in the flashy position players—quarterbacks, running backs and wide receivers. I was never really a trenches kind of guy." Based on the survey results, many fans were not either.

Ray Didinger agreed that offensive linemen were not as respected when Brown played; if he played today, Ray seemed certain that Brown would be a household name. While 290-pound linemen are small nowadays, in the 1960s and 1970s, they were big. "He was a heavy-duty weight-lifter when lifting was not considered popular. Week in and week out, he overpowered his opponents on the defensive line that weighed between 240 and 260 pounds. He was very quick. He would knock one guy over and then get down the field and knock another guy over." Ray ranked Brown 23rd, while Merrill Reese placed big Bob 19th. "He had size, strength and technique; he was flawless. He overpowered the people that he blocked." Merrill was also influenced by Stan Walters' assessment of Brown: "Stan said that he was the greatest offensive lineman he ever saw."

Year	Team	Lg	G
1964	Eagles	NFL	14
1965	Eagles	NFL	14
1966	Eagles	NFL	14
1967	Eagles	NFL	8
1968	Eagles	NFL	14
1969	Los Angeles	NFL	14
1970	Los Angeles	NFL	14
1971	Oakland	NFL	10
1972	Oakland	NFL	14
1973	Oakland	NFL	10
	Eagles Totals		64
	Career Totals		126

NFL Pro Bowl (1965–66, 1968–71)
Pro Football Hall of Fame (2004)

MARK ECKEL'S TOP 10

1. Wilt Chamberlain
2. Reggie White
3. Mike Schmidt
4. Steve Carlton
5. Chuck Bednarik
6. Donovan McNabb
7. Allen Iverson
8. Bobby Clarke
9. Bernie Parent
10. Julius Erving

70 Darryl Dawkins

RANK	POINTS	VOTES RECEIVED		RANK	POINTS	VOTES RECEIVED
1st	50	0		31st	20	0
2nd	49	0		32nd	19	0
3rd	48	0		33rd	18	0
4th	47	0		34th	17	2
5th	46	0		35th	16	1
6th	45	0		36th	15	1
7th	44	0		37th	14	0
8th	43	0		38th	13	0
9th	42	0		39th	12	0
10th	41	0		40th	11	2
11th	40	0		41st	10	1
12th	39	0		42nd	9	2
13th	38	0		43rd	8	0
14th	37	1		44th	7	1
15th	36	0		45th	6	0
16th	35	0		46th	5	0
17th	34	0		47th	4	1
18th	33	1		48th	3	1
19th	32	0		49th	2	3
20th	31	1		50th	1	0
21st	30	0		Not on List	0	79
22nd	29	0				
23rd	28	0				
24th	27	1		TOP 10 VOTES		0
25th	26	0		2ND 10 VOTES		3
26th	25	0		3RD 10 VOTES		3
27th	24	1		4TH 10 VOTES		6
28th	23	0		5TH 10 VOTES		9
29th	22	1		TOTAL VOTES		21
30th	21	0		TOTAL POINTS		309

▼ **TEAM**
Sixers

▼ **YEARS PLAYED**
1976–1982

▼ **POSITION**
Center

The year after Moses Malone bypassed college and went straight to the pros from high school, Darryl Dawkins, who attended Maynard Evans High School in Orlando, Florida, also chose to forego college. The Sixers saw enormous potential in Dawkins and picked him in the first round (fifth overall pick) of the 1975 draft. A few voters thought that Double D made a mistake by not gaining experience at the college level before turning pro, and consequently wasn't as good an NBA player as he could have been. "He had Shaq [Shaquille O'Neal] potential," said Joe Brown, "but never measured up. He didn't handle going straight to the pros well; he was too immature." Steve Danawitz didn't think that Dawkins learned the game the way that Malone did. "He didn't develop into what he could have been with his size and strength," said Frank Minch. Greg Veith came down the hardest on "Chocolate Thunder." "He made the least of his rather considerable skills and talents. If you gave Dawkins the 'want to' of Malone, he would have been a league-leading rebounder." Dawkins' rebounding stats were not impressive—he never grabbed as many as 700 boards in a season. (Malone, on the other hand, racked up 700 or more rebounds in 14 straight seasons, with an average of more than 1000 per season.)

Even though Double D wasn't in Malone's class as a player and he posted modest rebounding numbers, many voters thought highly of him. Bill Jakavick's interest in basketball was captivated by Darryl's "amazing talent" and "thunderous dunks." (Below, Andy Paul describes a particularly thunderous dunk by Dawkins.) Both Brent Saunders and Michael Brophy described him as dominant; Brent added that Darryl was tenacious under the basket and didn't want to give up a rebound to anybody. Paul Lightkep questioned Dawkins' intensity sometimes, but on the whole had favorable comments: "He had incredible skills. He got the job done a lot of nights. He had a tremendous impact on the Sixers." Joe Fee said Dawkins was powerful under the basket, which helped him to compile a very good field-goal percentage. Dawkins was second in the NBA in that category twice (1978 and 1981). Brent Saunders, Paul Lightkep and Paul Lalley also mentioned Dawkins' colorful personality as a reason why they cast their votes for him. As Brent said, Dawkins was "someone you talked about."

As an adult, I have reflected many times on the challenges of going through life as a 76ers fan. However, I wouldn't have traded the memories for anything else.

Being able to experience an NBA game, in-person, is usually a thrill for most young boys as they have the chance to see some kind of acrobatic act by any player with the basketball. On December 5, 1979, this 11-year-old boy saw something at a 76ers game that remains in NBA history.

Chocolate Thunder, an alien from the planet Lovetron, or as most fans know him, Darryl Dawkins, was an awesome sight to behold. Having been one of the first players in NBA history to be drafted directly from high school into the NBA (as the 76ers' number five pick in 1975), his raw playing ability was exciting to me. Although he often made mistakes on the basketball court, he was a crowd favorite.

CRASH...BANG...BOOM...the sound of glass breaking is what I remember the most. The fans cheered and screamed as Darryl Dawkins, while performing one of his dunks during the game, slammed a basketball into the hoop and broke the glass backboard. Pieces of glass fell to the ground and the players scrambled to get to the other end of the court. The game was stopped by the referees. Unfortunately for the NBA, this backboard-breaking event had occurred 23 days before as Chocolate Thunder broke a backboard in Kansas City during a game. But this backboard event was definitely fortunate for me.

Having had season tickets to the 76ers for several years, my dad had the opportunity to meet some of the other people who also had season tickets in the surrounding rows in our section. One of these individuals happened to be a vice president for the 76ers at the time—and he was at the game with us when Darryl Dawkins broke the backboard. While the game was being delayed due to the cleanup and the need for the 76ers staff to locate a new backboard, I noticed the 76ers VP speaking to one of the security guards. Being a curious 11-year-old, I watched every step that the security guard took after walking away from our section. He walked behind our section and down the aisle of the next section that took him to the floor of the Spectrum. He walked onto the court, spoke to another security guard for a minute, then reached down onto the court and grabbed what appeared to be a piece of the broken glass from the backboard. He walked from the court, back up the steps and over to our section, and handed the piece of glass to me. WOW! I had a real piece of an NBA backboard, one that Darryl Dawkins broke. I was going to show this to all of my friends—and I did. The rest of the game didn't matter. I don't even know who won the game. My greatest memory of this event was thinking that I was the coolest kid in school the next day and that it was very cool that my dad knew the VP of the 76ers.

In a year when the premiere of *Star Trek: The Motion Picture* was released, I find it appropriate that Chocolate Thunder, the alien from Lovetron, created his own news story.

—ANDY PAUL

Year	Team	Lg	G	Min	FGM	FGA	FGP	FTM	FTA	FTP	AST	REB	Pts	PPG
1975–76	Sixers	NBA	37	165	41	82	.500	8	24	.333	3	49	90	2.4
1976–77	Sixers	NBA	59	684	135	215	.628	40	79	.506	24	230	310	5.3
1977–78	Sixers	NBA	70	1722	332	577	.575	156	220	.709	85	555	820	11.7
1978–79	Sixers	NBA	78	2035	430	831	.517	158	235	.672	128	631	1018	13.1
1979–80	Sixers	NBA	80	2541	494	946	.522	190	291	.653	149	693	1178	14.7
1980–81	Sixers	NBA	76	2088	423	697	.607	219	304	.720	109	545	1065	14.0
1981–82	Sixers	NBA	48	1124	207	367	.564	114	164	.695	55	305	528	11.0
1982–83	New Jersey	NBA	81	2093	401	669	.599	166	257	.646	114	420	968	12.0
1983–84	New Jersey	NBA	81	2417	507	855	.593	341	464	.735	123	541	1357	16.8
1984–85	New Jersey	NBA	39	972	192	339	.566	143	201	.711	45	181	527	13.5
1985–86	New Jersey	NBA	51	1207	284	441	.644	210	297	.707	77	251	778	15.3
1986–87	New Jersey	NBA	6	106	20	32	.625	17	24	.708	2	19	57	9.5
1987–88	Utah-Detroit	NBA	6	33	2	9	.643	6	15	.400	2	5	10	3.5
1988–89	Detroit	NBA	14	48	9	19	.474	9	18	.500	1	7	27	1.9
Sixers Totals			448	10359	2062	3715	.555	885	1317	.672	553	3008	5009	11.8
Career Totals			726	17235	3477	6079	.572	1777	2593	.685	917	4432	8733	12.0

71 Jerry Sisemore

RANK	POINTS	VOTES RECEIVED
1st	50	0
2nd	49	0
3rd	48	0
4th	47	0
5th	46	0
6th	45	0
7th	44	0
8th	43	0
9th	42	0
10th	41	0
11th	40	0
12th	39	0
13th	38	0
14th	37	0
15th	36	0
16th	35	0
17th	34	1
18th	33	1
19th	32	0
20th	31	0
21st	30	0
22nd	29	0
23rd	28	0
24th	27	0
25th	26	0
26th	25	0
27th	24	0
28th	23	0
29th	22	1
30th	21	1

RANK	POINTS	VOTES RECEIVED
31st	20	0
32nd	19	0
33rd	18	0
34th	17	2
35th	16	1
36th	15	1
37th	14	2
38th	13	0
39th	12	3
40th	11	2
41st	10	0
42nd	9	1
43rd	8	0
44th	7	0
45th	6	2
46th	5	2
47th	4	0
48th	3	1
49th	2	2
50th	1	1
Not on List	0	76

TOP 10 VOTES	0
2ND 10 VOTES	2
3RD 10 VOTES	2
4TH 10 VOTES	11
5TH 10 VOTES	9
TOTAL VOTES	24
TOTAL POINTS	300

▼ **TEAM**
Eagles

▼ **YEARS PLAYED**
1973–1984

▼ **POSITION**
Offensive Tackle/Guard

The Eagles were one win away from their first Super Bowl when they met the Cowboys, who had played in three of the five previous Super Bowls, in the NFC Championship Game following the 1980 season. On the second play from scrimmage, Wilbert Montgomery raced 42 yards for a touchdown, which set the tone for the Eagles' 20-7 win. A key block, which helped open up a lane for Wilbert, was thrown by tackle Jerry Sisemore. It was par for the course, according to Merrill Reese. "He was an outstanding tackle on the right side, a powerful force. He created huge holes." Mike Koob wholeheartedly agreed with Merrill. "He is the best tackle the Eagles have ever had, period. He was a statue; he protected Jaws year after year." Big, strong and powerful were the words that Cliff Patterson used to describe Sisemore. "He would plow people over." Dave Beck pointed to Sisemore's durability—he played 12 years with the Birds and rarely missed a game.

Gordie Jones and Mike DiColla thought Sisemore was one of the better Eagles players on the losing teams of the mid-1970s. "When the Eagles were bad," said Gordie, "he gave them respectability and solidified things. He stayed there for the years when they became good." Mike: "He was a rock on a lot of poor teams, and one of the leaders on their Super Bowl team."

Harvey Feldman and Mark Voigt were both of the opinion that offensive linemen don't get the respect they deserve. Harvey thought that Sisemore was important to the Eagles' successes during the Vermeil era, and included him on his list. But Mark described offensive linemen during the time that Sisemore played as unsung heroes who don't make lists like these. He passed on Sisemore. Bob Anderson thought that Sisemore was not as good as his longtime fellow lineman Stan Walters, while Jon Grisdale rendered the opinion that Sisemore was better than Jon Runyan, but wasn't as good as Bob Brown. "It wasn't even close."

Year	Team	Lg	G
1973	Eagles	NFL	13
1974	Eagles	NFL	14
1975	Eagles	NFL	14
1976	Eagles	NFL	14
1977	Eagles	NFL	14
1978	Eagles	NFL	16
1979	Eagles	NFL	16
1980	Eagles	NFL	16
1981	Eagles	NFL	16
1982	Eagles	NFL	7
1983	Eagles	NFL	14
1984	Eagles	NFL	2
	Eagles Totals		156
	Career Totals		156

NFL Pro Bowl (1979, 1981)

MICHAEL BARKANN'S TOP 10

1. Wilt Chamberlain
2. Allen Iverson
3. Julius Erving
4. Bobby Clarke
5. Charles Barkley
6. Reggie White
7. Mike Schmidt
8. Pete Rose
9. Tom Gola
10. Richie Ashburn

Curt Simmons

RANK	POINTS	VOTES RECEIVED
1st	50	0
2nd	49	0
3rd	48	0
4th	47	0
5th	46	0
6th	45	0
7th	44	0
8th	43	0
9th	42	0
10th	41	0
11th	40	0
12th	39	0
13th	38	0
14th	37	0
15th	36	0
16th	35	1
17th	34	1
18th	33	0
19th	32	0
20th	31	0
21st	30	0
22nd	29	0
23rd	28	0
24th	27	1
25th	26	0
26th	25	1
27th	24	0
28th	23	0
29th	22	0
30th	21	1
31st	20	1
32nd	19	0
33rd	18	0
34th	17	0
35th	16	0
36th	15	1
37th	14	1
38th	13	1
39th	12	2
40th	11	0
41st	10	2
42nd	9	1
43rd	8	0
44th	7	1
45th	6	1
46th	5	1
47th	4	2
48th	3	1
49th	2	2
50th	1	0
Not on List	0	78

TOP 10 VOTES	0
2ND 10 VOTES	2
3RD 10 VOTES	3
4TH 10 VOTES	6
5TH 10 VOTES	11
TOTAL VOTES	22
TOTAL POINTS	290

▼ TEAM
Phillies

▼ YEARS PLAYED
1947–1950, 1952–1960

▼ POSITION
Pitcher

In the final disastrous days of the 1964 season, Gene Mauch's Phillies lost 10 games in a row, virtually ensuring their elimination from the National League pennant race, after they held a lofty six and a half game lead less than two weeks earlier. The pitcher who downed the Phillies for loss number 10 in a row was southpaw Curt Simmons of the Cardinals, who overtook the Phillies to win the pennant that year. Simmons won 18 games for the Redbirds that season, second to Bob Gibson on the staff. The Cardinals went on to beat the Yankees in the World Series that year. It was ironic that Simmons dealt the '64 Phillies their final blow because he had spent parts of 13 seasons in a Phillies uniform before he was sent to the Cardinals in a 1960 trade.

Neil Goldstein and Jon Grisdale both thought that when Simmons was a Phillie, he was a good complement to staffmate Robin Roberts. Jon compared the Roberts/Simmons righty-lefty one-two punch to Jim Bunning and Chris Short from the 1960s. Simmons won 14 games or more in a season for the Phillies five times and ranks fifth on their all-time wins list. Simmons' 17 wins for the pennant-taking 1950 Phillies earned him a spot on Jerry McDonough's top 50. Had Simmons not missed five weeks of the season due to two separate military interruptions, he probably would have been a 20-game winner. Jerry recalled a certain player who described Simmons as the toughest pitcher he ever faced: Hank Aaron. "Simmons would throw Aaron breaking balls and get him to ground out."

Simmons' banner season for the Cardinals in 1964 was a big reason that neither Bob Cinalli nor Fred Schumacher included Simmons on their lists. "He was a hell of a pitcher for the Cardinals," said Bob. "He had his best days after he was traded to St. Louis," said Fred. "Overall, he never quite reached his potential in Philadelphia." Simmons' 18 wins in '64 became his single-season high, and his 2.48 ERA the year before for the Cardinals was the lowest of his career.

The most memorable game I ever attended, not counting the Eagles game in which the inebriated Tony Martin (was that his name?) screwed up the words to The National Anthem and almost fell off his platform, was a Phillies game at Connie Mack Stadium against the Reds. I was still in high school (1958) and went with my best friend, Bruce Gordon. It was Curt Simmons' tenth and final year in the Phillies' starting rotation. We had upper deck seats above the left field bleachers very close to the foul pole. The game was close throughout, and the Phillies entered the bottom of the ninth two behind—5-3, maybe. (If this is beginning to sound like "Casey at the Bat," hang on.) I cannot remember how many outs there were when Pancho Herrara and then someone else reached base. Out of the dugout came Stan Lopata to pinch-hit. He was pinch-hitting because he had been on the disabled list and this was going to be his first at-bat in about a month. By now you have guessed the rest. He slugged a home run about 20 feet inside the left field foul pole that landed in the bleachers, and the crowd went nuts.

—**HARVEY FELDMAN**

Year	Team	Lg	G	W	L	CG	SH	IP	H	BB	SO	ER	ERA
1947	Phillies	N.L.	1	1	0	1	0	9	5	6	9	1	1.00
1948	Phillies	N.L.	31	7	13	7	0	170	169	108	86	92	4.87
1949	Phillies	N.L.	38	4	10	2	0	131.1	133	55	83	67	4.59
1950	Phillies	N.L.	31	17	8	11	2	214.2	178	88	146	81	3.40
1951	Military service												
1952	Phillies	N.L.	28	14	8	15	6	201.1	170	70	141	63	2.82
1953	Phillies	N.L.	32	16	13	19	4	238	211	82	138	85	3.21
1954	Phillies	N.L.	34	14	15	21	3	253	226	98	125	79	2.81
1955	Phillies	N.L.	25	8	8	3	0	130	148	50	58	71	4.92
1956	Phillies	N.L.	33	15	10	14	0	198	186	65	88	74	3.36
1957	Phillies	N.L.	32	12	11	9	2	212	214	50	92	81	3.44
1958	Phillies	N.L.	29	7	14	7	1	168.1	196	40	78	82	4.38
1959	Phillies	N.L.	7	0	0	0	0	10	16	0	4	5	4.50
1960	Phillies	N.L.	4	0	0	0	0	4	13	6	4	8	18.00
1960	St. Louis	N.L.	23	7	4	3	1	152	149	31	63	45	2.66
1961	St. Louis	N.L.	30	9	10	6	2	195.2	203	64	99	68	3.13
1962	St. Louis	N.L.	31	10	10	9	4	154	167	32	74	60	3.51
1963	St. Louis	N.L.	32	15	9	11	6	232.2	209	48	127	64	2.48
1964	St. Louis	N.L.	34	18	9	12	3	244	233	49	104	93	3.43
1965	St. Louis	N.L.	34	9	15	5	0	203	229	54	96	92	4.08
1966	S.L.-Chi. Cubs	N.L.	29	5	8	4	1	110.2	114	35	38	52	4.23
1967	Chi. Cubs	N.L.	17	3	7	3	0	82	100	23	31	45	4.94
1967	California	A.L.	14	2	1	1	1	34.2	44	9	13	10	2.60
	Phillies Totals		325	115	110	109	18	1939.2	1865	718	1052	789	3.66
	Career Totals		569	193	183	163	36	3348.10	3313	1063	1697	1318	3.54

National League All-Star (1952–53, 1957)
Member of World Champions (1964)

73 Gary Dornhoefer

RANK	POINTS	VOTES RECEIVED
1st	50	0
2nd	49	0
3rd	48	0
4th	47	0
5th	46	0
6th	45	0
7th	44	0
8th	43	0
9th	42	0
10th	41	0
11th	40	0
12th	39	0
13th	38	0
14th	37	1
15th	36	0
16th	35	0
17th	34	1
18th	33	0
19th	32	0
20th	31	1
21st	30	0
22nd	29	0
23rd	28	0
24th	27	0
25th	26	0
26th	25	1
27th	24	0
28th	23	0
29th	22	1
30th	21	0

RANK	POINTS	VOTES RECEIVED
31st	20	0
32nd	19	0
33rd	18	1
34th	17	0
35th	16	0
36th	15	1
37th	14	0
38th	13	1
39th	12	2
40th	11	0
41st	10	0
42nd	9	0
43rd	8	1
44th	7	0
45th	6	3
46th	5	0
47th	4	2
48th	3	1
49th	2	0
50th	1	2
Not on List	0	81

TOP 10 VOTES	0
2ND 10 VOTES	3
3RD 10 VOTES	2
4TH 10 VOTES	5
5TH 10 VOTES	9
TOTAL VOTES	19
TOTAL POINTS	258

▼ TEAM
Flyers

▼ YEARS PLAYED
1968–1978

▼ POSITION
Right Wing

As a rule, centers and wings are not considered good hockey players unless they rack up a lot of goals and assists. Gary Dornhoefer was arguably an exception to the rule. Dorny's season highs in goals and assists were modest, 30 and 49, respectively, and he cracked the 60 mark in points in just two seasons. But many voters felt that Dornhoefer, despite not having gaudy stats, was a valuable member of the Flyers team that won back-to-back Stanley Cups. "He was scrappy at the offensive end," said Mike Rad. "He would screen out goalies and tie up defensemen." Bill McElroy also saluted Dornhoefer's offensive contributions. "He is still referred to as the quintessential slot man on the power play. He just planted himself in the slot and could not be moved." Rob Betts: "He would do anything to help the team. He played hard. He scored clutch goals." Like the game-winner in Game 7 of the conference semifinals against the Rangers in 1974.

Bill Jakavick and John Senkow thought Dornhoefer epitomized the type of player that Philly fans admire. "He was a Philly blue-collar player," said Bill. "He had a great attitude and commanded great respect from other players." John: "He was a tough, gritty, physical player that Philly fans love."

Many voters didn't think that Dorny's fan appeal or the intangibles that he brought to the table were enough to earn himself a spot on a best athletes list. "He was a good player, but not an all-timer" (Bob Kelly). "He was a solid role player, he would not hurt the team, but was not good enough for the list" (John Mitchell). "He was an essential member of the Stanley Cup teams, but was not a star player" (Bob Anderson). "He was good, but did not take over games like [other wings on the Flyers teams]" (Ned Hark).

No voter went to the lengths that Greg Veith did in summing up Dornhoefer's strengths and weaknesses. "He was a workman-like winger who was best known for hanging out in front of the net and taking a vicious pounding in order to harass the goalie. Could he absorb punishment in unusually large doses? Yes. Was he extremely helpful to the team? Yes. But his skill sets were rather limited; he couldn't skate well, didn't shoot hard, and was not a clever passer."

Year	Team	Lg	Gm	G	A	Pts	PM
1963–64	Boston	NHL	32	12	10	22	20
1964–65	Boston	NHL	20	0	1	1	13
1965–66	Boston	NHL	10	0	1	1	2
1967–68	Flyers	NHL	65	13	30	43	134
1968–69	Flyers	NHL	60	8	16	24	80
1969–70	Flyers	NHL	65	26	29	55	96
1970–71	Flyers	NHL	57	20	20	40	93
1971–72	Flyers	NHL	75	17	32	49	183
1972–73	Flyers	NHL	77	30	49	79	168
1973–74	Flyers	NHL	57	11	39	50	125
1974–75	Flyers	NHL	69	17	27	44	102
1975–76	Flyers	NHL	74	28	35	63	128
1976–77	Flyers	NHL	79	25	34	59	85
1977–78	Flyers	NHL	47	7	5	12	62
Flyers Totals			725	202	316	518	1256
Career Totals			787	214	328	542	1291

NHL All-Star (1973, 1977)
Member of Stanley Cup Champions (1974–75)

Rick Tocchet

RANK	POINTS	VOTES RECEIVED
1st	50	0
2nd	49	0
3rd	48	0
4th	47	0
5th	46	0
6th	45	0
7th	44	0
8th	43	0
9th	42	0
10th	41	0
11th	40	0
12th	39	0
13th	38	0
14th	37	0
15th	36	0
16th	35	0
17th	34	0
18th	33	0
19th	32	0
20th	31	0
21st	30	1
22nd	29	1
23rd	28	0
24th	27	0
25th	26	0
26th	25	0
27th	24	0
28th	23	0
29th	22	1
30th	21	1
31st	20	1
32nd	19	0
33rd	18	0
34th	17	0
35th	16	1
36th	15	2
37th	14	0
38th	13	1
39th	12	1
40th	11	0
41st	10	0
42nd	9	0
43rd	8	2
44th	7	2
45th	6	1
46th	5	3
47th	4	0
48th	3	1
49th	2	2
50th	1	2
Not on List	0	77

TOP 10 VOTES	0
2ND 10 VOTES	0
3RD 10 VOTES	4
4TH 10 VOTES	6
5TH 10 VOTES	13
TOTAL VOTES	23
TOTAL POINTS	253

TEAM
Flyers

YEARS PLAYED
1985–1992, 2000–2002

POSITION
Right Wing

If Greg Veith were handed a Hockey Hall of Fame ballot, he would check the name of burly Rick Tocchet, who spent more than half of his nearly 20-year NHL career with the Flyers. "He was far better than Kerr, LeClair or Leach by duration or talent. He could score, fight and check." Mike Rad and Jason Garber also liked Tocchet, because he had the unique dual talent of being able to put the puck in the net, and take the gloves off and mix it up. "He was a combination of Bill Barber and Dave Schultz," said Mike. "He was a very good pure skater." Jason cited the numbers—Tocchet ranks 12th on the Flyers' all-time points list and first in penalty minutes. "Philly fans loved the guy. He played for the great teams in the 1980s [the Flyers made it to the finals in Tocchet's rookie season, 1985, and also 1987] and came back for our team in the late '90s and early '00s."

Bob Anderson agreed with Jason that Tocchet was popular in Philadelphia, but Bob didn't think that Rick was a standout player. "If you took him away from the Flyers, it wouldn't have made a difference. He wasn't fast or agile and he had an average shot." Gregg Asman was impressed with Tocchet's career numbers, but not enough to include him in his top 50. "His body of work is certainly better than what I think of his year-to-year accomplishments." Tocchet racked up nearly 1000 points and while he had a 100-point season for the Penguins, he never cracked the century mark for the Flyers. "Was he an elite player?" asked Gregg. "I don't think so."

John Clark felt that other Flyers players from the 1980s and early 1990s, including Tim Kerr and Brian Propp, got the edge over Tocchet. Ryan Kent thought Tocchet was a very good player but when compared to the likes of Eric Lindros, John LeClair and Ron Hextall, he didn't stack up.

Year	Team	Lg	Gm	G	A	Pts	PM
1985–86	Flyers	NHL	69	14	21	35	284
1986–87	Flyers	NHL	69	21	28	49	286
1987–88	Flyers	NHL	65	31	33	64	299
1988–89	Flyers	NHL	66	45	36	81	183
1989–90	Flyers	NHL	75	37	59	96	196
1990–91	Flyers	NHL	70	40	31	71	150
1991–92	Flyers	NHL	42	13	16	29	102
1991–92	Pittsburgh	NHL	19	14	16	30	49
1992–93	Pittsburgh	NHL	80	48	61	109	252
1993–94	Pittsburgh	NHL	51	14	26	40	134
1994–95	Los Angeles	NHL	36	18	17	35	70
1995–96	L.A.-Boston	NHL	71	29	31	60	181
1996–97	Boston-Wash.	NHL	53	21	19	40	98
1997–98	Phoenix	NHL	68	26	19	45	157
1998–99	Phoenix	NHL	81	26	30	56	147
1999–00	Phoenix	NHL	64	12	17	29	67
1999–00	Flyers	NHL	16	3	3	6	23
2000–01	Flyers	NHL	60	14	22	36	83
2001–02	Flyers	NHL	14	0	2	2	28
	Flyers Totals		621	232	276	508	1815
	Career Totals		1144	440	512	952	2970

NHL All-Star (1989–91, 1993)
Member of Stanley Cup Champions (1992)

Troy Vincent

RANK	POINTS	VOTES RECEIVED
1st	50	0
2nd	49	0
3rd	48	0
4th	47	0
5th	46	0
6th	45	0
7th	44	0
8th	43	0
9th	42	0
10th	41	0
11th	40	0
12th	39	0
13th	38	0
14th	37	1
15th	36	0
16th	35	0
17th	34	0
18th	33	0
19th	32	0
20th	31	0
21st	30	0
22nd	29	0
23rd	28	0
24th	27	0
25th	26	1
26th	25	1
27th	24	1
28th	23	0
29th	22	0
30th	21	0
31st	20	0
32nd	19	2
33rd	18	0
34th	17	0
35th	16	0
36th	15	1
37th	14	1
38th	13	0
39th	12	2
40th	11	0
41st	10	0
42nd	9	1
43rd	8	0
44th	7	1
45th	6	0
46th	5	3
47th	4	0
48th	3	1
49th	2	0
50th	1	1
Not on List	0	83

TOP 10 VOTES	0
2ND 10 VOTES	1
3RD 10 VOTES	3
4TH 10 VOTES	6
5TH 10 VOTES	7
TOTAL VOTES	17
TOTAL POINTS	238

▼ TEAM
Eagles

▼ YEARS PLAYED
1996–2003

▼ POSITION
Cornerback

Eagles fans were breathlessly anticipating a victory and trip to the Super Bowl when the Birds faced Tampa Bay in the NFC Championship Game in January 2003. Instead, they were greatly disappointed as the Birds were dumped by the Bucs 27-10 in the final game at Veterans Stadium. A year later, once again the Eagles were on the verge of making it to the big game, but they were upset by Carolina 14-3. In the opinion of Mike Koob, one of the players who came up small in those championship game losses was Troy Vincent. "He was vastly overrated," insisted Mike. Rob Betts, who has been an Eagles season ticket holder with Mike since the Dick Vermeil years, also thought Vincent was overrated. "He would play not to get beaten deep on an ESPN highlight-type play."

Other voters were not quite as critical as Rob and Mike, but didn't think that Vincent belonged in their top 50. "He was a solid corner, but got burned his fair share" (Randy Axelrod). "Good corners are nice to have, but top 50? He wasn't here long enough to make an impression on me" (Bill McElroy). "I compare all defensive backs to Eric Allen—and Troy was not as good" (Brent Saunders).

On the other hand, many voters complimented Vincent as both a player and person. Mark Eckel felt that Troy's work as Eagles starting cornerback for eight years earned him a 25th-place vote. Gordie Jones, who rated Vincent 27th, described him as a "lock-down corner." "He was very consistent," said Gordie. "He made big plays and he was a good guy, an ambassador to the team. He was a mentor to younger guys like Sheldon Brown and Lito Sheppard." Steve Kennedy ranked Troy 32nd, noting that in this passing-oriented era Troy was one of the best cornerbacks at defending against the pass." Dave Myers also thought highly of Vincent. "He was a Pro Bowl player year-in and year-out. He gave a solid, workman-like effort. He had size and speed. He was a starting cornerback on three straight Eagles teams that made it to the NFC Championship Game." In John

Bergmann's opinion, during Vincent's time as an Eagle, he was a leader on the team and one of the best cornerbacks in football.

Vincent's credentials with the Birds were impressive. He was a Pro Bowl selection for five straight years; only Reggie White and Pete Pihos have registered more than five consecutive Pro Bowl appearances for the Eagles. Vincent led the Birds in interceptions three times (1999, 2000 and 2001) and was tied for team lead in 1997, 1998 and 2003. In 1996, James Willis intercepted a Troy Aikman pass four yards deep in the end zone, returned it to the Eagles' 10-yard line and then lateraled the ball back to Vincent, who ran 90 yards for a memorable touchdown.

Year	Team	Lg	Games	Int	Yds	TD	Sacks
1992	Miami	NFL	15	2	47	0	0
1993	Miami	NFL	13	2	29	0	0
1994	Miami	NFL	13	5	113	1	0
1995	Miami	NFL	16	5	95	1	0
1996	Eagles	NFL	16	3	144	1	0
1997	Eagles	NFL	16	3	14	0	0
1998	Eagles	NFL	13	2	29	0	1
1999	Eagles	NFL	14	7	91	0	1
2000	Eagles	NFL	16	5	34	0	1
2001	Eagles	NFL	15	3	0	0	1.5
2002	Eagles	NFL	15	2	1	0	0
2003	Eagles	NFL	13	3	28	0	0
2004	Buffalo	NFL	7	1	8	0	1
2005	Buffalo	NFL	16	4	78	0	0
2006	Washington	NFL	7	0	0	0	0
	Eagles Totals		118	28	341	1	4.5
	Career Totals		205	47	711	3	5.5

NFL Pro Bowl (1999–03)

76 Tony Taylor

RANK	POINTS	VOTES RECEIVED		RANK	POINTS	VOTES RECEIVED
1st	50	0		31st	20	1
2nd	49	0		32nd	19	0
3rd	48	0		33rd	18	0
4th	47	0		34th	17	1
5th	46	0		35th	16	1
6th	45	0		36th	15	1
7th	44	0		37th	14	0
8th	43	0		38th	13	0
9th	42	0		39th	12	0
10th	41	0		40th	11	0
11th	40	1		41st	10	2
12th	39	0		42nd	9	1
13th	38	0		43rd	8	0
14th	37	0		44th	7	1
15th	36	0		45th	6	1
16th	35	0		46th	5	0
17th	34	0		47th	4	0
18th	33	0		48th	3	1
19th	32	0		49th	2	2
20th	31	0		50th	1	2
21st	30	0		Not on List	0	82
22nd	29	0				
23rd	28	1				
24th	27	0		TOP 10 VOTES	0	
25th	26	1		2ND 10 VOTES	1	
26th	25	0		3RD 10 VOTES	3	
27th	24	1		4TH 10 VOTES	4	
28th	23	0		5TH 10 VOTES	10	
29th	22	0		TOTAL VOTES	18	
30th	21	0		TOTAL POINTS	237	

▼ **TEAM**
Phillies

▼ **YEARS PLAYED**
1960–1971, 1974–1976

▼ **POSITION**
Second Baseman

When asked why he declined to include Tony Taylor in his top 50, Ken Miller lamented, "The Phillies in the 1960s were nothing but a heartache to me." You and thousands of other Phillies fans, too, Ken. There was not only the heartache of 1964, but in 1961, the team suffered through a miserable 23-game losing streak. Tony T., who was a Phillie throughout the 1960s, endured both of those low points in the team's history. Taylor was the Phils' starting second baseman for most of the decade, but also saw some playing time at the other three infield positions.

Mike Koob felt that Tony was one of the most identifiable Phillies players of that era, as well as a fan favorite. Jim Schloth and Steve Van Allen remembered Tony for his good glove at second base. Jon Grisdale considered Taylor a "scrappy player" and a "tough out." Doug Brown described him as a clutch hitter with some power. (That is well illustrated by Doug's story below.)

The hearts of many Phillies fans were broken when the team dealt Taylor to the Tigers in 1971 for two pitchers, Carl Cavanaugh and Mike Fremuth; neither ever made it to the majors. But when the Tigers released Taylor after the 1973 season, the Phillies signed him, and it was his pinch-hitting over the next two-plus seasons that drew the most comments. Fans at the Vet began to give Tony a standing ovation whenever he emerged from the dugout as a pinch-hitter. He led the National League with 17 pinch-hits in 1975 and added 12 more in 1976. "He was a folk hero when he returned from Detroit," said John Mitchell. "He had a love affair with the city," said Steve Van Allen. Dave Beck looked at Taylor's overall performance: "He wasn't an All-Star with glitzy numbers but a team player who provided consistency and leadership." Dave was right—Tony only made it to one All-Star Game (1960), and while his numbers were not glitzy on a season-by-season basis, they were quite impressive over the long haul. Tony is on the Phillies' all-time top 10 list in a number of categories, including games played, hits and stolen bases.

Knocks on Tony: Mike Rad didn't include Taylor because he considered him a little above average and didn't have much power. Ned Hark and Bill McElroy felt that Tony did not stack up with other Phillies second basemen such as Dave Cash, Manny Trillo and Juan Samuel.

On a hot afternoon in early August 1970, my father, my brother, a friend and I ventured down to Connie Mack Stadium in North Philadelphia for a game between the hapless Phillies and the Giants (who would finish third to the Big Red Machine in the N.L. West) in the final season before the opening of Veterans Stadium. The Phils were managed by feisty Frank Lucchesi and the Giants by Charlie Fox. Aging superstars Willie Mays and Willie McCovey were featured in the Giants' line-up. The pre-Carlton/Schmidt/Luzinski (and post-Allen) Phillies featured the likes of Don Money, Deron Johnson and Johnny Briggs.

A little-known pitcher, Lowell Palmer, took the mound for the Phillies. I don't remember much of what happened until the bottom of the ninth. I'm sure I had a 25-cent hot dog and 25-cent Coke; maybe some peanuts or Cracker Jacks. By Saam, Bill Campbell and Richie Ashburn were in the broadcast booth for what would turn out to be a classic and memorable finish to an otherwise ordinary and meaningless baseball game.

The Phillies went into the bottom of the ninth trailing 6-3. Larry Hisle led off with a double to left-center; Doc Edwards (the bullpen coach activated due to all the catcher injuries that year) singled with Hisle stopping at third; Terry Harmon pinch-hit for a walk, loading the bases. Up comes a hometown favorite and reliable clutch hitter, number 8, Tony Taylor. TT crossed himself before digging into the batters' box and looked 60 feet and six inches away at Mike Davison, in to try to earn a save for the Giants. On a 1-1 count, Tony slammed a high fastball into left-center, heading toward the huge Coca-Cola billboard on top of the roof. Tony's amazing shot (he was not known as a power hitter) landed in the upper deck and when he finished circling the bases, the Phillies had won 7-6. By the ninth inning many of the paltry crowd of 10,201 had left, but the four of us and the others still scattered throughout the ballpark were glad we stayed.

—DOUG BROWN

Year	Team	Lg	G	AB	R	H	HR	RBI	SB	Avg	SLG
1958	Chi. Cubs	N.L.	140	497	63	117	6	27	21	.235	.314
1959	Chi. Cubs	N.L.	150	624	96	175	8	38	23	.280	.393
1960	Chi. Cubs	N.L.	19	76	14	20	1	9	2	.263	.421
1960	Phillies	N.L.	127	505	66	145	4	35	24	.287	.370
1961	Phillies	N.L.	106	400	47	100	2	26	11	.250	.323
1962	Phillies	N.L.	152	625	87	162	7	43	20	.259	.342
1963	Phillies	N.L.	157	640	102	180	5	49	23	.281	.367
1964	Phillies	N.L.	154	570	62	143	4	46	13	.251	.316
1965	Phillies	N.L.	106	323	41	74	3	27	5	.229	.319
1966	Phillies	N.L.	125	434	47	105	5	40	8	.242	.346
1967	Phillies	N.L.	132	462	55	110	2	34	10	.238	.312
1968	Phillies	N.L.	145	547	59	137	3	38	22	.250	.311
1969	Phillies	N.L.	138	557	68	146	3	30	19	.262	.339
1970	Phillies	N.L.	124	439	74	132	9	55	9	.301	.462
1971	Phillies	N.L.	36	107	9	25	1	5	2	.234	.299
1971	Detroit	A.L.	55	181	27	52	3	19	5	.287	.414
1972	Detroit	A.L.	78	228	33	69	1	20	5	.303	.404
1973	Detroit	A.L.	84	275	35	63	5	24	9	.229	.338
1974	Phillies	N.L.	62	64	5	21	2	13	0	.328	.484
1975	Phillies	N.L.	79	103	13	25	1	17	3	.243	.340
1976	Phillies	N.L.	26	23	2	6	0	3	0	.261	.304
	Phillies Totals		1669	5799	737	1511	51	461	69	.261	.346
	Career Totals		2195	7680	1005	2007	75	598	234	.261	.352

National League All-Star (1960)

Dave Schultz

RANK	POINTS	VOTES RECEIVED	RANK	POINTS	VOTES RECEIVED
1st	50	0	31st	20	0
2nd	49	0	32nd	19	0
3rd	48	0	33rd	18	1
4th	47	0	34th	17	0
5th	46	0	35th	16	1
6th	45	0	36th	15	2
7th	44	0	37th	14	1
8th	43	0	38th	13	0
9th	42	0	39th	12	1
10th	41	0	40th	11	3
11th	40	0	41st	10	1
12th	39	0	42nd	9	2
13th	38	0	43rd	8	0
14th	37	0	44th	7	0
15th	36	0	45th	6	2
16th	35	0	46th	5	1
17th	34	0	47th	4	1
18th	33	0	48th	3	1
19th	32	0	49th	2	3
20th	31	0	50th	1	4
21st	30	0	Not on List	0	74
22nd	29	0			
23rd	28	0			
24th	27	1			
25th	26	0			
26th	25	0			
27th	24	1			
28th	23	1			
29th	22	0			
30th	21	0			

TOP 10 VOTES	0
2ND 10 VOTES	0
3RD 10 VOTES	2
4TH 10 VOTES	9
5TH 10 VOTES	15
TOTAL VOTES	26
TOTAL POINTS	232

▼ **TEAM**
Flyers

▼ **YEARS PLAYED**
1972–1976

▼ **POSITION**
Left Wing

It has been more than 30 years since the Flyers electrified the city by winning back-to-back Stanley Cups, and in the opinion of Adam Kimelman, the two players whom Philadelphia fans think of most from that team are Bobby Clarke and . . . not Bernie Parent, not Bill Barber, not Rick MacLeish . . . but Dave Schultz. "He dropped the hammer," said Adam. "He personified the intimidating presence of the Flyers." Dave Myers admitted that Schultz was not a great talent, but thought he was perfect for the Broad Street Bullies team. "He embodied what that team was about. He epitomized Philadelphia athletes: an athlete who did the dirty work and would protect his players." Likewise, Bob Chazin conceded that Schultz was not a great skater or scorer, but included "the Hammer" for his role as enforcer and protector of teammates. "If somebody picked on Clarke, Schultz would go after that player the next shift." Bill McElroy and Mike Rad thought Schultz could do more than slug it out with goons from other teams. Mike: "Even if he couldn't fight, he would have made it as a player. He had skill; he was underrated." Bill: "He brought a toughness and skill (20-goal scorer one season) that the Flyers are still trying to emulate." Sentimentality was the driving force behind Paul Troy's inclusion of Schultz in his top 50. "Any list of top Philadelphia athletes must include Dave Schultz."

As passionate as some voters were that Schultz was worthy of a spot on the list, others were equally emphatic that he did not belong. Rob Betts had especially strong opinions on the subject. "People who put him on their lists are idiots. I enjoyed seeing Schultz fight [Blackhawks defenseman] Keith Magnuson as much as anybody, but he was not a great hockey player. They wouldn't have won the Cup without Bernie; they would have without Schultz." Terry Bickhart said there were plenty of other tough guys on the Flyers who were better players than Schultz, like Bob Kelly. Mike DiColla lumped Schultz into the same category as Kelly and Don Saleski: goons who were entertaining to watch, but not blessed with superior hockey skills. Joe Fee also scoffed at people who voted for Schultz. "I think it's hilarious that Schultz made [voters'] lists. He played four years and did nothing but fight."

For the record, Schultz averaged 13 goals, 16 assists and 346 penalty minutes during his four years in Philadelphia. That's a lot more fighting than scoring. But he has two Stanley Cup rings.

Year	Team	Lg	Gm	G	A	Pts	PM
1971–72	Flyers	NHL	1	0	0	0	0
1972–73	Flyers	NHL	76	9	12	21	259
1973–74	Flyers	NHL	73	20	16	36	348
1974–75	Flyers	NHL	76	9	17	26	472
1975–76	Flyers	NHL	71	13	19	32	307
1976–77	Los Angeles	NHL	76	10	20	30	232
1977–78	Los Angeles	NHL	8	2	0	2	27
1977–78	Pittsburgh	NHL	66	9	25	34	378
1978–79	Pittsburgh	NHL	47	4	9	13	157
1978–79	Buffalo	NHL	28	2	3	5	86
1979–80	Buffalo	NHL	13	1	0	1	28
	Flyers Totals		297	51	64	115	1386
	Career Totals		535	79	121	200	2294

Member of Stanley Cup Champions (1974–75)

78 Andre Waters

RANK	POINTS	VOTES RECEIVED
1st	50	0
2nd	49	0
3rd	48	0
4th	47	0
5th	46	0
6th	45	0
7th	44	0
8th	43	0
9th	42	0
10th	41	0
11th	40	0
12th	39	0
13th	38	0
14th	37	0
15th	36	0
16th	35	0
17th	34	0
18th	33	0
19th	32	0
20th	31	1
21st	30	0
22nd	29	0
23rd	28	0
24th	27	0
25th	26	0
26th	25	0
27th	24	0
28th	23	0
29th	22	0
30th	21	0
31st	20	1
32nd	19	2
33rd	18	1
34th	17	2
35th	16	1
36th	15	0
37th	14	0
38th	13	0
39th	12	1
40th	11	1
41st	10	1
42nd	9	0
43rd	8	1
44th	7	0
45th	6	1
46th	5	2
47th	4	2
48th	3	1
49th	2	2
50th	1	0
Not on List	0	80

TOP 10 VOTES	0
2ND 10 VOTES	1
3RD 10 VOTES	0
4TH 10 VOTES	9
5TH 10 VOTES	10
TOTAL VOTES	20
TOTAL POINTS	229

▼ **TEAM**
Eagles

▼ **YEARS PLAYED**
1984–1993

▼ **POSITION**
Safety

Of all the players on the Eagles' punishing defense in the Buddy Ryan/Rich Kotite era, nobody had more of a reputation as a hitter than Andre Waters. On *Monday Night Football* telecasts, broadcaster Dan Dierdorf used to criticize Waters as "dirty" and "a cheap shot artist." Jon Grisdale couldn't have agreed less. "There is no such thing as a cheap shot." Grisdale said that because Andre was on the small side (5'11", 190 lbs.), he hit low, but that was not cheap. "He was a good tackler," said Jon, "in bounds or out of bounds." Bill McElroy liked Waters for the same reasons. "Other teams hated him because he always went for the other running backs' legs." Cliff Patterson described Andre as a vicious hitter.

Why was Waters so eager to lay a hit on an opposing player? "The fear factor," said Brent Saunders. "He wasn't scared of anybody." But some opposing players were scared of him, said Ralph Antonelli. "Wide receivers thought twice about heading into his area." Ralph, as well as Andy Paul, described Waters as one of the leaders of the Eagles' defense. "His big hits rallied his teammates," said Andy.

Mark Eckel pointed out a key fact in support of his decision not to include Waters in his top 50. "He never went to a Pro Bowl." Mike Sielski also took a pass on Andre. "He was not considered the best at his position in the league." Andre was a personal favorite of Fran Garvin; Fran liked Waters because he was a "bad ass." But when Fran sized up other Eagles defensive backs—Eric Allen, Wes Hopkins and Troy Vincent—Waters fell short. Ditto Randy Axelrod. "Brian Dawkins and Hopkins were better safeties."

Tom Walter and Dennis Brady put Andre in the overrated category. "He was a big hitter, but made mistakes," said Tom. "He wasn't that good of a strong safety," said Dennis. "Other players on the team made him better."

Year	Team	Lg	G	Int	Yds	TD	Sacks
1984	Eagles	NFL	16	0	0	1	0
1985	Eagles	NFL	16	0	0	0	0
1986	Eagles	NFL	16	6	39	0	2
1987	Eagles	NFL	12	3	63	0	0
1988	Eagles	NFL	16	3	19	0	0.5
1989	Eagles	NFL	16	1	20	0	1
1990	Eagles	NFL	14	0	0	0	0
1991	Eagles	NFL	16	1	0	0	0
1992	Eagles	NFL	6	1	23	0	0
1993	Eagles	NFL	9	0	0	0	0
1994	Arizona	NFL	12	0	0	0	0
1995	Arizona	NFL	8	0	0	0	0
	Eagles Totals		137	15	164	1	3.5
	Career Totals		157	15	164	1	3

ANDY MUSSER'S TOP 10

1. Wilt Chamberlain
2. Steve Carlton
3. Mike Schmidt
4. Chuck Bednarik
5. Bobby Clarke
6. Julius Erving
7. Robin Roberts
8. Reggie White
9. Norm Van Brocklin
10. Richie Ashburn

79

Pete Pihos

RANK	POINTS	VOTES RECEIVED
1st	50	0
2nd	49	0
3rd	48	0
4th	47	0
5th	46	0
6th	45	0
7th	44	0
8th	43	0
9th	42	0
10th	41	0
11th	40	0
12th	39	0
13th	38	0
14th	37	1
15th	36	0
16th	35	0
17th	34	0
18th	33	0
19th	32	0
20th	31	0
21st	30	1
22nd	29	0
23rd	28	0
24th	27	0
25th	26	0
26th	25	0
27th	24	1
28th	23	1
29th	22	0
30th	21	1

RANK	POINTS	VOTES RECEIVED
31st	20	0
32nd	19	0
33rd	18	0
34th	17	0
35th	16	0
36th	15	0
37th	14	0
38th	13	3
39th	12	1
40th	11	0
41st	10	2
42nd	9	0
43rd	8	2
44th	7	0
45th	6	0
46th	5	1
47th	4	0
48th	3	0
49th	2	0
50th	1	2
Not on List	0	84

TOP 10 VOTES	0
2ND 10 VOTES	1
3RD 10 VOTES	4
4TH 10 VOTES	4
5TH 10 VOTES	7
TOTAL VOTES	16
TOTAL POINTS	229

▼ TEAM
Eagles

▼ YEARS PLAYED
1947–1955

▼ POSITION
Offensive/Defensive End

The Eagles have featured many outstanding receivers over the years, but only two have been enshrined in the Pro Football Hall of Fame: Tommy McDonald and Pete Pihos. Despite his Hall of Fame admission, Pihos' name recognition was not strong, especially among the younger voters. But many pollsters, including Gordie Jones, John Senkow and Neil Goldstein, who either saw Pihos play or were well aware of his Hall of Fame career, included him in their top 50. Gordie also cited Pihos' many Pro Bowl appearances; Pete was a Pro Bowler in each of his last six seasons. Fred Schumacher watched Pihos haul in passes at Shibe Park/Connie Mack Stadium and remembered the receiver's excellence. "He could start for the Eagles today. He was a 'real' football player, not like the specialists we have today."

Ray Didinger rattled off some of Pihos' accomplishments and explained why he is well deserving of his Hall of Fame plaque, and why Ray ranked him 21st. "He was the number one receiver in all of football three straight years (1953-55). He had great stats—high touchdown totals, even though the Eagles did not have great quarterbacks (Tommy Thompson, Adrian Burk and Bobby Thomason) when running was in vogue, which made his stats more impressive." Ray added that in 1952, the Eagles decided to switch Pihos to defensive end (he still continued to get some playing time on offense as well) and Pete responded by being named All-Pro.

Pihos' knack for scoring touchdowns was especially amazing, considering the length of the NFL season. They only played 12-game seasons back in Pete's day, but he caught 10 or more touchdown passes in a season three times. To give you an indication of how impressive that is, consider this: Dallas Cowboys receiver Michael Irvin played 12 years in the league when the season was 16 games, and although he caught 750 passes in his career, he only had one 10-touchdown season.

Some voters were Eagles fans back in Pihos' day, but opted not to include him on their lists. Bob Cinalli explained his choice: "He was a good receiver, but not in Tommy McDonald's category. The roles of ends were different in those days; receiving was secondary to blocking. He played on the 1948 and 1949 championship teams, but [Jack] Ferrante stood out more as a receiver." Ferrante was another standout receiver from that time; he led the Birds in receptions twice, and in the '49 championship season, Ferrante outdid Pihos in yards and touchdowns and matched him in receptions.

Jerry McDonough recalled Pihos' teammate Steve Van Buren as the dominant offensive player from those Eagles championship teams. "He was the biggest offensive star in the NFL," said Jerry. Van Buren had two 1000-yard seasons on the ground, and was the NFL's career rushing leader when he retired in 1951.

Year	Team	Lg	G	Rec	Yds	Avg	TD
1947	Eagles	NFL	12	23	382	16.6	7
1948	Eagles	NFL	12	46	766	16.7	11
1949	Eagles	NFL	11	34	484	14.2	4
1950	Eagles	NFL	12	38	447	11.8	6
1951	Eagles	NFL	12	35	536	15.3	5
1952	Eagles	NFL	12	12	219	18.3	1
1953	Eagles	NFL	12	63	1049	16.7	10
1954	Eagles	NFL	12	60	872	14.5	10
1955	Eagles	NFL	12	62	864	13.9	7
	Eagles Totals		107	373	5619	15.1	61
	Career Totals		107	373	5619	15.1	61

Member of NFL Champions (1948–49)
NFL Pro Bowl (1950–55)
Pro Football Hall of Fame (1970)

80

Barry Ashbee

RANK	POINTS	VOTES RECEIVED		RANK	POINTS	VOTES RECEIVED
1st	50	0		31st	20	2
2nd	49	0		32nd	19	0
3rd	48	0		33rd	18	3
4th	47	0		34th	17	0
5th	46	0		35th	16	0
6th	45	0		36th	15	1
7th	44	0		37th	14	0
8th	43	0		38th	13	1
9th	42	0		39th	12	0
10th	41	0		40th	11	0
11th	40	0		41st	10	1
12th	39	0		42nd	9	0
13th	38	0		43rd	8	0
14th	37	0		44th	7	0
15th	36	0		45th	6	0
16th	35	0		46th	5	1
17th	34	0		47th	4	1
18th	33	0		48th	3	1
19th	32	1		49th	2	0
20th	31	0		50th	1	1
21st	30	0		Not on List	0	86
22nd	29	0				
23rd	28	0				
24th	27	0		**TOP 10 VOTES**	0	
25th	26	1		**2ND 10 VOTES**	1	
26th	25	0		**3RD 10 VOTES**	1	
27th	24	0		**4TH 10 VOTES**	7	
28th	23	0		**5TH 10 VOTES**	5	
29th	22	0		**TOTAL VOTES**	14	
30th	21	0		**TOTAL POINTS**	203	

▼ TEAM
Flyers

▼ YEARS PLAYED
1971–1974

▼ POSITION
Defenseman

Except for a very brief stint with the Bruins in his mid-20s, Barry Ashbee did not break into the NHL until he was 30. After four years with the Flyers, his career was cut short when he suffered an eye injury in the 1974 semifinals against the Rangers; three years later, his life was cut short by leukemia.

Michael Beirne and Bob Anderson ruled out Ashbee because of the brevity of his playing days in Philadelphia. "He was a career minor leaguer; he only had three good seasons," said Bob. (Ashbee logged more than a decade in the minors.) "He was a one-role player, to keep the likes of [Boston's high-scoring center] Phil Esposito out of the slot." Jon Grisdale defined Ashbee's role the same way as Bob, but felt that Barry's was such an important role in the Flyers' first championship that he deserved a top 50 spot. Many others felt that despite Ashbee's short length of service, his impact was significant. Paul Lightkep: "He was a class guy, a rock on the Flyers during the pre-Stanley Cup years and for the first Stanley Cup." Mike DiColla: "He was an excellent defenseman who was very influential during his years with the Flyers. He's a piece of the Flyers' foundation." Dave Myers: "He was tougher than the Watsons [Joe and Jimmy], more representative of Philly sports than they were." Glenn Young, Ashbee's biggest ally, described the confidence he had when Barry was in the game: "I just felt safe when he was on the ice. I knew he would never outstickhandle anyone and he would never stray far from the net. But I also saw him stop shots with his face to make Bernie's job easier."

Mike Rad agreed with the voters who said that Ashbee was a good defenseman, but he excluded number 4 for his lack of offense. "If he had to cross center ice, he was lost in the desert with no oasis." Ned Hark felt that while Ashbee may have been a fit on the Flyers when Bobby Clarke was the captain and center, he wouldn't have lasted long on the team with Bobby as general manager. "He's the type of player that Clarke would have traded after a year or two."

Year	Team	Lg	Gm	G	A	Pts	PM
1965–66	Boston	NHL	14	0	3	3	14
1970–71	Flyers	NHL	64	4	23	27	44
1971–72	Flyers	NHL	73	6	14	20	75
1972–73	Flyers	NHL	64	1	17	18	106
1973–74	Flyers	NHL	69	4	13	17	52
	Flyers Totals		270	15	67	82	277
	Career Totals		284	15	70	85	291

Member of Stanley Cup Champions (1974)
Number 4 retired by Flyers

81

Clyde Simmons

RANK	POINTS	VOTES RECEIVED		RANK	POINTS	VOTES RECEIVED
1st	50	0		31st	20	0
2nd	49	0		32nd	19	1
3rd	48	0		33rd	18	0
4th	47	0		34th	17	0
5th	46	0		35th	16	0
6th	45	0		36th	15	1
7th	44	0		37th	14	0
8th	43	0		38th	13	0
9th	42	0		39th	12	3
10th	41	0		40th	11	0
11th	40	0		41st	10	0
12th	39	0		42nd	9	0
13th	38	0		43rd	8	0
14th	37	0		44th	7	0
15th	36	0		45th	6	2
16th	35	0		46th	5	0
17th	34	0		47th	4	0
18th	33	0		48th	3	1
19th	32	0		49th	2	0
20th	31	0		50th	1	1
21st	30	0		Not on List	0	86
22nd	29	0				
23rd	28	0				
24th	27	0		TOP 10 VOTES		0
25th	26	1		2ND 10 VOTES		0
26th	25	0		3RD 10 VOTES		5
27th	24	0		4TH 10 VOTES		5
28th	23	3		5TH 10 VOTES		4
29th	22	1		TOTAL VOTES		14
30th	21	0		TOTAL POINTS		203

▼ TEAM
Eagles

▼ YEARS PLAYED
1986–1993

▼ POSITION
Defensive End

On the Eagles' all-time sacks leader board, Clyde Simmons ranks second to Hall of Famer Reggie White. Clyde was the team leader in that category in 1989 and 1992 and second to White four times. Why did Simmons rack up so many sacks? According to several voters, it was Reggie's presence. "One of the reasons he got so many sacks is that he played alongside Reggie, who was getting double- and triple-teamed," said Mike Sielski. "He was never considered the best defensive end in the league." Gordie Jones and John Mitchell agreed. "Without Reggie on the other side," said Gordie, "Clyde isn't as good a player."

Rob Betts and Mike Koob took it one step further: Simmons' sack totals were inflated, not only because he played alongside Reggie White, but also because Clyde and Jerome Brown were linemates. "He was a byproduct of Jerome and Reggie," said Mike. "When he followed Buddy Ryan to Arizona, he wasn't as good." Along the same lines, Brent Saunders thought that Simmons fell short when compared to Reggie and Jerome.

Wait a minute, screamed a few voters, Clyde didn't pile up all those sacks just because he played next to two outstanding linemen. Let's give him his due. "He never got the recognition which he deserved with Reggie and Jerome on the defensive line with him," said Mark Voigt. Fran Garvin and Randy Axelrod both said Simmons was underrated. "He was a sack artist," added Randy. Lee Fiederer and Ryan Kent both mentioned that Clyde was a part of one of the NFL's great defenses. As Lee pointed out, in 1991, the Eagles were first against the run and the pass. "It all starts on the line," said Lee. "Clyde was a force." Ryan: "He was one of the poster boys for one of the best defenses of all time. Aside from the '85 Bears and the '00 Ravens, the '91 Eagles are hands down the best defense ever. . . He was one of the faces of that tenacious defense, something the city of Philadelphia and Eagles organization are extremely proud of."

Year	Team	Lg	G	Int	Yds	TD	Sacks
1986	Eagles	NFL	16	0	0	0	2
1987	Eagles	NFL	12	0	0	0	6
1988	Eagles	NFL	16	0	0	0	8
1989	Eagles	NFL	16	1	60	1	15.5
1990	Eagles	NFL	16	0	0	1	7.5
1991	Eagles	NFL	16	0	0	1	13
1992	Eagles	NFL	16	0	0	0	19
1993	Eagles	NFL	16	1	0	0	5
1994	Arizona	NFL	16	0	0	0	6
1995	Arizona	NFL	16	1	25	1	11
1996	Jacksonville	NFL	16	0	0	0	7.5
1997	Jacksonville	NFL	16	0	0	0	8.5
1998	Cincinnati	NFL	16	0	0	0	5
1999	Chicago	NFL	16	0	0	0	7
2000	Chicago	NFL	16	0	0	0	0.5
	Eagles Totals		124	2	60	3	76
	Career Totals		236	3	85	4	121

NFL Pro Bowl (1991–92)
Scored touchdown on fumble return

JODY McDONALD'S TOP 10

1. Wilt Chamberlain
2. Mike Schmidt
3. Julius Erving
4. Reggie White
5. Steve Carlton
6. Bobby Clarke
7. Chuck Bednarik
8. Bernie Parent
9. Billy Cunningham
10. Robin Roberts

82

Chet Walker

RANK	POINTS	VOTES RECEIVED
1st	50	0
2nd	49	0
3rd	48	0
4th	47	0
5th	46	0
6th	45	0
7th	44	0
8th	43	0
9th	42	0
10th	41	0
11th	40	0
12th	39	0
13th	38	0
14th	37	0
15th	36	0
16th	35	0
17th	34	0
18th	33	1
19th	32	0
20th	31	0
21st	30	0
22nd	29	0
23rd	28	0
24th	27	1
25th	26	0
26th	25	0
27th	24	1
28th	23	0
29th	22	0
30th	21	0

RANK	POINTS	VOTES RECEIVED
31st	20	0
32nd	19	0
33rd	18	0
34th	17	1
35th	16	1
36th	15	1
37th	14	1
38th	13	1
39th	12	0
40th	11	0
41st	10	1
42nd	9	0
43rd	8	0
44th	7	1
45th	6	1
46th	5	0
47th	4	1
48th	3	1
49th	2	0
50th	1	1
Not on List	0	86

TOP 10 VOTES	0
2ND 10 VOTES	1
3RD 10 VOTES	2
4TH 10 VOTES	5
5TH 10 VOTES	6
TOTAL VOTES	14
TOTAL POINTS	190

▼ TEAM
Sixers

▼ YEARS PLAYED
1964–1969

▼ POSITION
Forward

Smooth. Very smooth. That is the way several voters, including Andy Musser, Michael Beirne and Cliff Patterson, described Chet Walker, one of the starting forwards on the 1967 World Champion Sixers. Andy ranked Walker 18th and considered him one of the key players on that great team. "He could shoot, rebound and play defense." That he could. He averaged 19 points a game in that amazing season in which the Sixers won 68 games, and then stepped it up in the postseason, averaging 21.7 points in the Sixers' 15 contests. Michael liked Walker's jump shot. "With Wilt, he was lethal." Cliff imitated Walker's patented turnaround jumper when playing on the Philly courts with his buddies in the late 1960s.

Jim Schloth recalled Walker's nickname: "Chet the Jet." Jim added, "He was instant offense on a great team." Dan McCarthy and Gordie Jones were also wowed by Chet's offense. Gordie described him as an explosive, versatile player with a terrific shot. Dan fondly remembered Walker's 10-foot turnaround jump shot.

Chet may have been victimized in the voting by being overshadowed by his teammates on the Sixers—Wilt, Hal Greer and Billy Cunningham are Hall of Famers, and as good as Walker's career was, he didn't make the Hall. "He didn't stand out like Cunningham or Greer," said Bill Jakavick. John Mitchell: "He was a good forward, but Cunningham was better. He also had good years with the Bulls." Walker played six years each in Philadelphia and Chicago, and the numbers indicate that Walker was better with the Bulls. He averaged 16.8 points a game for the Sixers, but bumped it up to 20.6 for Chicago. One of the reasons for the increase in his average was that Walker transformed himself from a good foul shooter for the Sixers (74.5%) to a great one for the Bulls (85.4%). He was the NBA's best foul shooter in 1971.

Year	Team	Lg	G	Min	FGM	FGA	FGP	FTM	FTA	FTP	AST	REB	Pts	PPG
1962–63	Syracuse	NBA	78	1992	352	751	.469	253	362	.699	83	561	957	12.3
1963–64	Sixers	NBA	76	2775	492	1118	.440	330	464	.711	124	784	1314	17.3
1964–65	Sixers	NBA	79	2187	377	936	.403	288	388	.742	132	528	1042	13.2
1965–66	Sixers	NBA	80	2603	443	982	.451	335	468	.716	201	636	1221	15.3
1966–67	Sixers	NBA	81	2691	561	1150	.488	445	581	.766	188	660	1567	19.3
1967–68	Sixers	NBA	82	2623	539	1172	.460	387	533	.726	157	607	1465	17.9
1968–69	Sixers	NBA	82	2753	554	1145	.484	369	459	.804	144	640	1477	18.0
1969–70	Chicago	NBA	78	2726	596	1249	.477	483	568	.850	192	604	1675	21.5
1970–71	Chicago	NBA	81	2927	650	1398	.465	480	559	.859	179	588	1780	22.0
1971–72	Chicago	NBA	78	2588	619	1225	.505	481	568	.847	178	473	1719	22.0
1972–73	Chicago	NBA	79	2455	597	1248	.478	376	452	.832	179	395	1570	19.9
1973–74	Chicago	NBA	82	2661	572	1178	.486	439	502	.875	200	406	1583	19.3
1974–75	Chicago	NBA	76	2452	524	1076	.487	413	480	.860	169	432	1461	19.2
	Sixers Totals		480	15632	2966	6503	.456	2154	2893	.745	946	3855	8086	16.8
	Career Totals		1032	33433	6876	14628	.470	5079	6384	.796	2126	7314	18831	18.2

NBA All-Star (1964, 1966–67, 1970–71, 1973–74)
Member of NBA Champions (1967)

83 Manny Trillo

RANK	POINTS	VOTES RECEIVED
1st	50	0
2nd	49	0
3rd	48	0
4th	47	0
5th	46	0
6th	45	0
7th	44	0
8th	43	0
9th	42	0
10th	41	0
11th	40	0
12th	39	0
13th	38	1
14th	37	0
15th	36	0
16th	35	0
17th	34	0
18th	33	0
19th	32	0
20th	31	0
21st	30	0
22nd	29	1
23rd	28	0
24th	27	0
25th	26	0
26th	25	0
27th	24	1
28th	23	0
29th	22	0
30th	21	1

RANK	POINTS	VOTES RECEIVED
31st	20	0
32nd	19	1
33rd	18	0
34th	17	0
35th	16	0
36th	15	2
37th	14	0
38th	13	0
39th	12	0
40th	11	0
41st	10	1
42nd	9	0
43rd	8	1
44th	7	0
45th	6	1
46th	5	1
47th	4	0
48th	3	0
49th	2	0
50th	1	0
Not on List	0	89

TOP 10 VOTES	0
2ND 10 VOTES	1
3RD 10 VOTES	3
4TH 10 VOTES	3
5TH 10 VOTES	4
TOTAL VOTES	11
TOTAL POINTS	190

▼ TEAM
Phillies

▼ YEARS PLAYED
1979–1982

▼ POSITION
Second Baseman

Trivia question: When the Phillies beat the Astros in the epic, hard-fought, five-game League Championship Series in 1980 in which the last four games went into extra innings, who was named MVP of the series? It was not one of the superstars like Schmidt, Carlton or Rose, but Manny Trillo. The scrappy second baseman hit .381 in the series, and in the decisive fifth game, which the Phillies won 8-7 in 10 innings after trailing 5-2 through seven innings, Trillo went 3-5 with a triple and two RBIs and he threw a runner out at the plate. Trillo's outstanding performance in that memorable series paved the way for the Phillies' long-awaited first world championship. Many voters picked Trillo, in large part, because of his phenomenal series against Houston. Bryan Davis picked his all-time favorite Phillie 13th because, in addition to the great LCS, he was a vital part of the 1980 Phillies team. Bob Kelly thought that Trillo was a clutch hitter and one of the best second basemen of his time. Ned Hark compared Trillo to Sixer Bobby Jones: a quiet, unassuming player who was a key part of a championship team.

There were also plenty of raves about Trillo's defense. "He was the Phillies' best defensive second baseman ever" (Dennis Brady). "His fielding was second to none" (Dan Brown). "He was an excellent fielder with a cannon arm" (Mike Mastalski). Trillo won three Gold Gloves for the Phillies.

The reasons for not including Trillo fell into three categories. First, he wasn't a Phillie for long enough, just four years (Gregg Asman, Frank Minch). Trillo suited up for seven teams during his 17 years in the majors, so his time in Philadelphia only comprised a small piece of his career. Second, he wasn't enough of an impact player (Bob Bookbinder, Gregg Asman). Bob thought that Bowa, Schmidt and Carlton were bigger contributors to the Phillies. Bob Anderson felt that Trillo was a key member of the '80 Phillies, but not a star. Third, Trillo wasn't as good as other Phillies second basemen. Joe Brown, for example, said that he would have rated Dave Cash higher than Trillo.

Year	Team	Lg	G	AB	R	H	HR	RBI	SB	Avg	SLG
1973	Oakland	A.L.	17	12	0	3	0	3	0	.250	.417
1974	Oakland	A.L.	21	33	3	5	0	2	0	.152	.152
1975	Chi. Cubs	N.L.	154	545	55	135	7	70	1	.248	.316
1976	Chi. Cubs	N.L.	158	582	42	139	4	59	17	.239	.311
1977	Chi. Cubs	N.L.	152	504	51	141	7	57	3	.280	.377
1978	Chi. Cubs	N.L.	152	552	53	144	4	55	0	.261	.332
1979	Phillies	N.L.	118	431	40	112	6	42	4	.260	.357
1980	Phillies	N.L.	141	531	68	155	7	43	8	.292	.412
1981	Phillies	N.L.	94	349	37	100	6	36	10	.287	.395
1982	Phillies	N.L.	149	549	52	149	0	39	8	.271	.319
1983	Cleveland	A.L.	88	320	33	87	1	29	1	.272	.328
1983	Montreal	N.L.	31	121	16	32	2	16	0	.264	.380
1984	San Fran.	N.L.	98	401	45	102	4	36	0	.254	.342
1985	San Fran.	N.L.	125	451	36	101	3	25	2	.224	.288
1986	Chi. Cubs	N.L.	81	152	22	45	1	19	0	.296	.382
1987	Chi. Cubs	N.L.	108	214	27	63	8	26	0	.294	.444
1988	Chi. Cubs	N.L.	76	164	15	41	1	14	2	.250	.299
1989	Cincinnati	N.L.	17	39	3	8	0	0	0	.205	.205
	Phillies Totals		502	1860	197	516	19	160	30	.277	.369
	Career Totals		1780	5950	598	1562	61	571	56	.263	.345

Member of World Champions (1974, 1980)
National League All-Star (1977, 1981–82)
National League Gold Glove (1979, 1981–82)

National League Championship Series MVP (1980)
American League All-Star (1983)

Brian Westbrook

RANK	POINTS	VOTES RECEIVED
1st	50	0
2nd	49	0
3rd	48	0
4th	47	0
5th	46	0
6th	45	0
7th	44	0
8th	43	0
9th	42	0
10th	41	0
11th	40	0
12th	39	0
13th	38	0
14th	37	0
15th	36	0
16th	35	0
17th	34	0
18th	33	1
19th	32	0
20th	31	0
21st	30	0
22nd	29	1
23rd	28	0
24th	27	0
25th	26	0
26th	25	1
27th	24	0
28th	23	0
29th	22	0
30th	21	1

RANK	POINTS	VOTES RECEIVED
31st	20	0
32nd	19	0
33rd	18	1
34th	17	0
35th	16	1
36th	15	1
37th	14	0
38th	13	0
39th	12	0
40th	11	0
41st	10	1
42nd	9	0
43rd	8	0
44th	7	1
45th	6	0
46th	5	0
47th	4	0
48th	3	1
49th	2	1
50th	1	0
Not on List	0	89

TOP 10 VOTES	0
2ND 10 VOTES	1
3RD 10 VOTES	3
4TH 10 VOTES	3
5TH 10 VOTES	4
TOTAL VOTES	11
TOTAL POINTS	179

Patrick Dooley aptly sized up Brian Westbrook in one word: *electric*. "When was the last time you saw a combination of elusive moves, breakaway speed and pure power in one package—not to mention his receiving capabilities. He is the reason the Eagles made it as far as they did the past few years." In 2003, Westbrook's first season as a starter, he scored seven touchdowns rushing, four receiving, and returned two punts for touchdowns, including an 84-yarder with less than two minutes left in the game to beat the Giants. Joe Gribb and John Bergmann also thought that Westbrook has been paramount to the Eagles. Joe believed that Westbrook has been more of an impact player for the Eagles than Donovan McNabb, as well as former Eagles Randall Cunningham and Mike Quick. "With T.O. and Westbrook on the field [in 2004], the Eagles were the best team in football," said Joe. (Well, second best.) "When Donovan was hurt [in 2002], the Eagles still made it to the NFC Championship Game with A.J. Feeley [at quarterback]." John described Westbrook as the most important member of the Eagles in the past few years, especially during their run to the Super Bowl. "Without him, the offense is stale and ineffective."

Other accolades about Brian came from Greg Geier and Andy Paul. Greg maintained, "He is a better version of Wilbert Montgomery." Andy added, "He is explosive—one of the top three Eagles multi-purpose players [ever]. He reminds me of Keith Byars."

Westbrook's short tenure, his tendency to get injured, and his lower ranking than other Eagles running backs were cited by several people who did not include him on their lists. Bob Bookbinder touched on these reasons when he explained why he passed on Westbrook. After acknowledging Brian's "great quickness and athleticism," Bob said: "I didn't put him on the list because I was factoring a number of things: how long he has been an Eagle, his key injuries, he is not an every-down running back that can grind out three to five yards whenever needed. There are days when he looks too small to be on the field. I think Westbrook has not yet contributed consistently at the level of a star player." Mike Mastalski hung the "injury-prone" label on Westbrook and said that he is not as good as Wilbert. Dennis Brady remembered that unlike Westbrook, Timmy Brown did not miss any downs. Bob Chazin thought of Westbrook as a clone of Timmy ("fast through the hole"), but without enough tenure. Fran Garvin also nixed Westbrook for his short tenure and said that he only included short-tenured athletes on his list if they made a huge impact. Fran listed Moses Malone, Norm Van Brocklin and Pete Rose as examples.

Year	Team	Lg	G	Att	Rushing Yds	Avg	TD	Rec	Receiving Yds	Avg	TD
2002	Eagles	NFL	15	46	193	4.2	0	9	86	9.6	0
2003	Eagles	NFL	15	117	613	5.2	7	37	332	9.0	4
2004	Eagles	NFL	13	177	812	4.6	3	73	703	9.6	6
2005	Eagles	NFL	12	156	617	4.0	3	61	616	10.1	4
2006	Eagles	NFL	15	240	1217	5.1	7	77	699	9.1	4
	Eagles Totals		70	736	3452	4.7	20	257	2436	9.7	14
	Career Totals		70	736	3452	4.7	20	257	2436	9.7	14

NFL Pro Bowl (2004)

85 Bill Bradley

RANK	POINTS	VOTES RECEIVED
1st	50	0
2nd	49	0
3rd	48	0
4th	47	0
5th	46	0
6th	45	0
7th	44	0
8th	43	0
9th	42	0
10th	41	0
11th	40	0
12th	39	0
13th	38	0
14th	37	0
15th	36	0
16th	35	0
17th	34	0
18th	33	0
19th	32	0
20th	31	0
21st	30	2
22nd	29	0
23rd	28	1
24th	27	0
25th	26	0
26th	25	0
27th	24	0
28th	23	0
29th	22	0
30th	21	0
31st	20	0
32nd	19	0
33rd	18	1
34th	17	0
35th	16	1
36th	15	0
37th	14	0
38th	13	0
39th	12	0
40th	11	1
41st	10	0
42nd	9	0
43rd	8	2
44th	7	1
45th	6	1
46th	5	1
47th	4	0
48th	3	2
49th	2	0
50th	1	1
Not on List	0	86

TOP 10 VOTES	0
2ND 10 VOTES	0
3RD 10 VOTES	3
4TH 10 VOTES	3
5TH 10 VOTES	8
TOTAL VOTES	14
TOTAL POINTS	174

▼ **TEAM**
Eagles

▼ **YEARS PLAYED**
1969–1976

▼ **POSITION**
Safety

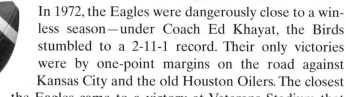

In 1972, the Eagles were dangerously close to a winless season—under Coach Ed Khayat, the Birds stumbled to a 2-11-1 record. Their only victories were by one-point margins on the road against Kansas City and the old Houston Oilers. The closest the Eagles came to a victory at Veterans Stadium that year was a 6-6 tie against the St. Louis Cardinals. The year before, the Eagles were eliminated from contention quickly, as they lost their first five games (by an average margin of 25 points), although they turned things around somewhat and finished the season at 6-7-1.

Those two seasons for the Eagles, though, were not complete disasters. Bill Bradley etched his name in the record book when he became the first NFL player in history to win the interception title two years in a row. He set an Eagles record in 1971 with 11 picks and came back the next season with nine more. He intercepted a few more passes in the years that followed, finishing with 34 career interceptions, which as Mike Koob recalled, ties him with Eric Allen atop the Birds' career interceptions list. A few voters gave Bradley credit for shining on a poor team. "He was a bright spot on a dismal team" (Dave Sautter). "He had a nose for the ball —he had a lot of interceptions on a team that stunk" (Frank Minch). "The Eagles were not competitive when Bill played. But to his credit, he was [often] at the top of the league in interceptions. Wes Hopkins and Eric Allen had vaunted defensive players around them. Bradley had Tim Rossovich" (Jim Schloth). "He was the agitator," said Jon Grisdale. "In your face. Other teams did not like him." Dave Beck described Bradley as an "intelligent, tough field general who knew the game well."

Dennis Brady voted for Bradley primarily for his knack to intercept. But Dennis gave Bradley extra credit because he also handled the team's punting duties in six of his eight years with the Eagles and returned punts in seven seasons. He broke one for 60 yards in 1972.

The reality, however, is that good players on winning teams get more consideration than very good players on losing teams. It certainly wasn't Bradley's fault that the Eagles did not post a winning record in any of his eight seasons, and usually finished in last or next-to-last place. But voters held it against Bill. "He was a token All-Pro on very poor teams," said Mike DiColla. "A true All-Pro is a star on a very good team." Greg Veith: "He was a nice player on a baaaaad team. He didn't do anything for me." Rob Betts referred to Bradley as a victim of his era; because the Eagles were not good in the early '70s, he didn't vote for Bill, nor did a lot of other voters. Rob also didn't think that Bradley had the athleticism of current players.

Year	Team	Lg	G	Int	Yds	TD
1969	Eagles	NFL	14	1	56	1
1970	Eagles	NFL	12	0	0	0
1971	Eagles	NFL	14	11	248	0
1972	Eagles	NFL	14	9	73	0
1973	Eagles	NFL	14	4	21	0
1974	Eagles	NFL	14	2	19	0
1975	Eagles	NFL	14	5	56	0
1976	Eagles	NFL	14	2	63	0
1977	St. Louis	NFL	4	0	0	0
	Eagles Totals		110	34	536	1
	Career Totals		114	34	536	1

NFL Pro Bowl (1971–73)

Eric Desjardins

RANK	POINTS	VOTES RECEIVED
1st	50	0
2nd	49	0
3rd	48	0
4th	47	0
5th	46	0
6th	45	0
7th	44	0
8th	43	0
9th	42	0
10th	41	0
11th	40	0
12th	39	0
13th	38	0
14th	37	0
15th	36	0
16th	35	1
17th	34	0
18th	33	0
19th	32	0
20th	31	0
21st	30	0
22nd	29	0
23rd	28	0
24th	27	0
25th	26	0
26th	25	0
27th	24	1
28th	23	0
29th	22	0
30th	21	1
31st	20	0
32nd	19	1
33rd	18	0
34th	17	0
35th	16	0
36th	15	1
37th	14	0
38th	13	1
39th	12	0
40th	11	2
41st	10	0
42nd	9	0
43rd	8	0
44th	7	1
45th	6	0
46th	5	0
47th	4	1
48th	3	3
49th	2	1
50th	1	2
Not on List	0	84

TOP 10 VOTES	0
2ND 10 VOTES	1
3RD 10 VOTES	2
4TH 10 VOTES	5
5TH 10 VOTES	8
TOTAL VOTES	16
TOTAL POINTS	173

▼ **TEAM**
Flyers

▼ **YEARS PLAYED**
1995–2006

▼ **POSITION**
Defenseman

When Eric Desjardins arrived in Philadelphia by way of a trade with Montreal in 1995, it didn't take long for him to send Flyers fans into a frenzy at the Spectrum. In the first game of the Eastern Conference Semifinals, Desjardins scored in over-time to beat the Rangers; the Flyers went on to beat the defending Stanley Cup Champions in four straight games. While not a prolific goal-scorer, Desjardins is second to Mark Howe in career goals—and assists—for a Flyers defenseman.

"He is one of the Flyers' three best defensemen ever," said Dennis Brady. "He [could] score and play defense." Joe Fee and Jeff Skow voted for Desjardins because of his abilities at both ends of the ice. Joe: "Eric racked up [more than] 500 points as a defenseman without sacrificing defense. Most defensemen who score don't have the plus-minus to go along with the points." Jeff: "He was a rock on defense for over a decade as the Flyers cycled through inept defense-men and 'head job' goalies. He was always the one constant when the Flyers couldn't score. He probably will never get his due in Philly because there is no Cup to show for it." Andy Dziedzic stressed the intangibles in voting for Desjardins: his hustle, superior skating and "involvement in every play." Bill McElroy labeled Desjardins "the best Flyer [from the mid-1990s to the mid-2000s]."

Those who left Desjardins off their lists were not critical of him—they just didn't characterize him as a great player. Mike Sielski acknowledged that Eric was the Flyers' best defenseman in recent years. "But he [was] not an elite defenseman like Mark Howe." Ned Hark put it about the same way. "He [was] good and steady, but not nearly the player that Mark Howe was." Mike Mastalski said that "while Desjardins [was] a consistent, team player, he [was] not a star." Ryan Kent agreed with this group of voters: "He [was] a very solid defenseman but not quite 'flashy' enough to make my list."

Year	Team	Lg	Gm	G	A	Pts	PM
1988–89	Montreal	NHL	36	2	12	14	26
1989–90	Montreal	NHL	55	3	13	16	51
1990–91	Montreal	NHL	62	7	18	25	27
1991–92	Montreal	NHL	77	6	32	38	50
1992–93	Montreal	NHL	82	13	32	45	98
1993–94	Montreal	NHL	84	12	23	35	97
1994–95	Montreal	NHL	9	0	6	6	2
1994–95	Flyers	NHL	34	5	18	23	12
1995–96	Flyers	NHL	80	7	40	47	45
1996–97	Flyers	NHL	82	12	34	46	50
1997–98	Flyers	NHL	77	6	27	33	36
1998–99	Flyers	NHL	68	15	36	51	38
1999–00	Flyers	NHL	81	14	41	55	32
2000–01	Flyers	NHL	79	15	33	48	50
2001–02	Flyers	NHL	65	6	19	25	24
2002–03	Flyers	NHL	79	8	24	32	35
2003–04	Flyers	NHL	48	1	11	12	28
2005–06	Flyers	NHL	45	4	20	24	56
		Flyers Totals	738	93	303	396	406
		Career Totals	1143	136	439	575	757

NHL All-Star (1992, 1996, 2000)
Member of Stanley Cup Champions (1993)

87 Stan Walters

RANK	POINTS	VOTES RECEIVED
1st	50	0
2nd	49	0
3rd	48	0
4th	47	0
5th	46	0
6th	45	0
7th	44	0
8th	43	0
9th	42	0
10th	41	0
11th	40	0
12th	39	0
13th	38	0
14th	37	0
15th	36	0
16th	35	0
17th	34	0
18th	33	0
19th	32	0
20th	31	0
21st	30	0
22nd	29	0
23rd	28	0
24th	27	0
25th	26	0
26th	25	0
27th	24	0
28th	23	0
29th	22	0
30th	21	0
31st	20	1
32nd	19	0
33rd	18	0
34th	17	1
35th	16	2
36th	15	1
37th	14	1
38th	13	0
39th	12	1
40th	11	1
41st	10	0
42nd	9	0
43rd	8	1
44th	7	3
45th	6	0
46th	5	1
47th	4	1
48th	3	0
49th	2	0
50th	1	2
Not on List	0	84

TOP 10 VOTES	0
2ND 10 VOTES	0
3RD 10 VOTES	0
4TH 10 VOTES	8
5TH 10 VOTES	8
TOTAL VOTES	16
TOTAL POINTS	161

▼ TEAM
Eagles

▼ YEARS PLAYED
1975–1983

▼ POSITION
Offensive Tackle

Rob Betts remembered listening to an Eagles broadcast when Stan Walters was incensed about an officiating call. "He was so fired up, he wanted to go down on the field and beat up an official." Merrill Reese calmly dissuaded his partner. "No, Stan." It was that passion and ferocity which Walters displayed on the field for nine years that earned him a spot on Rob's list. Merrill explained why his broadcasting partner for 14 years (1984-97) was such a good offensive tackle. "He had great feet and tremendous balance. He could protect the quarterback's blindside."

Bob Anderson likened Walters to Jon Runyan. "He often blocked the opposing team's best pass blocker. Runners ran to his side. He was very smart and mobile." Lee Fiederer: "He was one of the bright spots on a bad team who stuck around long enough when the Eagles became good." After Walters came over to the Eagles in a trade with the Bengals in 1975, the Eagles had losing records for three straight years, but before long, Walters was on the plane to New Orleans with his Eagles teammates to play the Raiders in the Super Bowl.

Ned Hark did not include Walters on his list, but paid him a compliment nonetheless. "Walters, [Jerry] Sisemore and [Guy] Morriss were great as a unit. But Stan wasn't great individually, not in the same category as Anthony Munoz [the Bengals' Hall of Fame offensive tackle]." The trio of Walters, Sisemore and Morriss was an anchor on the Birds' offensive line. Morriss played center and Walters and Sisemore started at tackle (Sisemore also played guard for two years) for a nine-year stretch (1975-83).

In passing on Walters, others compared him to his linemate Sisemore. Cliff Patterson thought Walters was crafty but believed Sisemore was stronger and more powerful. Dave Beck pointed out that Walters did not play as long in Philadelphia as Sisemore did. Walters was an Eagle for nine years; Sisemore played in Philly for 12 years.

Year	Team	Lg	Games
1972	Cincinnati	NFL	8
1973	Cincinnati	NFL	4
1974	Cincinnati	NFL	14
1975	Eagles	NFL	14
1976	Eagles	NFL	14
1977	Eagles	NFL	14
1978	Eagles	NFL	16
1979	Eagles	NFL	16
1980	Eagles	NFL	16
1981	Eagles	NFL	16
1982	Eagles	NFL	9
1983	Eagles	NFL	12
		Eagles Totals	127
		Career Totals	153

NFL Pro Bowl (1978–79)

CHRIS WHEELER'S TOP 10

1. Wilt Chamberlain
2. Mike Schmidt
3. Julius Erving
4. Bobby Clarke
5. Steve Carlton
6. Norm Van Brocklin
7. Reggie White
8. Pete Rose
9. Bernie Parent
10. Jim Bunning

88 Mark Recchi

RANK	POINTS	VOTES RECEIVED
1st	50	0
2nd	49	0
3rd	48	0
4th	47	0
5th	46	0
6th	45	0
7th	44	0
8th	43	0
9th	42	0
10th	41	0
11th	40	0
12th	39	0
13th	38	0
14th	37	0
15th	36	0
16th	35	0
17th	34	0
18th	33	0
19th	32	0
20th	31	0
21st	30	0
22nd	29	0
23rd	28	0
24th	27	0
25th	26	1
26th	25	0
27th	24	0
28th	23	0
29th	22	0
30th	21	0

RANK	POINTS	VOTES RECEIVED
31st	20	1
32nd	19	0
33rd	18	0
34th	17	0
35th	16	1
36th	15	0
37th	14	0
38th	13	0
39th	12	1
40th	11	0
41st	10	1
42nd	9	3
43rd	8	1
44th	7	1
45th	6	0
46th	5	3
47th	4	2
48th	3	2
49th	2	0
50th	1	2
Not on List	0	81

TOP 10 VOTES	0
2ND 10 VOTES	0
3RD 10 VOTES	1
4TH 10 VOTES	3
5TH 10 VOTES	15
TOTAL VOTES	19
TOTAL POINTS	157

▼ **TEAM**
Flyers

▼ **YEARS PLAYED**
1992–1995, 1999–2004

▼ **POSITION**
Right Wing

Joe Fee didn't mince words when he stated his case for Mark Recchi, the key player in the trade that brought John LeClair and Eric Desjardins to the Flyers from Montreal in 1995. "Anyone who overlooked Recchi [made a big mistake]. What he did to launch Lindros' career is huge. Nobody else on the team those first two years had a clue how to play the game the right way. There were a few players with talent, but [they] weren't too bright. Throw in a single-season franchise record for points [Recchi's 123 points in 1994 is the highest ever for a Flyer] and solid second tour of duty [he led the Flyers in points three seasons during his second stint] and there's no argument."

According to some voters, however, there *is* an argument as to whether Recchi belongs on a list of top Philadelphia athletes. Randy Axelrod said he was never overly impressed with Recchi, and the Flyers floundered when he was there. The Flyers first obtained Recchi in a trade with the Penguins in February '92; Philadelphia failed to make the playoffs that season for the third year in a row. They also sat out the postseason in '93 and '94, despite Recchi's consecutive 100-point seasons. "Once the Flyers got LeClair," said Randy, "the Flyers improved." In '95, they were back in the playoffs, and they won their first two series before bowing to New Jersey in the Eastern Conference Finals. "He was one-dimensional," added Randy. "He didn't play defense." Although Recchi played about eight seasons with the Flyers, Bob Anderson didn't think of him as a Flyer because he was so well-traveled. Also, he played on Stanley Cup winners for two different teams: the Penguins in 1991 and the Hurricanes in 2006. Paul Troy credited Recchi for playing hard, but thought he was often injured.

Joe Fee wasn't the only Recchi enthusiast. Steve Kennedy felt that Recchi was a fan favorite and a good enough player for his several years in Philly to earn a spot in his top 50. Sean Bergin voted for Recchi because he was a good goal scorer and was tough; in evaluating Flyers wings, Sean gave Recchi the nod over Rick Tocchet and

Rod Brind'Amour. Jason Garber's main reason for including Recchi on his list: he has Hall of Fame potential. Jason's point is well taken; Recchi racked up more career points than Bobby Clarke, although less than half were with the Flyers.

Year	Team	Lg	Gm	G	A	Pts	PM
1988–89	Pittsburgh	NHL	15	1	1	2	0
1989–90	Pittsburgh	NHL	74	30	37	67	44
1990–91	Pittsburgh	NHL	78	40	73	113	48
1991–92	Pittsburgh	NHL	58	33	37	70	78
1991–92	Flyers	NHL	22	10	17	27	18
1992–93	Flyers	NHL	84	53	70	123	95
1993–94	Flyers	NHL	84	40	67	107	46
1994–95	Flyers	NHL	10	2	3	5	12
1994–95	Montreal	NHL	39	14	29	43	16
1995–96	Montreal	NHL	82	28	50	78	69
1996–97	Montreal	NHL	82	34	46	80	58
1997–98	Montreal	NHL	82	32	42	74	51
1998–99	Montreal	NHL	61	12	35	47	28
1998–99	Flyers	NHL	10	4	2	6	6
1999–00	Flyers	NHL	82	28	63	91	50
2000–01	Flyers	NHL	69	27	50	77	33
2001–02	Flyers	NHL	80	22	42	64	46
2002–03	Flyers	NHL	79	20	32	52	35
2003–04	Flyers	NHL	82	26	49	75	47
2005–06	Carolina	NHL	20	4	3	7	12
	Flyers Totals		602	232	395	627	388
	Career Totals		1256	484	781	1265	848

NHL All-Star (1991, 1993–94, 1997–00)
Member of Stanley Cup Champions (1991, 2006)

Keith Jackson

RANK	POINTS	VOTES RECEIVED		RANK	POINTS	VOTES RECEIVED
1st	50	0		31st	20	0
2nd	49	0		32nd	19	0
3rd	48	0		33rd	18	1
4th	47	0		34th	17	0
5th	46	0		35th	16	1
6th	45	0		36th	15	1
7th	44	0		37th	14	0
8th	43	0		38th	13	0
9th	42	0		39th	12	0
10th	41	0		40th	11	1
11th	40	0		41st	10	1
12th	39	0		42nd	9	0
13th	38	0		43rd	8	0
14th	37	0		44th	7	0
15th	36	0		45th	6	0
16th	35	0		46th	5	0
17th	34	0		47th	4	1
18th	33	1		48th	3	0
19th	32	0		49th	2	1
20th	31	0		50th	1	1
21st	30	0		Not on List	0	89
22nd	29	0				
23rd	28	0				
24th	27	0		TOP 10 VOTES		0
25th	26	0		2ND 10 VOTES		1
26th	25	0		3RD 10 VOTES		2
27th	24	1		4TH 10 VOTES		4
28th	23	0		5TH 10 VOTES		4
29th	22	0		TOTAL VOTES		11
30th	21	1		TOTAL POINTS		155

▼ TEAM
Eagles

▼ YEARS PLAYED
1988–1991

▼ POSITION
Tight End

On New Year's Eve, 1988, the Eagles traveled to Chicago to play their first postseason game in seven years. The game would become known as "the Fog Bowl" as a heavy fog rolled in toward the end of the first half, making it difficult for the players to see each other. The Eagles lost the game 20-12, their first of three straight opening-round playoff losses under Buddy Ryan. In the first half, when the fog had not yet set in, tight end Keith Jackson dropped an easy touchdown pass in the end zone from Randall Cunningham. "Jackson's drop changed the game," said Greg Veith. "The Eagles well may have won if he caught it." Greg thought that during the four years Jackson was with the Eagles, he was a very good player, but not great. "He never wowed me. For a guy who came into the league with credentials to stretch the defense, how many long gains did he produce?" In Jackson's first three years with the Birds, he caught almost 200 passes, but none for longer than 41 yards. In 1991, his fourth and final season in Philly, he broke loose for a 73-yarder. But then, as Dave Myers lamented, Jackson whined his way out of Philadelphia; he signed with Miami in 1992. "The Eagles drafted him out of Oklahoma and made him the player he was," said Dave, who thought Jackson was a good tight end but not a dominating player. Cliff Patterson agreed: Jackson, while good, was not in the dominating category like other Eagles from that time, such as Reggie White and Randall Cunningham.

Jackson received especially harsh criticism when Mike Koob and Bob Anderson were asked about him. "The most overrated tight end in history in the NFL" was Mike Koob's assessment. Bob called Jackson "a big waste of talent" who never made a tough catch and didn't block much.

Reasonable minds will differ, though, and many voters found a place on their lists for Jackson. "He was the Eagles' best tight end in recent years," said Greg Geier, "better than John Spagnola, Chad Lewis or L.J. Smith." Merrill Reese took it a step further. "He was the greatest tight end in the history of the franchise. He was a tremendous receiving tight end, making catches over the middle, rarely dropping balls; he was a great target, had speed, and could run over people." Nobody was more impressed with Jackson's athleticism than Michael Barkann, who ranked Keith 18th. "He had size, speed, could block and catch. He ran great pass routes. He was a great weapon; he could have been as good as [the Giants' great tight end] Mark Bavaro. He was underused; he would have been better if he had a quarterback other than Randall." Brent Saunders and Sean Bergin also brought up Bavaro when asked about Jackson. Brent: "He and Bavaro redefined the tight end position. Linebackers couldn't cover him and if teams put a safety on him, he'd knock him right over." Sean: "He and Bavaro were pioneers among tight ends. He was awesome, a standout in terms of talent. He and Randall had such a connection."

Year	Team	Lg	G	Rec	Yds	Avg	TD
1988	Eagles	NFL	16	81	869	10.7	6
1989	Eagles	NFL	14	63	648	10.3	3
1990	Eagles	NFL	14	50	670	13.4	6
1991	Eagles	NFL	16	48	569	11.9	5
1992	Miami	NFL	13	48	594	12.4	5
1993	Miami	NFL	15	39	613	15.7	6
1994	Miami	NFL	16	59	673	11.4	7
1995	Green Bay	NFL	9	13	142	10.9	1
1996	Green Bay	NFL	16	40	505	12.6	10
	Eagles Totals		60	242	2756	11.4	20
	Career Totals		129	441	5283	12.0	49

NFC Rookie of the Year (1988)
NFL Pro Bowl (1988–90, 1992, 1996)
Member of Super Bowl Champions (1996)

90 Tom Woodeshick

RANK	POINTS	VOTES RECEIVED
1st	50	0
2nd	49	0
3rd	48	0
4th	47	0
5th	46	0
6th	45	0
7th	44	0
8th	43	0
9th	42	0
10th	41	0
11th	40	0
12th	39	0
13th	38	0
14th	37	0
15th	36	0
16th	35	0
17th	34	0
18th	33	0
19th	32	0
20th	31	0
21st	30	1
22nd	29	0
23rd	28	0
24th	27	0
25th	26	0
26th	25	0
27th	24	0
28th	23	0
29th	22	0
30th	21	0

RANK	POINTS	VOTES RECEIVED
31st	20	1
32nd	19	0
33rd	18	1
34th	17	1
35th	16	0
36th	15	1
37th	14	0
38th	13	1
39th	12	1
40th	11	1
41st	10	0
42nd	9	0
43rd	8	0
44th	7	0
45th	6	1
46th	5	0
47th	4	0
48th	3	0
49th	2	0
50th	1	1
Not on List	0	90

TOP 10 VOTES	0
2ND 10 VOTES	0
3RD 10 VOTES	1
4TH 10 VOTES	7
5TH 10 VOTES	2
TOTAL VOTES	10
TOTAL POINTS	143

▼ TEAM
Eagles

▼ YEARS PLAYED
1963–1971

▼ POSITION
Running Back

Jerry McDonough recalled a typical series by the Eagles in the woeful years of 1967-69: Woodeshick off right tackle, Woodeshick off left tackle, swing pass to Woodeshick, punt. Tom Woodeshick led the team in rushing in each of those three seasons, but the Birds were just 12-28-2 over the three years; in 1968, the Eagles started the season 0-11, and finished 2-12. (If the Eagles could have remained winless, they would have taken Heisman Trophy winner O.J. Simpson; instead, they chose running back Leroy Keyes, who was the third pick. Keyes rushed for 368 yards in his short and unimpressive four-year career in Philadelphia.)

In addition to Jerry, other voters like Bill McElroy and Rob Betts thought that while Woodeshick was a respectable running back, he didn't make the cut because the Eagles were so bad during his prime. Rob added that several running backs since then have been better, including Wilbert Montgomery, Keith Byars, Duce Staley and Brian Westbrook.

Woodeshick's efforts did not go unnoticed by many pollsters. Cliff Patterson called him "the most recognized Eagles player of that time." Chuck Wolf described Woodeshick as scrappy and dependable, adding that he was always a guarantee for some small yardage when needed. Doug Brown liked Woodeshick because he was a really tough fullback; it was Woodeshick's toughness, said Steve Van Allen, that Philly fans loved. Doug also pointed out that after his playing days ended, Woodeshick did some bartending at Dirty Frank's, a Center City watering hole.

Fred Warren pointed to Woodeshick's longevity—he played nine years in Philadelphia; no running back has ever worn Eagles green longer. (Jim Parmer was also a running back with the Eagles for nine years, 1948-56.)

In compiling his top 50 list, Jim Angelichio gave more weight to players with heart and soul than to players with pure talent and strong stats, and for that reason Woodeshick got the nod from him.

Year	Team	Lg	G	Att	Rushing Yds	Avg	TD	Rec	Receiving Yds	Avg	TD
1963	Eagles	NFL	14	5	18	3.6	0	1	-3	-3.0	0
1964	Eagles	NFL	13	37	180	4.9	2	4	12	3.0	0
1965	Eagles	NFL	12	28	145	5.2	0	6	86	14.3	0
1966	Eagles	NFL	14	85	330	3.9	4	10	118	11.8	1
1967	Eagles	NFL	14	155	670	4.3	6	34	391	11.5	4
1968	Eagles	NFL	14	217	947	4.4	3	36	328	9.1	0
1969	Eagles	NFL	12	186	831	4.5	4	22	177	8.0	0
1970	Eagles	NFL	6	52	254	4.9	2	6	28	4.7	0
1971	Eagles	NFL	11	66	188	2.8	0	6	36	6.0	1
1972	St. Louis	NFL	4	5	14	2.8	0	1	2	2.0	0
Eagles Totals			110	831	3563	4.3	21	125	1173	9.4	6
Career Totals			114	836	3577	4.3	21	126	1175	9.3	6

NFL Pro Bowl (1968)

George McGinnis

RANK	POINTS	VOTES RECEIVED		RANK	POINTS	VOTES RECEIVED
1st	50	0		31st	20	0
2nd	49	0		32nd	19	1
3rd	48	0		33rd	18	0
4th	47	0		34th	17	0
5th	46	0		35th	16	0
6th	45	0		36th	15	1
7th	44	0		37th	14	0
8th	43	0		38th	13	1
9th	42	1		39th	12	0
10th	41	0		40th	11	0
11th	40	0		41st	10	0
12th	39	0		42nd	9	1
13th	38	0		43rd	8	1
14th	37	0		44th	7	0
15th	36	0		45th	6	0
16th	35	0		46th	5	0
17th	34	0		47th	4	0
18th	33	0		48th	3	1
19th	32	0		49th	2	1
20th	31	0		50th	1	0
21st	30	0		Not on List	0	91
22nd	29	0				
23rd	28	0				
24th	27	1		TOP 10 VOTES		1
25th	26	0		2ND 10 VOTES		0
26th	25	0		3RD 10 VOTES		1
27th	24	0		4TH 10 VOTES		3
28th	23	0		5TH 10 VOTES		4
29th	22	0		TOTAL VOTES		9
30th	21	0		TOTAL POINTS		138

▼ **TEAM**
Sixers

▼ **YEARS PLAYED**
1976–1978

▼ **POSITION**
Forward

The Sixers had just started to turn the corner in 1974 and 1975. Although they posted losing records, they played respectably, after the nine-win nightmare in '73. A key move in bringing the Sixers to the next level, many voters felt, was the signing of free-agent George McGinnis. The Sixers drafted big George in the second round of the '73 draft, but he chose to remain in his hometown with the ABA's Pacers, with whom he had just completed his second season. However, after four years in the ABA, McGinnis was ready to move to the NBA. "[The signing of McGinnis] signaled [owner] Harold Katz's commitment to winning a championship," said Rod Smith. "He was the first arrival to a team which eventually became great. He was physical, a good rebounder, who for a big man got up and down the court and played both ends consistently. He made the players around him better with his unselfish play."

In McGinnis' first year, the Sixers made the playoffs, although they lost to the Buffalo Braves in the first round. In 1977, McGinnis helped lead the Sixers to the NBA finals, which they lost to Bill Walton's Portland Trailblazers in six games. "He turned the program around," said Dan Brown. "He brought the Sixers back from the dead," agreed Joe Brown. "He was a star." Joe also liked McGinnis' personality and that he was entertaining in an interview. Mike Rad wished that McGinnis played in Philadelphia for 10 years instead of just three. (He was traded to Denver in 1978 in the deal that brought Bobby Jones to the Sixers.) "He was a pure shooter. When he was on he was on, and he was good defensively."

If McGinnis had remained a Sixer for longer than three years, undoubtedly his name would have appeared on more voters' lists. Many people, including Cliff Patterson, Paul Lightkep and John Surbeck, thought that George's tenure in Philadelphia was too short. John Mitchell went into more detail in explaining why he passed on McGinnis. "He was the first fix after the 9-73 season, and helped the Sixers become respectable, but he came up small in the playoffs. He needed the ball, and after Doc came [in '77, McGinnis' second year], they couldn't co-exist. He was not as good as advertised."

McGinnis did come up small in the playoffs, especially the '77 finals. Greg Veith: "I disqualified McGinnis for his miserable showing in the series versus Portland."

Year	Team	Lg	G	Min	FGM	FGA	FGP	FTM	FTA	FTP	AST	REB	Pts	PPG
1971–72	Indiana	ABA	73	2179	465	999	.465	298	462	.645	137	711	1234	16.9
1972–73	Indiana	ABA	82	3347	868	1755	.495	517	778	.665	205	1022	2261	27.6
1973–74	Indiana	ABA	80	3266	789	1686	.468	488	715	.683	267	1197	2071	25.9
1974–75	Indiana	ABA	79	3193	873	1934	.451	545	753	.724	495	1126	2353	29.8
1975–76	Sixers	NBA	77	2946	647	1552	.417	475	642	.740	359	967	1769	23.0
1976–77	Sixers	NBA	79	2769	659	1439	.458	372	546	.681	302	911	1690	21.4
1977–78	Sixers	NBA	78	2533	588	1270	.463	411	574	.716	294	810	1587	2.3
1978–79	Denver	NBA	76	2552	603	1273	.474	509	765	.665	283	864	1715	22.6
1979–80	Den.-Ind.	NBA	73	2208	400	886	.451	270	488	.553	333	699	369	13.2
1980–81	Indiana	NBA	69	1845	348	768	.453	207	385	.538	210	528	903	13.1
1981–82	Indiana	NBA	76	1341	141	378	.373	72	159	.453	204	398	354	4.7
Sixers Totals			853	28583	4192	7940	.528	2005	2537	.790	6212	2538	10429	12.2
Career Totals			1101	34845	4906	9374	.523	2331	2938	.793	7392	3088	12195	11.1

Member of ABA Champions (1972–73)
ABA Playoffs MVP (1973)
ABA All-Star (1973–75)
ABA co-MVP (1975)
NBA All-Star (1976–77, 1979)
Number 30 retired by Pacers

92 Steve Mix

RANK	POINTS	VOTES RECEIVED
1st	50	0
2nd	49	0
3rd	48	0
4th	47	0
5th	46	0
6th	45	0
7th	44	0
8th	43	0
9th	42	0
10th	41	0
11th	40	0
12th	39	0
13th	38	0
14th	37	0
15th	36	0
16th	35	0
17th	34	0
18th	33	0
19th	32	0
20th	31	0
21st	30	0
22nd	29	0
23rd	28	0
24th	27	0
25th	26	1
26th	25	0
27th	24	1
28th	23	0
29th	22	0
30th	21	0

RANK	POINTS	VOTES RECEIVED
31st	20	1
32nd	19	0
33rd	18	0
34th	17	0
35th	16	0
36th	15	0
37th	14	0
38th	13	1
39th	12	0
40th	11	0
41st	10	1
42nd	9	1
43rd	8	3
44th	7	0
45th	6	1
46th	5	0
47th	4	0
48th	3	0
49th	2	1
50th	1	0
Not on List	0	89

TOP 10 VOTES	0
2ND 10 VOTES	0
3RD 10 VOTES	2
4TH 10 VOTES	2
5TH 10 VOTES	7
TOTAL VOTES	11
TOTAL POINTS	134

▼ **TEAM**
Sixers

▼ **YEARS PLAYED**
1974–1982

▼ **POSITION**
Forward

For four years, it didn't look like Steve Mix's pro basketball career was going anywhere. Drafted by the Pistons in 1969, Mix saw little playing time for two-plus seasons in Detroit, had a cup of coffee with the ABA's Nuggets, and was out of basketball for an entire season. A less determined player might have thrown in the towel, but Mix didn't give up. The Sixers acquired him in 1973, and coach Gene Shue, in the rebuilding mode, put him in the starting lineup. He remained in Philly for nine years, although his playing time decreased after the Sixers signed Julius Erving in 1977.

Rob Neducsin and Fran Garvin liked Mix because he was a bright spot on some bad Sixers teams; in Mix's first two years in town, Shue's squad won only 25 and 34 games. Rob was a Mix fan because he was an overachiever who played hard every night. Fran didn't think that Mix got much recognition, even though he was an All-Star (in 1975). Joe Gribb: "Mix gave you that old-fashioned forward that every team needs, but few have, the post player with the good shot from 'Mixville.'" (Mix's favorite spot on the floor was about 18 feet from the basket along the right baseline; broadcaster Bill Campbell dubbed the area "Mixville.") Glenn Young was another Mix supporter: "Mix did everything so fundamentally well that I was amazed he could get so many points, rebounds and defensive stops when his competitors seemed to be far superior athletes." While Mix was a competent scorer and rebounder, he was especially adept at stealing the ball. Mix held the Sixers' single-season steals record until Allen Iverson broke it nearly 30 years later.

The consensus among those voters who didn't include Mix is that he was a cut below star quality. "He hustled, but he wasn't a dominating player" (Frank Minch). "He was a tough, good player but he wasn't great" (Paul Lightkep). "He was the same caliber player as Mike Gminski and Hersey Hawkins—good, but not good enough" (Lee Fiederer). "He was a productive player on bad teams; on good teams, he was an average player who didn't hurt you too much. He made the most of his rather limited abilities" (Greg Veith).

Year	Team	Lg	G	Min	FGM	FGA	FGP	FTM	FTA	FTP	AST	REB	Pts	PPG
1969–70	Detroit	NBA	18	276	48	100	.480	23	39	.590	15	64	119	6.6
1970–71	Detroit	NBA	35	731	111	249	.446	68	89	.764	34	164	290	8.3
1971–72	Detroit	NBA	9	108	16	48	.333	7	12	.583	4	23	39	4.3
1971–72	Denver	ABA	1	4	1	1	1	0	0	0	0	1	2	2.0
1973–74	Sixers	NBA	82	2969	495	1042	.475	228	288	.792	152	864	1218	14.9
1974–75	Sixers	NBA	46	1748	280	582	.481	159	205	.776	99	500	719	15.6
1975–76	Sixers	NBA	81	3039	421	844	.499	287	351	.818	216	662	1129	13.9
1976–77	Sixers	NBA	75	1958	288	551	.523	215	263	.817	152	376	791	1.5
1977–78	Sixers	NBA	82	1819	291	560	.520	175	220	.795	174	297	757	9.2
1978–79	Sixers	NBA	74	1269	265	493	.538	161	201	.801	121	293	691	9.3
1979–80	Sixers	NBA	81	1543	363	703	.516	207	249	.831	149	290	937	11.6
1980–81	Sixers	NBA	72	1327	288	575	.501	200	240	.833	114	264	776	1.8
1981–82	Sixers	NBA	75	1235	202	399	.506	136	172	.791	93	225	541	7.2
1982–83	L.A. Lakers-Mil.	NBA	58	809	137	283	.484	75	88	.852	70	137	350	6.0
Sixers Totals			668	16907	2893	5749	.503	1768	2189	.808	1270	3771	7559	11.3
Career Totals			788	18831	3205	6429	.499	1941	2417	.803	1393	4160	8357	1.6

NBA All-Star (1975)

93 Keith Primeau

RANK	POINTS	VOTES RECEIVED		RANK	POINTS	VOTES RECEIVED
1st	50	0		31st	20	0
2nd	49	0		32nd	19	0
3rd	48	0		33rd	18	0
4th	47	0		34th	17	0
5th	46	0		35th	16	1
6th	45	0		36th	15	0
7th	44	0		37th	14	1
8th	43	0		38th	13	0
9th	42	0		39th	12	0
10th	41	0		40th	11	1
11th	40	0		41st	10	0
12th	39	0		42nd	9	0
13th	38	0		43rd	8	0
14th	37	0		44th	7	0
15th	36	0		45th	6	1
16th	35	0		46th	5	0
17th	34	0		47th	4	1
18th	33	0		48th	3	1
19th	32	0		49th	2	0
20th	31	0		50th	1	1
21st	30	0		Not on List	0	90
22nd	29	0				
23rd	28	0				
24th	27	0				
25th	26	0				
26th	25	1				
27th	24	2				
28th	23	0				
29th	22	0				
30th	21	0				

TOP 10 VOTES	0
2ND 10 VOTES	0
3RD 10 VOTES	3
4TH 10 VOTES	3
5TH 10 VOTES	4
TOTAL VOTES	10
TOTAL POINTS	128

▼ **TEAM**
Flyers

▼ **YEARS PLAYED**
2000–2006

▼ **POSITION**
Center

Keith Primeau's amazing performance in the 2004 playoffs generated a flurry of compliments from the voters. After scoring only seven goals during the regular season, Primeau pumped in nine goals and added seven assists in the Flyers' pursuit of a third Stanley Cup, which ended when Tampa Bay beat the Flyers in seven games in the Eastern Conference Finals. Primeau's hat trick against Toronto in Game 5 of the Eastern Conference Semifinals was one of his many great games during the playoffs. Mike Sielski compared Primeau's postseason performance in 2004 to Lenny Dykstra's effort in the '93 postseason and Allen Iverson's heroics in the 2001 playoffs. "But," Mike said, "his overall body of work was not good enough to make the list." Randy Axelrod passed on Primeau for the same reason. "He was great in the '04 playoffs, but hasn't done much else."

Other voters, including Jim Schloth, Mike DiColla and Michael Beirne, cited Primeau's outstanding play in the '04 playoffs as a primary reason for including him. Mike also described Primeau as a "hard-nosed, take-charge player." Michael recalled Keith's dramatic game-winning goal against the Penguins in the five-overtime marathon, Game 4 of the 2000 Eastern Conference Semifinals, which tied the series against Pittsburgh at two. Michael also gave Primeau points for his leadership role, as did Sean Bergin. Sean added: "He meshed well with the working man; he [was] not a prima donna." Bob Kelly agreed: "He [was] a blue-collar, Philly-type player." Bob also described Primeau as a great team player and a top defensive center.

Here's how Joe Fee explained why Primeau didn't make his top 50: "Inspirational? Absolutely. Dominant? Briefly. Consistent? Nope. Productive? Not enough." Other reasons voters provided in declining to pick big Keith: "He [was] not the scorer that Kerr or LeClair was" (Mike Mastalaski). "He [was] injury-prone and inconsistent" (Bill McClain). "He [was] a good player, but big and lumbering and typical of a Bobby Clarke player in recent years" (Lee Fiederer).

Covering the Flyers since 2002, I've spent a lot of time at the Wachovia Center. The crowds there always have been regarded as "corporate," not like the rowdy, raucous old days at the Spectrum. But the new building and the people that fill it can get loud when the mood strikes them. One night in particular stands out: April 22, 2004. It was Game 1 of the conference semifinals against the Toronto Maple Leafs. The Leafs had eliminated the Flyers from the playoffs the year before, and they were a team that sent a little shudder through the collective spine of the fan base. But Marcus Ragnarsson's goal early in the second period broke a 1-1 tie, and when Simon Gagne scored the insurance goal with just under five minutes left in the third period, the building shook like no other time since I've been covering games. I felt the balcony-level press box sway, something I never felt before and haven't felt since. Just an amazing moment.

—ADAM KIMELMAN

Year	Team	Lg	Gm	G	A	Pts	PM
1990–91	Detroit	NHL	58	3	12	15	106
1991–92	Detroit	NHL	35	6	10	16	83
1992–93	Detroit	NHL	73	15	17	32	152
1993–94	Detroit	NHL	78	31	42	73	173
1994–95	Detroit	NHL	45	15	27	42	99
1995–96	Detroit	NHL	74	27	25	52	168
1996–97	Carolina	NHL	75	26	25	51	161
1997–98	Carolina	NHL	81	26	37	63	110
1998–99	Carolina	NHL	78	30	32	62	75
1999–00	Flyers	NHL	23	7	10	17	31
2000–01	Flyers	NHL	71	34	39	73	76
2001–02	Flyers	NHL	75	19	29	48	128
2002–03	Flyers	NHL	80	19	27	46	93
2003–04	Flyers	NHL	54	7	15	22	80
2005–06	Flyers	NHL	9	1	6	7	6
Flyers Totals			312	87	126	213	414
Career Totals			909	266	353	619	1541

NHL All-Star (1999, 2004)

94 Norm Snead

RANK	POINTS	VOTES RECEIVED
1st	50	0
2nd	49	0
3rd	48	0
4th	47	0
5th	46	0
6th	45	0
7th	44	0
8th	43	0
9th	42	0
10th	41	0
11th	40	0
12th	39	0
13th	38	0
14th	37	0
15th	36	0
16th	35	1
17th	34	0
18th	33	0
19th	32	0
20th	31	0
21st	30	0
22nd	29	0
23rd	28	1
24th	27	0
25th	26	0
26th	25	0
27th	24	0
28th	23	0
29th	22	1
30th	21	0

RANK	POINTS	VOTES RECEIVED
31st	20	0
32nd	19	0
33rd	18	0
34th	17	0
35th	16	0
36th	15	0
37th	14	0
38th	13	2
39th	12	0
40th	11	0
41st	10	0
42nd	9	0
43rd	8	1
44th	7	0
45th	6	1
46th	5	0
47th	4	0
48th	3	0
49th	2	0
50th	1	0
Not on List	0	93

TOP 10 VOTES	0
2ND 10 VOTES	1
3RD 10 VOTES	2
4TH 10 VOTES	2
5TH 10 VOTES	2
TOTAL VOTES	7
TOTAL POINTS	125

▼ TEAM
Eagles

▼ POSITION
Quarterback

▼ YEARS PLAYED
1964–1970

When the subject of regrettable trades by Philadelphia teams is discussed, Phillies fans are quick to recall the 1981 trade in which they sent future Hall of Famer Ryne Sandberg (and Larry Bowa) to the Cubs for Ivan DeJesus. The blood of Sixers fans still boils when discussing the deal in which they parted with Moses Malone after the 1986 season in exchange for, among others, Jeff Ruland. Bill McElroy is among the many Eagles fans who hasn't forgotten the 1965 deal in which the Birds swapped quarterback Sonny Jurgensen, who later made the Hall of Fame, with the Redskins for Norm Snead. Bill made an understatement when he said, "We got the wrong end of the Jurgensen/Snead trade."

In explaining why he didn't pick Snead, Terry Bickhart had these comments: "He was hard-nosed but the Eagles were bad for most of the years that he was quarterback. It wasn't all his fault." Snead held the starting job for seven years during which the Eagles had just one winning season. Cliff Patterson and Neil Goldstein were less diplomatic than Terry. "He was the best quarterback they had," said Cliff, "but he wasn't that good." Neil: "He was a very average quarterback, and was slow afoot."

Norm incurred the wrath of the Philly fans during his seven years as the Birds' number one quarterback. But he had his supporters. Patrick Dooley was especially emphatic in his defense of Snead. "I don't care what anyone else says. I liked his style and professional demeanor while playing on less than great teams. I remember him as a very, very good pocket passer." Chuck Wolf: "He was scrappy and dependable." Jon Grisdale said that Snead was resented by the Philadelphia fans because of the Jurgensen trade. But, Jon pointed out, he had a lousy offensive line, except for Bob Brown, who Jon remembers as often helping up Snead following a sack. Dave Bristowe really went to bat for Stormin' Norman: "Snead had a long career as a quarterback starting in the early 1960s through the mid-1970s—when the game seemed more real than it is today—and I thought some of his best years were with the Eagles. It seemed like a great trade for the Eagles, sending Jurgensen to the Redskins for Snead, who was somewhat fresh to the league and on his way to being in his prime. He had some good seasons with the Eagles statistically, but the Eagles did not always seem to come through on the defensive side, unfortunately. Any quarterback who played in the 1960s and played as long as Snead did deserves high ranking in my book. The game was so different then in terms of toughness and spirit. His record and dedication show this." As Dave mentioned, Snead compiled some good stats. His 29 touchdown passes in 1967 tied for second in the NFL and included a four-touchdown game against the Saints. He was third in the league in passing yards twice. In 1969, Snead tossed five TDs in a game against the Steelers. He had eight 300-yard games as an Eagle.

Year	Team	Lg	G	Att	Comp	Pct	Yds	TD	Int
1961	Washington	NFL	14	375	172	45.9	2337	11	22
1962	Washington	NFL	14	354	184	52.0	2926	22	22
1963	Washington	NFL	14	363	175	48.2	3043	13	27
1964	Eagles	NFL	12	283	138	48.8	1906	14	12
1965	Eagles	NFL	11	288	150	52.1	2346	15	13
1966	Eagles	NFL	10	226	103	45.6	1275	8	11
1967	Eagles	NFL	14	434	240	55.3	3399	29	24
1968	Eagles	NFL	11	291	152	52.2	1655	11	21
1969	Eagles	NFL	13	379	190	50.1	2768	19	23
1970	Eagles	NFL	14	335	181	54.0	2323	15	20
1971	Minnesota	NFL	7	75	37	49.3	470	1	6
1972	N.Y. Giants	NFL	14	325	196	60.3	2307	17	12
1973	N.Y. Giants	NFL	10	235	131	55.7	1483	7	22
1974	N.Y.G.-S.F.	NFL	8	159	97	61.0	983	5	8
1975	San Francisco	NFL	9	189	108	57.1	1337	9	10
1976	N.Y. Giants	NFL	3	42	22	52.4	239	0	4
	Eagles Totals		85	2236	1154	51.6	15672	111	124
	Career Totals		178	4353	2276	52.3	30797	196	257

NFL Pro Bowl (1963, 1965, 1972)

95 Luke Jackson

RANK	POINTS	VOTES RECEIVED
1st	50	0
2nd	49	0
3rd	48	0
4th	47	0
5th	46	0
6th	45	0
7th	44	0
8th	43	0
9th	42	0
10th	41	0
11th	40	0
12th	39	0
13th	38	0
14th	37	0
15th	36	0
16th	35	0
17th	34	0
18th	33	0
19th	32	0
20th	31	0
21st	30	0
22nd	29	1
23rd	28	0
24th	27	0
25th	26	0
26th	25	0
27th	24	0
28th	23	0
29th	22	0
30th	21	1
31st	20	0
32nd	19	1
33rd	18	0
34th	17	0
35th	16	0
36th	15	0
37th	14	1
38th	13	0
39th	12	0
40th	11	0
41st	10	0
42nd	9	0
43rd	8	1
44th	7	2
45th	6	1
46th	5	1
47th	4	1
48th	3	1
49th	2	0
50th	1	0
Not on List	0	89

TOP 10 VOTES	0
2ND 10 VOTES	0
3RD 10 VOTES	2
4TH 10 VOTES	2
5TH 10 VOTES	7
TOTAL VOTES	11
TOTAL POINTS	123

▼ **TEAM**
Sixers

▼ **YEARS PLAYED**
1965–1972

▼ **POSITION**
Forward

Knee injuries cut short the careers of many outstanding Philadelphia athletes—Billy Cunningham, Mike Quick and Darren Daulton, to name a few. Luke Jackson was headed toward being outstanding when he tore up his knee. When Jackson broke into the NBA in 1965, he had an auspicious first year: he made the NBA's All-Rookie team and led the Sixers in rebounds. He kept up the good work by finishing second on the team to Chamberlain in boards in each of the next three seasons. Then, early in the 1969 season, Jackson sustained a devastating knee injury. He came back to play three more seasons, although he was not nearly as productive. However, Jackson's performance in those first four years was strong enough that numerous voters included him on their lists.

Andy Musser and Mark Voigt used the same phrase to describe Jackson: the prototypical power forward. Mark described him as "an underappreciated star on the greatest basketball team of all time, the 1966-67 Sixers." (Fans of the great Celtics teams of the 1960s, which ran off eight straight NBA titles, the '72 Lakers [69-13] and the '96 Bulls [72-10] might not agree with Mark's assessment of the '67 Sixers.) Andy admired Jackson's determination and fortitude in coming back to play following his injury, albeit not at the same level. Gordie Jones, Jim Schloth and Jon Grisdale also thought that Jackson's rebounding prowess for those few years made him top-50-worthy. Gordie: "He was the enforcer—he rooted down in the post and pounded away." Jim: "He was a big, physical, unselfish team player when big men dominated by scoring, not defending." Jon: "He was one of the best rebounders the Sixers have ever had."

Because Jackson's career was abbreviated, most voters passed on him. "He was an important part of some very good teams," said Terry Bickhart, "but he wasn't around long enough to have an impact." Doug Brown commended Jackson for being a starter on a championship team, and for being likable, but on the whole didn't think that he had a distinguished career. Also, Doug described Jackson as "very slow," a point noted as well by Chuck Wolf.

If Luke hadn't sustained his injury and maintained the same level of play that he had his first four years, undoubtedly he would have finished high on John Mitchell's list. John declined picking Luke because of the brevity of his career, but described him, in his prime, as a "monster power forward who would have beaten up Dennis Rodman." John also recalled a compliment paid to Luke by his teammate, Wilt Chamberlain: "He was the second strongest player in the league." The strongest, according to Wilt? Wilt himself, of course.

MERRILL REESE'S TOP 10

1. Wilt Chamberlain
2. Julius Erving
3. Reggie White
4. Robin Roberts
5. Chuck Bednarik
6. Bobby Clarke
7. Richie Ashburn
8. Bernie Parent
9. Harold Carmichael
10. Steve Carlton

Year	Team	Lg	G	Min	FGM	FGA	FGP	FTM	FTA	FTP	AST	REB	Pts	PPG
1964–65	Sixers	NBA	76	2590	419	1013	.414	288	404	.713	93	980	1126	14.8
1965–66	Sixers	NBA	79	1966	246	614	.401	158	214	.738	132	676	650	8.2
1966–67	Sixers	NBA	81	2377	386	882	.438	198	261	.759	114	724	970	12.0
1967–68	Sixers	NBA	82	2570	401	927	.433	166	231	.719	139	872	968	11.8
1968–69	Sixers	NBA	25	840	145	332	.437	69	97	.711	54	286	359	14.4
1969–70	Sixers	NBA	37	583	71	181	.392	60	81	.741	50	198	202	5.5
1970–71	Sixers	NBA	79	1774	199	529	.376	131	189	.693	148	568	529	6.7
1971–72	Sixers	NBA	63	1083	137	346	.396	92	133	.692	88	309	366	5.8
Sixers Totals			522	13783	2004	4824	.415	1162	1610	.722	818	4613	5170	9.9
Career Totals			522	13783	2004	4824	.415	1162	1610	.722	818	4613	5170	9.9

NBA All-Star (1965)
Member of NBA Champions (1967)

Joe Watson

RANK	POINTS	VOTES RECEIVED		RANK	POINTS	VOTES RECEIVED
1st	50	0		31st	20	0
2nd	49	0		32nd	19	0
3rd	48	0		33rd	18	1
4th	47	0		34th	17	0
5th	46	0		35th	16	1
6th	45	0		36th	15	0
7th	44	0		37th	14	0
8th	43	0		38th	13	0
9th	42	0		39th	12	0
10th	41	0		40th	11	1
11th	40	0		41st	10	1
12th	39	0		42nd	9	0
13th	38	0		43rd	8	0
14th	37	0		44th	7	1
15th	36	0		45th	6	1
16th	35	0		46th	5	1
17th	34	0		47th	4	1
18th	33	0		48th	3	1
19th	32	0		49th	2	1
20th	31	0		50th	1	1
21st	30	0		Not on List	0	88
22nd	29	0				
23rd	28	0				
24th	27	0		TOP 10 VOTES		0
25th	26	0		2ND 10 VOTES		0
26th	25	0		3RD 10 VOTES		1
27th	24	1		4TH 10 VOTES		3
28th	23	0		5TH 10 VOTES		8
29th	22	0		TOTAL VOTES		12
30th	21	0		TOTAL POINTS		107

When asked his opinion of Joe Watson, Gregg Asman prefaced his answer by offering an apology to hockey fans and Watson supporters. "It is hard enough to include hockey players on a list of great athletes when you compare them to football and basketball players. But Joe Watson is not even in a league with Bob Dailey, Behn Wilson or Brad McCrimmon." Dailey played in two All-Star Games and was a member of the '80 Flyers' team, which lost in the Finals. Wilson was also on that 1980 squad and was an All-Star once. McCrimmon was picked for one All-Star team during his years in Philadelphia (although he didn't play), and was a member of the Flyers club that advanced to the Finals against Edmonton in 1985 and 1987.

Was Joe in their league? While Dailey, Wilson and McCrimmon weren't goal-scoring machines, they scored more goals than Watson. Joe did make two All-Star teams, though, and most importantly was part of the Flyers team that won consecutive Stanley Cups. A key part, some felt. Joe's biggest supporter was Paul Troy, who ranked him 27th. "He was a steady, reliable anchor on defense for championship teams." Steve Van Allen liked Watson because he was a "tough, gritty defenseman." Bill McElroy compared Watson to a longtime New Jersey Devils defenseman and future Hall of Famer: "He was a 'stay at home' defenseman for Stanley Cup Champions. [Along with Ed Van Impe] we had two Scott Stevenses a generation ago."

On the whole, though, Watson was overshadowed by other Flyers as well as other athletes. Ed Brittingham thought Watson was crucial to the Flyers teams that relied on heart as much as talent, but said that with such a large pool of athletes, there wasn't room for Joe on his list. "If this was the top 125, he would be more than entitled to a spot." Mike Rad agreed that Watson was a tough defenseman, but struck Joe because of his lack of offense. Watson scored just 36 goals in his 11 seasons in Philadelphia. Conversely, Watson's teammate on the Boston Bruins during his rookie year, Bobby Orr, scored more than 36 goals in one season three times. Joe did score one particularly memorable goal and it was not one of his 36 regular-season goals, nor one of his three goals in the postseason. It came in a 1976 exhibition contest against the Soviet Red Army team. Watson scored a short-handed goal, which proved to be the game-winner in a 4-1 Flyers victory.

Year	Team	Lg	Gm	G	A	Pts	PM
1966–67	Boston	NHL	69	2	13	15	38
1967–68	Flyers	NHL	73	5	14	19	56
1968–69	Flyers	NHL	60	2	8	10	14
1969–70	Flyers	NHL	54	3	11	14	28
1970–71	Flyers	NHL	57	3	7	10	50
1971–72	Flyers	NHL	65	3	7	10	38
1972–73	Flyers	NHL	63	2	24	26	46
1973–74	Flyers	NHL	74	1	17	18	34
1974–75	Flyers	NHL	80	6	17	23	42
1975–76	Flyers	NHL	78	2	22	24	28
1976–77	Flyers	NHL	77	4	26	30	39
1977–78	Flyers	NHL	65	5	9	14	22
1978–79	Colorado	NHL	16	0	2	2	12
	Flyers Totals		746	36	162	198	397
	Career Totals		835	38	178	216	447

NHL All-Star (1974, 1977)
Member of Stanley Cup Champions (1974–75)

Paul Holmgren

RANK	POINTS	VOTES RECEIVED
1st	50	0
2nd	49	0
3rd	48	0
4th	47	0
5th	46	0
6th	45	0
7th	44	0
8th	43	0
9th	42	0
10th	41	0
11th	40	0
12th	39	0
13th	38	0
14th	37	0
15th	36	0
16th	35	0
17th	34	0
18th	33	0
19th	32	0
20th	31	0
21st	30	0
22nd	29	0
23rd	28	0
24th	27	0
25th	26	1
26th	25	0
27th	24	0
28th	23	0
29th	22	0
30th	21	1
31st	20	0
32nd	19	0
33rd	18	0
34th	17	0
35th	16	1
36th	15	0
37th	14	0
38th	13	0
39th	12	2
40th	11	1
41st	10	0
42nd	9	0
43rd	8	1
44th	7	0
45th	6	0
46th	5	0
47th	4	0
48th	3	0
49th	2	0
50th	1	0
Not on List	0	93

TOP 10 VOTES	0
2ND 10 VOTES	0
3RD 10 VOTES	2
4TH 10 VOTES	4
5TH 10 VOTES	1
TOTAL VOTES	7
TOTAL POINTS	106

▼ TEAM
Flyers

▼ YEARS PLAYED
1976–1984

▼ POSITION
Right Wing

Right before the 1976-77 season, the Flyers traded Dave Schultz to the Los Angeles Kings. The Flyers needed a tough guy to replace Schultz, and Paul Holmgren filled the bill. Just three weeks after the trade, Schultz returned to the Spectrum in a Kings uniform, and Holmgren, a Flyers rookie, got the best of "the Hammer" in a fight. Holmgren frequently took off the gloves as he racked up 1600 penalty minutes, second on the Flyers' all-time list behind Rick Tocchet. Gordie Jones liked Holmgren because he typified the Flyers' "take the body" style, and put points on the board. Michael Brophy saw the same value in Holmgren as Gordie—a tough player with skill. "He epitomized the soul of the Flyers," said Mike DiColla. "He wasn't a standout, but he was always around." Terry Bickhart was another big Holmgren supporter. "He wasn't spectacular, but was the type of blue-collar player that Philly fans appreciated. He went to work every day. The Flyers stayed good over all those years because of players like him."

The Flyers indeed were very good when Holmgren was in town, playing about .640 hockey during his eight-year stay. Clearly, 1980 was the season in the sun for Paul. He helped the Flyers compile an incredible 35-game unbeaten streak, the longest in professional sports history in North America. Holmgren had his only 30-goal season, and in the postseason, which ended with the finals defeat to the Islanders, he scored 10 goals and added 10 assists.

Holmgren, though, did too much fighting and not enough scoring to suit many voters. "He was nothing more than a role player," said Joe Fee. "Just because you can fight doesn't make you a great hockey player. Should we include Dave Brown on this list, too?" The author's namesake was a noted brawler during his 11 years in Philly, piling up 250 or more penalty minutes in a season twice. Paul Troy also made a reference to Brownie in discounting Holmgren. "He was an enforcer, but his production was closer to Dave Brown's than Tim Kerr's." Brown's season high in goals was just 12; Kerr, on the other hand, ran off four straight 50-goal seasons. John Mitchell and Bob Anderson also didn't think Holmgren was good enough. John: "He was talented, but he could have been better. He didn't materialize as well as he could have. He didn't put up the numbers." Bob: "He wasn't a good scorer, wasn't an All-Star [Holmgren appeared in one All-Star Game], and wasn't essential to the Flyers of that period."

Year	Team	Lg	Gm	G	A	Pts	PM
1975–76	Flyers	NHL	1	0	0	0	2
1976–77	Flyers	NHL	59	14	12	26	201
1977–78	Flyers	NHL	62	16	18	34	190
1978–79	Flyers	NHL	57	19	10	29	168
1979–80	Flyers	NHL	74	30	35	65	267
1980–81	Flyers	NHL	77	22	37	59	306
1981–82	Flyers	NHL	41	9	22	31	183
1982–83	Flyers	NHL	77	19	24	43	178
1983–84	Flyers	NHL	52	9	13	22	105
1983–84	Minnesota	NHL	11	2	5	7	46
1984–85	Minnesota	NHL	16	4	3	7	38
	Flyers Totals		500	138	171	309	1600
	Career Totals		527	144	179	323	1684

NHL All-Star (1981)

John Bunting

RANK	POINTS	VOTES RECEIVED
1st	50	0
2nd	49	0
3rd	48	0
4th	47	0
5th	46	0
6th	45	0
7th	44	0
8th	43	0
9th	42	0
10th	41	0
11th	40	0
12th	39	0
13th	38	0
14th	37	0
15th	36	0
16th	35	0
17th	34	0
18th	33	0
19th	32	0
20th	31	0
21st	30	0
22nd	29	0
23rd	28	1
24th	27	0
25th	26	0
26th	25	0
27th	24	0
28th	23	0
29th	22	0
30th	21	0
31st	20	0
32nd	19	0
33rd	18	1
34th	17	1
35th	16	0
36th	15	0
37th	14	0
38th	13	0
39th	12	1
40th	11	0
41st	10	0
42nd	9	0
43rd	8	2
44th	7	1
45th	6	0
46th	5	0
47th	4	0
48th	3	0
49th	2	2
50th	1	0
Not on List	0	91

TOP 10 VOTES	0
2ND 10 VOTES	0
3RD 10 VOTES	1
4TH 10 VOTES	3
5TH 10 VOTES	5
TOTAL VOTES	9
TOTAL POINTS	102

▼ TEAM
Eagles

▼ YEARS PLAYED
1972–1982

▼ POSITION
Linebacker

Bill Bergey was the leader of the Eagles' defense for several years and he made the Pro Bowl four times in a five-year stretch for the Birds. According to Wayne Smith, one of the players instrumental in making Bergey better was unsung linebacker John Bunting. "It was the era of Bergey and Bunting that I started following Eagles games. In those lean years before Dick Vermeil, the defense was the only part of the team that was worth watching. Bergey was the focus (and well deserved) but it seemed to me that if the play popped outside, it was Bunting making the play. As tight ends became a bigger part of every team's passing game, Bunting had the skills to cover them. It wasn't until Seth Joyner that there was a better Eagle outside linebacker. Like Bergey, John came back from a major injury [he injured his knee in 1978, requiring several months of rehabilitation] to fuel their run to the Super Bowl. I feel it was his play that made Bergey better."

Joe Brown acknowledged that Bunting wasn't in Bergey's class, but liked John because he had a good, long, consistent career, and had good character. Bunting was a starting outside linebacker for 10 years; few Birds linebackers have matched his longevity. Harvey Feldman also had positive things to say about the Eagles' tenth-round pick from the University of North Carolina. "He always seemed to make clutch plays. He was smart and was always where he belonged, unlike Seth Joyner, for example."

Bunting's longevity and role on the Super Bowl team were not enough in most voters' eyes. "He was a role player, not outstanding" (Mike Koob). "He was stable, but not dominating" (Frank Minch). "He was a solid linebacker, but nothing sensational, and not that athletic" (John Mitchell). Andy Paul didn't think Bunting was nearly as good a linebacker as Bergey, Joyner or Jeremiah Trotter. Rob Betts added the names of three other Eagles linebackers who had a leg up on Bunting: Jerry Robinson, William Thomas and Carlos Emmons.

Year	Team	Lg	Games	Int	Yds	Sacks
1972	Eagles	NFL	14	1	45	0
1973	Eagles	NFL	7	0	0	0
1974	Eagles	NFL	14	2	23	0
1975	Eagles	NFL	14	1	6	0
1976	Eagles	NFL	14	0	0	0
1977	Eagles	NFL	14	0	0	0
1978	Eagles	NFL	6	1	9	0
1979	Eagles	NFL	15	2	13	0
1980	Eagles	NFL	16	0	0	0
1981	Eagles	NFL	9	0	0	0
1982	Eagles	NFL	9	1	0	3
	Eagles Totals		132	8	96	3
	Career Totals		132	8	96	3

RAY DIDINGER'S TOP 10

1. Wilt Chamberlain
2. Chuck Bednarik
3. Bobby Clarke
4. Mike Schmidt
5. Julius Erving
6. Steve Carlton
7. Robin Roberts
8. Bernie Parent
9. Reggie White
10. Tommy McDonald

Rod Brind'Amour

RANK	POINTS	VOTES RECEIVED
1st	50	0
2nd	49	0
3rd	48	0
4th	47	0
5th	46	0
6th	45	0
7th	44	0
8th	43	0
9th	42	0
10th	41	0
11th	40	0
12th	39	0
13th	38	0
14th	37	0
15th	36	0
16th	35	0
17th	34	0
18th	33	0
19th	32	0
20th	31	0
21st	30	0
22nd	29	0
23rd	28	1
24th	27	0
25th	26	0
26th	25	0
27th	24	0
28th	23	0
29th	22	0
30th	21	0

RANK	POINTS	VOTES RECEIVED
31st	20	0
32nd	19	0
33rd	18	0
34th	17	1
35th	16	0
36th	15	0
37th	14	0
38th	13	0
39th	12	2
40th	11	2
41st	10	0
42nd	9	0
43rd	8	0
44th	7	0
45th	6	1
46th	5	1
47th	4	0
48th	3	0
49th	2	0
50th	1	0
Not on List	0	92

TOP 10 VOTES	0
2ND 10 VOTES	0
3RD 10 VOTES	1
4TH 10 VOTES	5
5TH 10 VOTES	2
TOTAL VOTES	8
TOTAL POINTS	102

▼ **TEAM**
Flyers

▼ **YEARS PLAYED**
1992–2000

▼ **POSITION**
Center/Left Wing

In 2006, Rod Brind'Amour did what Flyers fans sorely wished he could have done when he played in Philadelphia: he helped his team, the Carolina Hurricanes, win the Stanley Cup. Ned Hark may have included Brindy if he was part of a parade down Broad Street, but chose not to, although he agreed that Brind'Amour had good numbers. Bob Anderson didn't think Rod's numbers were as good as they should have been. "He had tons of ice time, but he didn't accumulate a lot of points. His stats were not impressive enough, especially based on as much ice time as he had. He was supposed to make a difference in Philly, but didn't." Bob paid Brind'Amour a parting compliment: "Fans loved him—he was a Philly-type player who got his uniform dirty." Randy Axelrod agreed that Brind'Amour was a fan favorite, but didn't think that earned him a place on the list. "He was more popular than great." Paul Troy commended Rod for playing hard, but didn't think he was productive enough for top 50 inclusion.

Nevertheless, the man who ranks fourth in career points among Flyers centers had his share of supporters. John Bergmann described Brind'Amour as a clubhouse leader who did all the dirty work and made his teammates better. Tom Walter picked Brindy because he was all over the ice and made big plays. Mike DiColla liked Brind'Amour because he was opportunistic—he was a player who had a knack for being in the right place at the right time. Andy Dziedzic and Jeff Skow went to the greatest lengths in justifying their pick of Brind'Amour. Andy: "Brindy was a maniac on the ice and his face showed it. He had no fear and seemed to be in on every play. I am a big fan of players that have heart and will not blink an eye when they are asked to play when they are injured." Jeff: "He was consistent, hard-nosed and clutch. He was a guy who was easy to like. I remember a lot of games yelling at Renberg, Therien and Gratton for half-hearted performances, but I never had to yell at Brind'Amour. He always delivered hard checks and short-handed goals to get the team going. He is the guy that every team needs." Especially Carolina.

Year	Team	Lg	Gm	G	A	Pts	PM
1989–90	St. Louis	NHL	79	26	35	61	46
1990–91	St. Louis	NHL	78	17	32	49	93
1991–92	Flyers	NHL	80	33	44	77	100
1992–93	Flyers	NHL	81	37	49	86	89
1993–94	Flyers	NHL	84	35	62	97	85
1994–95	Flyers	NHL	48	12	27	39	33
1995–96	Flyers	NHL	82	26	61	87	110
1996–97	Flyers	NHL	82	27	32	59	41
1997–98	Flyers	NHL	82	36	38	74	54
1998–99	Flyers	NHL	82	24	50	74	47
1999–00	Flyers	NHL	12	5	3	8	4
1999–00	Carolina	NHL	33	4	10	14	22
2000–01	Carolina	NHL	79	20	36	56	47
2001–02	Carolina	NHL	81	23	32	55	40
2002–03	Carolina	NHL	48	14	23	37	37
2003–04	Carolina	NHL	78	12	26	38	28
2005–06	Carolina	NHL	78	31	39	70	68
		Flyers Totals	633	235	366	601	563
		Career Totals	1187	382	599	981	944

NHL All-Star (1992)
Member of Stanley Cup Champions (2006)

Jimmy Watson

RANK	POINTS	VOTES RECEIVED
1st	50	0
2nd	49	0
3rd	48	0
4th	47	0
5th	46	0
6th	45	0
7th	44	0
8th	43	0
9th	42	0
10th	41	0
11th	40	0
12th	39	0
13th	38	0
14th	37	0
15th	36	0
16th	35	0
17th	34	0
18th	33	0
19th	32	0
20th	31	0
21st	30	0
22nd	29	0
23rd	28	0
24th	27	0
25th	26	0
26th	25	0
27th	24	0
28th	23	1
29th	22	0
30th	21	0

RANK	POINTS	VOTES RECEIVED
31st	20	0
32nd	19	0
33rd	18	0
34th	17	2
35th	16	1
36th	15	0
37th	14	0
38th	13	0
39th	12	0
40th	11	0
41st	10	0
42nd	9	0
43rd	8	1
44th	7	1
45th	6	0
46th	5	0
47th	4	1
48th	3	0
49th	2	2
50th	1	1
Not on List	0	90

TOP 10 VOTES	0
2ND 10 VOTES	0
3RD 10 VOTES	1
4TH 10 VOTES	3
5TH 10 VOTES	6
TOTAL VOTES	10
TOTAL POINTS	97

▼ **TEAM**
Flyers

▼ **YEARS PLAYED**
1973–1982

▼ **POSITION**
Defenseman

When Bernie Parent was tending goal impeccably for the Flyers in the glory years, he had a strong stable of defensemen in front of him. According to Tom Walter and John Senkow, Jimmy Watson, the younger brother of Joe, was the cream of the crop. "He was a good puck carrier and also strong defensively," said Tom. "He had a long career and a few All-Star Game appearances." Five, in fact, as John pointed out, in a six-year period (1975-80). An impressive accomplishment indeed—Bobby Clarke is the only other Flyer to play in five All-Star Games over a six-year stretch.

John also did his homework by pointing out that in 1979, Watson led the NHL in the important plus/minus category, finishing the year at plus 53. Jimmy earned the votes of Ralph Antonelli and Harvey Feldman because he was such a good team player. "Also, he could score some goals," said Ralph. Not nearly as many as Mark Howe or Eric Desjardins, but he ranked higher on the Flyers' career goals list than Stanley Cup teammates Ed Van Impe, Barry Ashbee and brother Joe.

Even though Jimmy Watson scored more goals than Van Impe, Ashbee and his brother and made more All-Star teams than those three defensemen, the consensus, as reflected by how Jimmy finished in the voting, which Paul Lightkep echoed, is that as a Philadelphia athlete, Jimmy was a shade behind the other three. "He didn't have quite as much of an impact on the Stanley Cup teams as Ashbee, Van Impe or Joe Watson," said Paul. A few other voters, including Rob Betts, John Mitchell, Bob Kelly and Dave Myers, used words like "steady" and "solid" to describe the younger Watson, but decided he wasn't good enough for the list. "He wasn't a standout," said Bob. "He didn't embody the Flyers as much as other players," said Dave.

Year	Team	Lg	Gm	G	A	Pts	PM
1972–73	Flyers	NHL	4	0	1	1	5
1973–74	Flyers	NHL	78	2	18	20	44
1974–75	Flyers	NHL	68	7	18	25	72
1975–76	Flyers	NHL	79	2	34	36	66
1976–77	Flyers	NHL	71	3	23	26	35
1977–78	Flyers	NHL	71	5	12	17	62
1978–79	Flyers	NHL	77	9	13	22	52
1979–80	Flyers	NHL	71	5	18	23	51
1980–81	Flyers	NHL	18	2	2	4	6
1981–82	Flyers	NHL	76	3	9	12	99
		Flyers Totals	613	38	148	186	492
		Career Totals	613	38	148	186	492

NHL All-Star (1975–78, 1980)
Member of Stanley Cup Champions (1974–75)

About the Author

Dave Brown has co-authored two books with former Philadelphia athletes: *The Baseball Trivia Quiz Book* with Phillies reliever Mitch "The Wild Thing" Williams and *Jim McMahon's In-Your-Face Book of Pro Football Trivia* with Eagles quarterback Jim McMahon. He lives in the Downingtown area with his wife Kim and their two sons, Alex and Jack.